Praise for

"The subtitle of this book says it is for 'Scrum Managers,' however, its guidance and advice extend to anyone associated with an agile (Scrum) team. It will also certainly help team members better understand their relationship to the work ScrumMasters, agile coaches, and project managers do for the team. And, beyond this, the book can be valuable to anyone working in a coaching capacity with any group of people, expanding the book's application beyond agile-based efforts."

—Scott Duncan, Agile Coach

"Lyssa explains brilliantly how skills from professional coaching can be applied to coaching agile software development teams. What I love about this book is how Lyssa brings practical advice to life by relating it to everyday experiences we all recognize. An essential guide for every agile manager's bookshelf."

—Rachel Davies, author of Agile Coaching

"As I read this book I could actually hear Lyssa's voice, guiding me and sparking precious 'a-ha moments.' This truly is the next best thing to having an experienced and wise coach sitting by your side, helping you be the best coach you can be for your team."

—Kris Blake, agile coach

"Lyssa Adkins presents agile coaching in a gentle style with firm underpinnings. She resolves the paradox of how coaching can help a team to self-organize, and shows how a nurturing environment can push teams to perform better than ever."

—Bill Wake, Industrial Logic, Inc.

"I love Lyssa's three qualities of an agile coach—loving, compassionate, uncompromising—sweet. Every chapter offers a compelling blend of philosophy and action, framework and freedom, approach and avoidance, as any agile book should. *Coaching Agile Teams* is a good candidate to become dog-eared on my desktop rather than looking good on my bookshelf. The depth and quality of expertise that Lyssa sought, sampled, and sounded out along her own coaching journey have been synthesized in her own voice of experience."

—Christopher Avery, Responsibility Process mentor, www.LeadershipGift.com

"In my experience with agile projects, the agile coach is one of the most important roles to get right. *Coaching Agile Teams* by Lyssa Adkins gives the details and practical insights for what it takes to be a great agile coach."

—Dave Hendricksen, software architect, Thomson-Reuters

"I remember the first time I met Lyssa at a Scrum gathering in Orlando, and realized very quickly how inspirational she would become in the agile community. This book encapsulates her thoughts and ideas into a fantastic literary work that, I believe, fills a void in our community. We knew the role of a coach was needed, but for a long time we were not sure what that role actually was. We struggled as a community to explain what to do, when to do it, and what to do next. Lyssa not only collates all of the things we as coaches aspire to be, but has provided some great advice with realistic direction on how to be the best coach you can be for your team."

—*Martin Kearns, CSC + CST, Principal Consultant, Renewtek ply. Ltd.*

COACHING AGILE TEAMS

COACHING AGILE TEAMS

A Companion for ScrumMasters, Agile Coaches, and Project Managers in Transition

LYSSA ADKINS

✦✦Addison-Wesley

Upper Saddle River, NJ • Boston • Indianapolis • San Francisco
New York • Toronto • Montreal • London • Munich • Paris • Madrid
Capetown • Sydney • Tokyo • Singapore • Mexico City

Many of the designations used by manufacturers and sellers to distinguish their products are claimed as trademarks. Where those designations appear in this book, and the publisher was aware of a trademark claim, the designations have been printed with initial capital letters or in all capitals.

The author and publisher have taken care in the preparation of this book, but make no expressed or implied warranty of any kind and assume no responsibility for errors or omissions. No liability is assumed for incidental or consequential damages in connection with or arising out of the use of the information or programs contained herein.

The publisher offers excellent discounts on this book when ordered in quantity for bulk purchases or special sales, which may include electronic versions and/or custom covers and content particular to your business, training goals, marketing focus, and branding interests. For more information, please contact:

U.S. Corporate and Government Sales
(800) 382-3419
corpsales@pearsontechgroup.com

For sales outside the United States please contact:

International Sales
international@pearsoned.com

Visit us on the Web: informit.com/aw

Library of Congress Cataloging-in-Publication Data

Adkins, Lyssa.
  Coaching agile teams : a companion for ScrumMasters, agile coaches, and project managers in transition / Lyssa Adkins.
       p.   cm.
  Includes bibliographical references and index.
  ISBN-13: 978-0-321-63770-3
  ISBN-10: 0-321-63770-4 (pbk. : alk. paper) 1. Executive coaching. 2. Teams in the work-place. 3. Project management. I. Title.
  HD30.4.A35 2010
  658.3'124—dc22

                                                                      2010009922

Pearson Education, Inc.
Rights and Contracts Department
501 Boylston Street, Suite 900
Boston, MA 02116
Fax: (617) 671-3447

Illustrations in Figures 1.2 and 13.1–13.6 by Gail Cocker and Kathy Harman. All other illustrations by Gail Cocker.

ISBN-13: 978-0-321-63770-3
ISBN-10:   0-321-63770-4
Text printed in the United States on recycled paper at Courier in Stoughton, Massachusetts.
First printing, June, 2010

To emerging and experienced agile coaches alike—may you find something here to help you on your way.

Contents

Foreword by Mike Cohn

The buzz at the 2008 Scrum Gathering in Chicago was all about a presenter who was new to that conference. On Monday afternoon she presented a session called "The Road from Project Manager to Agile Coach." By Tuesday everyone was talking about it.

The reason that the presenter of that session—Lyssa Adkins, whose book you hold in your hands right now—created such a stir was the obvious passion, knowledge, and experience she brought to the critical topic of agile coaching. As a classically trained project manager and director of a large corporate project management office before discovering agile, Lyssa is the perfect guide for becoming a skilled agile coach.

Watching a great agile coach is like watching a magician. No matter how closely you watch, you can't quite figure out how she does it. In this book, magician/agile coach Lyssa Adkins takes us behind the curtain and shows us the tricks of her trade. What's even more amazing is that there is no sleight of hand or cards up her sleeve. What you'll find are simply wonderful techniques for guiding teams toward ever greater success.

Lyssa breaks down the magic of coaching into concrete terms. She not only explains the distinction between teaching, coaching, and advising, but she also shows us when and how to move between them. Lyssa provides guidance on how to choose between coaching one individual or the whole team. She also tells us how to identify coaching opportunities—chances to make a powerful impact on the team.

Guiding us past the white rabbits and black hats, Lyssa reveals how to initiate tough conversations using powerful questions designed to get team members talking constructively about a problem. This is one of my favorite parts of the book. Lyssa shares practical advice about collaboration—a rare find, because so many other books on the subject say merely that collaboration is necessary yet offer no advice on how to make it happen. But as important as all the tools she gives us is Lyssa's reminder that part of the coach's job is knowing when to sit back, observe, and let the team work things through.

Because we as agile coaches can fail, too, Lyssa presents a wonderful description of eight failure modes we can fall into. Early in my career I would often fall into the Expert and Hub failure modes. I can honestly say those are safely in my past, but I struggle still with acting in the Opinionator mode. Maybe you are occasionally a Spy, Seagull, or Butterfly, or perhaps you suffer from one of the other failure modes she describes. Fortunately, Lyssa also presents us with eight success modes to model. Read Chapter 11, "Agile Coach Failure, Recovery, and Success Modes," to see what mode you might be in.

Great agile coaches and ScrumMasters help their teams achieve more than those teams could ever achieve on their own. Becoming a skilled agile coach, like becoming a magician, starts with learning a set of techniques. From there it's a matter of practice, practice, and more practice. Though the practicing will be up to you, this wonderful book will get you started in the right direction by showing how a master agile coach performs her craft.

—Mike Cohn
Author of *Succeeding with Agile*
Boulder, Colorado

Foreword by Jim Highsmith

First and foremost, this is a great book! I get a chance to read many agile books, book proposals, and manuscripts, and too many are more of the same—a few good ideas here and there, but no solid contribution to the field. Lyssa Adkins' book is not more of the same.

I look for four things in agile books: Does the book contribute new ideas? Does the book organize existing ideas in new ways? Does the book extend existing ideas? Is the writing good? For example, Kent Beck's groundbreaking *Extreme Programming Explained* combined new ideas and organized existing ideas in new ways. Some people say there is nothing new in agile, but Kent's combination of specific practices and values was new. When I first received Mike Cohn's *Agile Estimating and Planning*, my response was, "How can there be a whole book on this topic? Wasn't it covered adequately in the Beck and Fowler's *Planning Extreme Programming*?" I realized quickly that Mike's book extended existing ideas in exciting new ways, plus added new ones.

Coaching Agile Teams builds an effective framework that organizes existing ideas and practices. Further, it extends existing ideas in thought-stimulating ways. Finally, the book is well written and compelling to read, and the ideas are practical and accompanied by experiential examples.

One of Lyssa's ideas that resonates with me is defining coaching by multiple roles: teacher, mentor, problem solver, conflict navigator, performance coach. This differentiation among roles brings depth to a coach's job. For example, mentors teach stuff—agile practices—whereas performance coaches encourage individuals and teams to learn about themselves. Lyssa's experience as a life coach brings this rich dimension to her coaching work and this book. Many agile "coaches" are mentors who teach agile practices. This book can help them become effective performance improvement coaches.

There are three audiences for this book: agile coaches, agile leaders, and individuals.

First, for everyone who considers themselves to be an agile coach, trainer, mentor, or facilitator, this book has a wealth of ideas, practices, and tidbits that can help them improve. For example, here's one thought-provoking quote from Lyssa, "A ScrumMaster who takes teams beyond getting agile practices up and running into their deliberate and joyful pursuit of high performance is an agile coach." In Chapter 10, "Coach as Collaboration Conductor," Lyssa explores cooperation and collaboration, a valuable differentiation for team performance improvement. Each of these ideas adds depth to the role of an agile coach.

The second audience for this book is anyone in a leadership position in an agile organization—manager, product owner, ScrumMaster, coach, project manager, or iteration manager. Although coaching is an agile coach's full-time job, it is a part-time job for all leaders. There is a lot written about self-organizing teams, but not as much on how to actually become a self-organizing team or how to help such a team emerge. Leaders influence the workplace environment, and Lyssa's book can help them facilitate the maturing of self-organizing teams, in large part, by being more agile themselves.

Finally, anyone who aspires to be an effective agile team member will benefit from reading this book. I am a fan of Christopher Avery, author of *Teamwork Is an Individual Skill: Getting Your Work Done When Sharing Responsibility*, who writes "To improve teamwork, I need to improve me" and "I am responsible for all the relationships within my project community." This means that improving team performance is not just the responsibility of the leader or coach but the responsibility of every team member. Lyssa's book can help individuals become agile self-coaches—improving their teams by improving themselves. Chapter 3, "Master Yourself," is as valid for individual team members as it is for agile coaches.

As you can see, I am an enthusiastic champion of this book. It goes on the bookshelf as one of my top ten agile books. *Coaching Agile Teams* focuses on what some would call *soft skills*, which we realize are usually harder to learn and apply than the so-called hard skills. For individuals, leaders, and coaches, there is a gold mine of ideas, practices, checklists, and thought gems in this book.

—Jim Highsmith
Director Agile Practice,
Cutter Consortium
Flagstaff, Arizona

Acknowledgments

Without Mike Cohn this book simply would not be. It took him about eight months to convince me to write it. And now, having written it and believing that it will bring more joy and meaning to people's work lives, I offer to Mike a big ol' bear hug of gratitude, only because I know that would embarrass him the most. My deepest thanks, Mike.

After Mike came Chris Guzikowski, editor at Addison-Wesley, who gave me the chance to write the book once I became convinced I should do so. Thanks, Chris. And then came the support of the talented authors and agile practitioners contributing books to the Mike Cohn Signature Series: Lisa Crispin, Janet Gregory, Clinton Keith, Roman Pichler, Kenny Rubin, and Jurgen Appelo. Knowing that each of you was going through many of the same things I was going through made the trip far less lonely.

Many thanks to my human muses, the women who helped me stay in the flow of ideas and turn a deaf ear to my inner saboteur: Sandra Enoch, my work/life coach; Beverly Johnson, my Phoenix Rising Yoga therapist; Eleanor Rouse, the mastermind of my local Women's Circle; and Kathy Harman, the one who kept encouraging me by finding tidbits in my writing to show me why coaches need this book. From the service of all these women, I draw great strength. Thank you, ladies. You and the music of B-Tribe kept it coming.

Without John Adkins, my husband and editor-in-residence, dear readers, you would simply have less content to read in this book. His willingness to do the heavy lifting in the final iterations of the chapters extended my ability to create new material and give you more. And, as the last round of edits came to a close, we could both see his mark on the book, and the book was made all the better for it. His English teacher mother would have been proud. And John, lover, the ways in which you contributed to this work are countless, every one of them deeply appreciated.

Lee Devin and his beloved wife, the talented director Abigail Adams, opened their theater and their hearts to me to allow me to experience true collaboration through the example of a troupe of actors working together in a start-up ensemble. That experience started the thinking and writing in earnest and "kicked things off" for this book quite nicely. Then, throughout it all, there was Lee—steadfast, insightful, experienced, brooking no excuses, even though the last word in a good tail kicking would always be "darlin'." As a first-time author, one could not wish for a better mentor.

Throughout the creation of the book, collaborations with new people and remembered moments with others provided the seeds of the stories that, I believe, make the book come alive. Thank you for those seeds Tobias Mayer, Kristen Blake, Ellen Braun, Aaron Sanders, Rich Sheridan, Michael Spayd, Mike Vizdos, and all of the coach apprentices and other agilists I have been blessed to see blossom.

Once the pieces of the book started to come together, reviewers appeared out of nowhere (OK, out of the Internet) to help make them even better. My sincere thanks to Bachan Anand, Brad Appleton, Suzanne Davenport, Rachel Davies, Scott Duncan, Scott Dunn, April Johnson, Robert Mead, Dan Mezick, Bent Myllerup, Michael Sahota, and Chris Sims.

Once pulled together, a group of experts was asked to review the book. Through their doubts and encouragements alike, the book became better yet again. Thank you, Ken Auer, Dave Hendricksen, Michael Feathers, Jim Highsmith, and Bill Wake.

Thanks to the founding agilists who created a way of working in which people find greater meaning in their work lives while producing amazing results for their companies and—now just emerging—the world. To Jeff Sutherland, Ken Schwaber, Alistair Cockburn, Kent Beck, Jim Highsmith, and many others, some known and others unknown, I offer my gratitude.

My special thanks to Jim Highsmith and Mike Cohn for contributing forewords to the book. When I was thinking about whom to invite to write a foreword for the book, Mike offered this advice, "Choose someone because you'd be thrilled to see their name on the cover of the book." Thrilled, indeed. Thanks, gentlemen.

Abiding love and thanks to my parents, Jeanette and John Clark, who continue to show me through their own example that hard work never killed anyone. Their hard work and sacrifices made possible this book and a life where I get to choose my work and work at it joyfully.

Last but never least, thanks to my daughter Kailey Adkins, who thought it quite normal that I should write a book. Her unwavering belief that I could do it (and would do it) helped make it so.

Introduction

These few pages of introduction were probably harder to write than most of the book. Bemoaning this fact to an agile coach colleague of mine, someone who was my coach apprentice a few years ago, I watched a slow smile creep across her face as she looked up at me and fed my words back to me. She said, with simplicity and clarity, "Take it to the team."

"Take it to the team," I repeated. How many times had I said that to her during her agile coach apprenticeship? Too many to count, as I helped her recover from command-and-control-ism and move into a world where she would routinely take problems to the team instead of solving them single-handedly.

So, when confronted with the problematic introduction text, "take it to the team" sounded like sage advice. I sent a note to the people who have been with me every step of the way while this book was coming to life and asked them what two things must be conveyed in the introduction. Their responses are interwoven with one another and my own ideas throughout the rest of this introduction.

This small example—this tiny reminder of what it is to be an agile coach—contains in it the purpose of this book. Perhaps you are like me, finding yourself recovering from some past way of working with teams and people that used to be successful but doesn't seem to work anymore. Or, perhaps you sense something ineffective, or even inhumane, in the way you have been trained to work with others. You want to change as you take up your agile leadership mantle but don't know where to start.

I've been recovering for many years now, yet the behaviors of the past linger. They hang around even though I find myself in a totally new agile landscape, full of freedom, accountability, and possibility. In this example, the need to take on the problem of the introduction single-handedly and solve it so that I can say "I did it all by myself" still clings to me even though it no longer serves me. I know this, yet I forget. And herein lies the practice of agile coaching: to constantly reawaken and refocus, so you can improve the span and impact of your coaching. Why? So that people become great agilists, teams create products that make them proud, and companies and nations reap the benefits of free and accountable teams living in a world of possibility from which both innovation and excellence arise.

The imperative to "constantly improve" means exposing ourselves to one good agile coaching idea after another and incorporating them into our daily responses as coaches to teams and people. This book serves up a wide variety of those good coaching ideas, some provocative and some practical. Some you will chew on for a long time, maybe even struggle with. Others you will adopt as yours right away. Expect both.

Why Is This Topic Important?

Most teams I see in my teaching and coaching use agile to achieve so-so results, usually in the form of mediocre products created faster. Yes, agile works for this, and perhaps it's better than what came before, but it's not the whole game. Look around and see that there is so much more to get! And agile coaches help people get it, but only if they hone their skills and keep improving.

Although I worked with agile teams as their coach, I constantly challenged myself with these questions: What is it, *really*, to be an agile coach? What does that mean for me? What else must I acquire? What must I let go?

This book offers answers to these questions. The answers came from agile frameworks themselves and from the allied disciplines that supplement the agile coach's toolkit quite naturally, such as facilitation, conflict mediation, collaboration, work/life coaching, and teaching. In this book, each chapter unfolds to bring you mind-sets and tools from these disciplines and others so that you can incorporate them in your coaching. The expected result? Teams that achieve astonishing results.

Who Is This Book For?

This is not a beginner text on agile frameworks and how to get the basics up and running. Throughout, I assume you know what agile is and how the practices work. If not, consult online references such as ScrumAlliance.org or mountaingoatsoftware.com.

I realize that my agile may not be your agile, but I'm betting that the core concepts of all agile frameworks shine through in the way I talk about agile in this book. My personal agile background started with Scrum and then, using Scrum as a backbone, mixed in other agile and nonagile tools and techniques. You'll see this reflected in the text.

You'll find this book to be tailor-made for you if you recognize any of the following:

- You've had a few experiences as a ScrumMaster, Extreme Programming (XP) coach, or other agile team lead, and it just doesn't seem to be working for you; or it's been good, but you sense that there's something *more*.

- Your job has become routine, and you notice the teams you coach seem to be going through the agile motions, too.

- Your teams get the agile practices and are doing well but not getting the fabulous results you were supposed to get.

- You are spread across many agile teams because your managers think agile coaching isn't a full-time job and you're not sure how to prove them wrong.

- You are not convinced that the agile coach role is right for you and want to get a real sense of it before diving in.

What Can You Achieve with This Book?

Let this book take you on a tour of the inner world of becoming an excellent agile coach. As you read it, notice the mountainous terrain of how an agile coach observes teams and people, frames thoughts about those observations, and processes personal biases and emotions. Pay attention as the book takes you to the wide-open plains of deciding to put observations and reflections into action (or nonaction) in the best service of agile teams in the unending quest to be better than we are today.

This book offers one person's approach, my approach, to building high-performance agile teams. It will not tell you "the way." Rather, through my journey, it will tell you one good way that will help you find your own path as a coach. I have used this pattern and the ideas in this book successfully while coaching many aspiring agile coaches, with the result that each coach found their path and, then, their unique voice.

Perhaps through this book you will see that the role of agile coach, successfully done, is more than getting the basic agile processes and principles instilled in a team. Perhaps this book will help teams know what to expect from a good (or great) agile coach so they can be specific about what they need when they don't get enough. Perhaps through this book middle and upper managers will see the job of agile coach as a time-consuming, energy-consuming, and valuable contribution so that the trend of having one agile coach split across many teams evaporates. Perhaps this book will set the aspiring agile coach on a personal journey toward enlightenment, where their motivation and intention is for the team rather than for themselves.

I accept all of these as stellar outcomes and the least of which I can imagine happening for you and the people you influence as you read this book and put its ideas into practice.

How Does This Book Work?

Each chapter of this book stands alone so that you may come to it when its message strikes home most. Perhaps you find yourself in a panic over something happening on a team and, scanning the table of contents, say to yourself, "A-ha! That's the one I need today." Or, in a reflective mood, you simply open the book to a random spot and start reading, trusting that the words on the page serve you best now. Feel free to read the book from cover to cover if you like. It will work that way, too. Just know that you don't have to travel any preset path, conventional or random, to use it well. Use this book as your companion along your journey, there when you need it and waiting patiently for you to come back when you're flying on your own and don't need its help in the moment.

The chapters contain "Things to Try" to assist as you move ideas into action, taking very sure steps toward better coaching. Because the chapters stand alone, references to other useful bits of the book appear in the "See Also" text found throughout the book. In addition, strategically placed thought-provoking quotations invite you to ruminate on the nature of remarkable agile coaching.

The book serves up its stories, secrets, and things to try in three sections and thirteen chapters:

Part I: It Starts with You

Chapter 1 *Will I Be a Good Coach?*	Who is this person we call an agile coach, and how do I know whether I am one already? What are the ten aspects of "native wiring" that predict success for an agile coach?
Chapter 2 *Expect High Performance*	The foundations that allow a high performance team to emerge are revealed and put in an agile team context. The secret? Expecting high performance.

Chapter 3 *Master Yourself*	Coaching starts with you, but it is not about you. It is about what you can bring to the team to help them get better. To do this, you must recover from command-and-control-ism and, then, master yourself.
Chapter 4 *Let Your Style Change*	The leadership style framework in this chapter helps coaches know which style to use as the team they coach evolves (and devolves).

Part II: Helping the Team Get More for Themselves

Chapter 5 *Coach as Coach-Mentor*	This chapter offers fundamentals of professional coaching in the setting of an agile team, along with the specifics of coaching whole teams as well as team members, product owners, and agile managers.
Chapter 6 *Coach as Facilitator*	Practical tools for facilitating conversations are offered, for standing meetings such as agile planning sessions, as well as for unstructured collaboration conversations.
Chapter 7 *Coach as Teacher*	Channel the best teacher you ever had—the one who was kind and hard, the one who knew you could do better and expected the best from you. Then, use the techniques in this chapter to teach agile, especially the roles in agile. Get ready to take advantage of common teachable moments such as team start-up, standing meetings, and those random perfect moments when agile just "clicks" for someone.
Chapter 8 *Coach as Problem Solver*	Viewing the team as an ecosystem surfaces the coach's role as "systems revealer," which, when done with the foundations of agile in mind, allows the team to move from simple recovery from problems into health and into vibrancy.
Chapter 9 *Coach as Conflict Navigator*	Conflict, as a useful element of a high-performing agile team, means that the coach helps the team navigate through conflict and into the desired state of constructive disagreement.

Chapter 10
Coach as Collabora-
tion Conductor

Building a team's collaboration muscle is an important aspect of the agile coach role, but only if we want astonishing results.

Part III: Getting More for Yourself

Chapter 11
Agile Coach Failure,
Recovery, and Success
Modes

Common failure and success modes in agile coaching are recognized and named in this chapter. Steps for recovering from the grips of failure modes are also offered, as this don't-take-yourself-too-seriously exploration of failure to success unfolds.

Chapter 12
When Will I Get
There?

A "road map" of abilities is served up in this chapter. It contains lists of skills, mind-sets, tools, and techniques, all of which can be helpful to indicate when you have successfully reached agile coachdom.

Chapter 13
It's Your Journey

Every coach's journey is different from the last, and the only Holy Grail to find in agile coaching is your best expression of the role. In this chapter, stories of other people's journeys inform and inspire you to see your coaching journey anew.

Are you ready to start? Well, what are you waiting for?

About the Author

Lyssa Adkins came to agile as a project leader with more than 15 years of project management success. Even with all that experience, nothing prepared her for the power and simplicity of agile done well.

She has coached many agile teams and been a master coach to many apprentice coaches over the past few years. Coaching coaches one-on-one and in small groups, Lyssa enjoys a front-row seat as remarkable agile coaches emerge and go on to entice the very best from the teams they coach.

Lyssa's agile experience, along with her professional coaching and training abilities, gives her the perspective needed to guide teams and agile leaders to harness agile as the competitive advantage weapon it was meant to be. She knows the transformation path is rocky. As a large-scale program manager and director of Project Management Offices turned agile coach and trainer, she has lived it herself. This makes her uniquely able to help others change their existing world to the agile world.

Lyssa holds triple certifications: Certified Scrum Trainer (CST), Project Management Professional (PMP), and Six Sigma Green Belt (SSGB). She is also a trained coactive coach.

For more information, visit coachingagileteams.com. You can also find Lyssa on Twitter as @lyssaadkins and by e-mail at lyssaadkins@cricketwing.com.

PART I

It Starts with You

Chapter **1**

Will I Be a Good Coach?

Even though I had about 15 years of managing projects by the time I encountered agile, nothing prepared me for the power and simplicity of agile done well. I didn't see it that way at first, however. When I was introduced to agile, I didn't believe it would work. My mental model of projects was that of a set of big machines that worked separately but in lockstep, each part producing a raw product to be ingested by another part of the machine and eventually spitting out a complete and finished product. In my world, project management was essential, serious business because project managers orchestrated the workings of the whole machine. Everything about getting projects done was complicated and big, and I was convinced it had to be this way. I couldn't imagine what a small team working together through plans of their own devising could possibly create. It just seemed too flimsy for getting "real work" done.

Thirty days later, after assisting a master agile coach get my first agile team up and running and watching how the team worked together, I was

---

By the time you finish this chapter, you will be able to answer these questions:

- Why does agile coaching matter?
- What other disciplines do agile coaches bring to their teams? Why?
- What does it mean that "being" an agile coach is as important as doing the job of an agile coach?
- How is an agile coach different from a ScrumMaster, project manager, or technical lead?
- How does one become an agile coach? How do I know when I'm "getting there"?
- What "native wiring" predicts success as an agile coach?

convinced that my perceptions of agile had been dead wrong and that my mental model of project management was simply outdated. Not only did the agile team start from scratch (an act that itself used to take 30 days in my previous world), but they built an important piece of functionality that was immediately usable and started returning hard-dollar value to the company right away. They had produced "real work," the kind that the project management machine would have taken many months to spit out. And, it was higher quality than what usually comes from the machine. And, the best part? They did it all in 30 days.

The kudos were amazing. Vice presidents came out of the woodwork to congratulate the team, sincerely thank them, and make sure the team understood the value of their work to the company—and to offer the next set of challenges. Just thirty days old, the team was more than ready to take on anything the company could throw their way. Highly and naturally motivated by their accomplishments together, they could see no limit to what they could achieve. Bring it on!

I want every new agile team to have an experience like this team did, or even better. I want standing agile teams to leverage agile to the full competitive advantage it was meant to provide, far exceeding all expectations with innovative products delivered when they matter most.

If teams are to have these kinds of stellar experiences with agile, they need coaches who can provide the right teaching, coaching, and mentoring to make it possible. This is where you come in.

Why Agile Coaching Matters

If you're like most of the aspiring agile coaches I work with, very little in your education or experience has properly prepared you for being an agile coach. You may wonder "What is my role in a self-organized team?" or "How do I help the team yet stay hands-off?" Many novice coaches respond by going too far to either extreme. To figure out how to coach from the center, providing just the right touch, you must first understand a few things about the world you coach in and the people you coach.

The problems we face today often don't stand up to the machine model many of us have used in the past. With the machine model, we believe that we can take any complex problem, break it down into its component parts, create each component more or less separately, and then bring them all back together in one final integration effort. This is how I ended up with programs running 19 simultaneous work streams to turn out one product. I know very few problems my teams face (today or yesterday) that lend themselves to this model. Instead, the problems they're asked to grapple with are slippery and have never been solved to people's satisfaction before. At the same time, the world feels far more uncertain than anyone can remember, and the latest change rocks us before we have even settled down from the last change. This is the world we work in.

Also, the people I coach want to know that they matter. They are no longer satisfied with being cogs in the machine. They want to know that what they put their effort and thought into yields something valuable and that their contributions to it are seen as valuable, too. The people I coach are not motivated by carrots and sticks; they are motivated by a sense of worth and purpose. "Why are we doing this anyway?" and "What good is it to anyone?" become pivotal questions for them as they seek meaning in their lives like never before. Look at how the people on our teams spend their personal time: going to yoga class, doing extreme sports, pursuing artistic endeavors, serving their communities, or engaging in intentional parenting. In short, they are exploring every facet of who they are in their quest to become fully integrated and complete human beings.

Agile coaching matters because it helps in both of these areas—producing products that matter in the real, complex, and uncertain world, and adding meaning to people's work lives. Agile is far more than an alternate project management methodology. It's great for that, but that is also the weakest expression of it. Done most powerfully (and simply), agile focuses us on the critical products to create and makes it possible for us to create them, one after another, most important after most important, in a way that allows us to meet our own high standard of excellence and pursue a vibrant personal purpose—but only when done well. This means teams need coaches who bring to them a clear view of agile done well and a host of other skills to make agile come alive for them.

The Agile Coaching Context

Agile itself is sufficient; coaching deepens it.

Described as lightweight, agile frameworks feature a small set of practices to teach, which makes it quick and easy to get teams up and running with them, at least with the basics. In my experience, getting a team using agile from scratch within a day not only is possible but is common. Agile is lightweight, fast, and simple—deceptively simple.

Agile is easy to get going yet hard to do well. Many reasons collude to make this so. Chief among them is that agile exposes the dirt people have been sweeping under the rug for years. Who wants to look at that? Yet, we must.

As a way of working, agile seems full of opposites: simple yet challenging, lightweight yet mighty, commonsensical yet subtle, easily accessible yet deep. To coach teams to do agile well, you need not add new artifacts, events, or roles to the agile framework you have chosen. Instead, find things that help express the challenging, mighty, subtle, and deep aspects of each element already present in the framework. Enter the allied disciplines.

The "Doing" of Agile Coaching

As Figure 1.1 illustrates, we can think of agile as a continuous backdrop—a set of values, practices, principles, and roles we uphold as we coach people to use agile well. To do this, we bring to them our skills in many allied disciplines, which allows us to step fully into the role as their agile coach. We become their facilitator, teacher, coach and mentor, conflict navigator, collaboration conductor, and problem solver. We bring to them other things we've learned that help express the challenging, mighty, subtle, and deep aspects of agile.

You will discover different disciplines and schools of thought than I did. That's why the model has room for what you learn. As you incorporate a new discipline and prove its usefulness with your agile teams, plop it in the "Your favorite goes here" spot. Make this model your own, and expand it as you learn new things. Share what you've learned with others so we can, together, continually advance the art of agile coaching.

This book explores each of these allied disciplines, contextualized for use in the agile world. For example, we don't bring the full intent of work/life coaching to agile teams because pursuing each person's individual agenda would overshadow the purpose of an agile team—to frequently produce real results that people find valuable. Instead, we use skills from work/life coaching to help each person become the best agilist they can become. Thus, we contextualize it for the agile world.

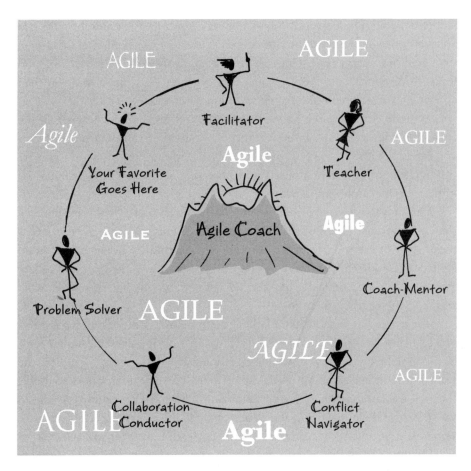

FIGURE 1.1 Agile provides the backdrop to which we bring other skills for the sake of deepening people's understanding and use of agile.

The "Being" of Agile Coaching

We just ran through a description of the many things the agile coach does, among them teach, facilitate, collaborate, and mentor. It adds up to a lot of things to do. Certainly, the doing matters. You must know your job as coach and your way around agile and be constantly searching for that next break-through idea for the team. Just as important as the "doing" part of agile coaching, though, is the "being" part.

Agile coaching is more about who you are and what behaviors you model than it is about any specific technique or idea you bring to the team. Throwing some very rough numbers at it, I would say that agile coaching is 40% doing and 60% being. The powerful (silent) influence you have because of who you are and how agile values shine through your every move should not be underestimated. It's potent stuff. Through your being, you exert a far-reaching and long-lasting impact on people, teams, and organizations, much more so than applying a whole textbook of agile techniques perfectly.

An agile coach models agile all the time, and just by *being* teaches all the time. This comes through in how you coach individuals on the team and how you interact with the team at large. It speaks clearly in how conscious you are of your actions and their impacts and how you take responsibility for those impacts, simply and transparently.

Through these ways of being, the coach also creates a living example of the depth and usefulness of agile, honoring the values that underlie it in every moment with every decision and through every action (or nonaction). A good agile coach walks the walk and, in so doing, creates a path the team can follow. As an agile coach, modeling the key behaviors of a good agilist, you *are* what you're trying to teach them to *be*.

You're not going to hit the mark all the time. You will make mistakes. You will lose your cool and yell. Your mind will wander during the stand-up meeting. You will skillfully manipulate people into doing what you think is right for the team. The most important thing you can do in the face of your mistake is to model the agile value of openness. Transparently and with humility, simply own up to the impact of the mistake, and apologize for it. Tell the team which agile value or principle your mistake undermined so they can learn from your example.

Imagine a team that admits mistakes, reinforces their shared values, forgives one another, and moves on. Do you think such a team would come up with astonishing ideas? I do.

Let's Get Our Language Straight

A ScrumMaster who takes teams beyond getting agile practices up and running into their deliberate and joyful pursuit of high performance is an agile coach. Notice the use of the plural—*teams*. That indicates an important ingredient needed to call oneself an agile coach: having coached multiple teams and having seen a range of possibilities and limitations and successes and failures across a variety of situations.

My bias for the term *agile coach* comes simply from my past experience. The company where I first learned agile used the role name, *agile coach*, as a way to keep their options open even though they were, at the core, a Scrum shop. Over time, the teams I coached used Scrum with lean, straight-up Six Sigma,

Extreme Programming practices, and user-centered design. *Agile coach* seemed a more accurate term for these situations.

AGILE MASH-UPS

When teams mashed up Scrum with something else, such as lean or user-centered design, they enjoyed success if they kept the Scrum framework mostly intact and the agile manifesto completely intact. When they let the Scrum framework and agile manifesto fall by the wayside as they sought a way of working that fit them best, they often struggled and sometimes outright failed.

Therein lies the seed of their downfall—finding a way of working that *fit them* best. In so doing, they often dismissed the inspect-and-adapt loop as superfluous, preferring to believe that they didn't need a formal structure to make themselves continuously improve. In so doing, they gave themselves tacit permission to sweep their dysfunctions under the rug (again). Had they kept the inspect-and-adapt loop alive, the various mash-ups of Scrum with other agile and nonagile methods would likely have been adapted until they succeeded. Heed the example.

This role name, *agile coach*, plays the field and keeps its options open. Should one agile framework be superseded by another, the more generic name will likely still be used in common conversation. And, it honors my previous experience of using Scrum as a base and adding other tools that make sense for the situation at hand. That's why I use it in this book.

Move Toward Agile Coaching

To become an agile coach, you'll need to journey on from where you are now. Even deeply experienced coaches find new places to venture when they learn from the ways their colleagues coach people, whole teams, and the organizations surrounding teams. They (and I) are still on the journey.

SEE ALSO Different coaches from different backgrounds share their personal coaching journeys in Chapter 13, "It's Your Journey."

Whether you are just starting or have been coaching for a while, your journey will be different from every other one before you. The journeys are different, but if you come from a similar background (ScrumMaster, project manager, or tech lead), some common street signs may be the same. Figure 1.2 shows some of those street signs, which are further explored in the sections that follow.

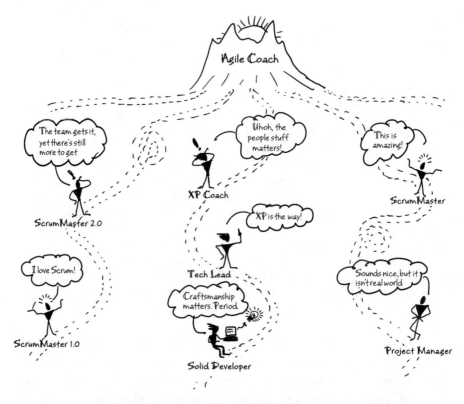

FIGURE 1.2 Although each person's journey to becoming an agile coach follows a different path, some of the street signs along the way may look familiar to those coming from similar backgrounds.

The Road from ScrumMaster to Agile Coach

A ScrumMaster gets a team up and running with Scrum practices and agile principles. For a while, these changes are all the team and company can absorb. In most organizations, working together in high-bandwidth communication within a short timebox to create real products through a team's shared commitment can be radical change enough. After a few sprints, though, the ScrumMaster often notices a significant depth to each of the Scrum practices.

For example, one could go on forever learning ways to set up a retrospective so that team members get a wholly new view of their work and come up with remarkable ideas for improving. By trying things others have blogged about, you could also help the team figure out the best methods for getting sprint planning done. And then there are conflicts and collaboration that arise, both of which many teams do not do well. And all the while the team throws you curveballs that call upon you to come up with new ideas to address what's happening on a daily basis.

The ScrumMaster dives into the Scrum depths and brings tools and techniques from many disciplines to help the team absorb Scrum's practices, principles, values, and roles. At the same time, the ScrumMaster realizes that a significant amount of time gets spent coaching people in the wider organization to support the team and become agile themselves.

Probably around this same time, the ScrumMaster starts up another team and will be the ScrumMaster across teams, which provides new perspectives. Patterns emerge, and the common impediments and glories of the teams become evident in new ways.

A COMMON PROGRESSION FROM SCRUMMASTER TO AGILE COACH

ScrumMaster turned agile coach =
    Certified ScrumMaster training +
    several team start-ups and ScrumMastering experiences +
    getting mentored by someone with more experience +
    adopting ideas from other allied disciplines +
    coaching people outside the team, not just holding the outsiders at bay +
    dealing with the organizational impediments around the teams

---

Since multiple teams are in play now, other people will step forward to try their hand at ScrumMastering. This causes the ScrumMaster to be newly born as a mentor, working with emerging ScrumMasters to help them learn the job and make the needed changes to get good at it. After a while of starting up new teams, ScrumMastering them, and then mentoring new ScrumMasters, the ScrumMaster has turned into an agile coach (or *Scrum coach* if you want to stick with Scrum parlance).

An agile (or Scrum) coach is

- Someone who appreciates the depths of agile practices and principles and can help teams appreciate them, too

- Someone who has faced the big dragons, organizational impediments, and has become a coach to managers and other outsiders in the course of addressing them

- Someone who can help management at all levels of the organization to understand the benefits of working agile
- Someone who has brought ideas from professional facilitation, coaching, conflict management, mediation, theater, and more, to help the team become a high-performance team—the way you always imagined a high-performance team could be when you allowed yourself to dream

The Road from Project Manager to Agile Coach

A project manager and an agile coach are not even as much alike as a house cat and a jaguar. They are simply not in the same family. A project manager plans and controls, supervising throughout. A coach guides. A project manager's success equals the success of the project. An agile coach's success equals the team's continual improvement and their pursuit of high performance. The two are focused on completely different things and thus act completely differently. For these reasons, the road from project manager to agile coach may be a bit longer than others. It was for me. And, it was the single best thing that has happened in my career.

The road starts with training in agile, whatever agile framework you plan to use. Then comes practice on teams, which leads to multiple teams in succession over time. While working with teams, it's important to be mentored by someone who has made the transition from project manager to agile coach. Many beliefs underlying plan-driven project management must be deprogrammed before one can become a successful agile coach, and a mentor can help you through the transition. Table 1.1 lists some of these.

TABLE 1.1   Core underpinnings of project management are replaced

Project management belief	Replaced with
We can plan the work and work the plan.	Planning is essential; plans are useless.*
The triple constraints can be traded off for one another to correct for unknowns.	Time and budget (people) are held constant. Only scope flexes.
The plan gets more accurate over time as we flesh out the project through phases of activity: requirements, design, development, testing, and so on.	A plan gets more accurate over time because it is constantly revised and trued up to the team's actual performance.

Project management belief	Replaced with
Delivering on time, within budget, and on scope equals success.	Clients getting the business value they need is the only measure of success.
Scope can be locked down with later discoveries being handled as change requests against the scheduled end date.	Scope remains flexible, and changes of any kind are welcomed even late in the project.
Controlling through the project plan is my job.	Controlling through a plan is not possible; releasing the team into the safety of agile is my only measure of control. So, I coach the team to use agile well.
Completing tasks and delivering deliverables indicate progress and value delivered.	Only delivered end products indicate progress and value delivered.

* After his presidency, Dwight D. Eisenhower said, "In preparing for battle, I have always found that plans are useless but planning is indispensable." Battles, like most projects, are unpredictable things that call for an empirical approach such as agile.

Generally, the underlying beliefs in plan-driven management are replaced with this simple fact: Gravity works.

Rock climbers know that gravity works. They understand it. They accept it. They plan for it. I was made newly aware of this as I hiked past a group of rock climbers in action, with all their gear deployed, ropes hanging down, and people clinging to the side of a vertical rock face far above me. As I later made my way around their cars in the parking area, I noticed a bumper sticker that said, simply, "Gravity Works." Yes, it does. Rock climbers know this and plan for it. So do agile coaches.

I use this metaphor to illustrate that, in our physical environment, some things are simply taken as a given. Constant. Always present. Undeniable. So, too, in our work environment.

Clients' needs change. Gravity.

What the team can do is known only to them and changes over time. Gravity.

The world moves at an unbelievably fast pace and creates situations no one could have foreseen. Gravity.

You cannot make a commitment on anyone else's behalf and expect committed behavior from them. Gravity.

Agile accepts gravity and accommodates its pull within its very practices and principles. Dealing with gravity is built in.

Project managers using plan-driven tactics attempt to defy gravity. So, throughout one's journey from project manager to agile coach, this central idea must be wrestled with and accepted: Gravity works.

A COMMON PROGRESSION FROM PROJECT MANAGER TO AGILE COACH

A project manager turned agile coach =

Agile training +

several ScrumMaster experiences (or the equivalent in your agile framework) +

getting mentored by someone who has made the transition from project manager to agile coach +

adopting ideas from other allied disciplines +

coaching people outside the team, not just holding the outsiders at bay +

dealing with the organizational impediments around the teams

As you progress, you will determine whether you want to make the transition to agile coach. Perhaps you are drawn to the product owner role because it includes work similar to the scoping and visioning you enjoyed as a project manager. Perhaps you want to be a team member as you dust off long-lost (but loved) skills. Or, perhaps you learn that agile coaching is perfect for you, so you dive in.

Maybe you decide that you will not make the transition and choose instead to continue using plan-driven skills with nonagile teams. Having worked agile, you have probably developed a keener sense of which projects are appropriate for a defined, plan-driven approach. Look for these, knowing that these projects will require you to try to defy gravity less.

Having a mentor help you through this change is critical. An agile coach mentor offers in-the-moment coaching to help you see how agile works and to bring it to your attention when you inadvertently fall back into your plan-driven mind-sets. These mind-sets run deep and come up in so many ways—in the need to tell team members what to do, in the built-in reaction to say "yes" to the client's latest interpretation of their requirements and then hope that the team can come through, or in committing to a date and informing the team afterward.

Many times, you, and even the team, will not realize your project management belief system has kicked in again until your mentor points it out and helps you see that an agile coach does none of this. Instead, an agile coach knows that the simple practices of agile done well have an answer for all of these situations and more. So, the coach focuses on getting teams to do agile well. The rest follows as a natural benefit.

The Road from Tech Lead to Agile Coach

Sometimes, agile coaching skills get added to one's bag of tricks as ways to further assist people developing their technical skills. The road from tech lead to agile coach falls into this category. Tech leads often start out as solid developers, honing the skills of their own software craftsmanship, and over time begin to mentor other developers. Along the way, new techniques and practices such as those from the discipline of Extreme Programming (XP) arise and get incorporated into the tech lead's repertoire. Pretty soon, the tech lead starts teaching others XP and working with them, side by side, to help them perform the practices well. The tech lead calls himself an XP coach, which looks a lot like being a basketball coach. The basketball coach knows the game inside and out; drills the basics into each player through teaching, repetition, and coaching; and then helps them add all that up to strategies that win games. The basketball coach's greatest assets are subject-matter expertise and the means to transfer that expertise to others. So, too, are the greatest assets of an XP coach.

Then, the teaching and mentoring expand across teams and take on the shape of helping excellence in software development emerge on a larger scale. At this scale, the problems inherent in the wider organization become barriers to advancing the cause of software craftsmanship. The tech lead realizes that being "head's up" to deal with these limitations and dysfunctions as bottlenecks can help many teams at once and proves an interesting challenge as it calls him to exercise a whole new set of skills such as facilitating the process and influencing others.

At some point, the tech lead starts using the term *agile coach* to describe himself. His work goes beyond teaching technical skills, although that remains the center of it, because he now also pays equal attention to the management framework surrounding the team and the "people stuff" that seems ever-present. When this agile coach can deftly navigate challenges inside and outside teams and move them into the pursuit of high performance on all levels, not just technical excellence, he has earned the title.

An Agile Coach Emerges

Regardless of the path you take or what background you came from, as you successfully work with agile teams, you begin to change. Telltale signs let you know that you are emerging as an agile coach. Table 1.2 lists some of these signs.

TABLE 1.2 Telltale signs that an agile coach is emerging

Coach will move away from	Coach will move toward
Coordinating individual contributions	Coaching the whole team for collaboration
Being a subject-matter expert	Being a facilitator *for* the team
Being invested in specific outcomes	Being invested in the team's overall performance
Knowing the answer	Asking the team for the answer
Directing	Letting the team find their own way
Driving	Guiding
Talk of deadlines and technical options	Talk of business value delivery
Talk of doing the optimal thing	Talk of doing the right thing for the business right now
Fixing problems	Taking problems to the team

What you do as the coach and what you talk about shift as you move from managing to coaching. When the behaviors on the right side of the table happen more often and start to come naturally, you are solidly on the road to becoming an agile coach. Keep going.

Native Wiring

Over time, I have noticed that the people who make resoundingly successful transitions into agile coaching have a few things in common—things they might not even recognize in themselves. Let's call these common characteristics *native wiring*. They seem to be present in the people I observe from the very beginning and cause me to predict, "Yes, he'll probably make it." Conversely, I notice their absence as I look back and consider why someone did not successfully make the transition to agile coach. And, sometimes I have been wrong, so use these as general guides, not rules.

I created this list by reflecting on my successful agile coach apprentices and what made the transition to agile coaching look smooth. Some of them had a trouble-free time becoming an agile coach, easy by comparison to my very arduous (and worthwhile) journey. Looking at the list now, I can see that I have adopted native wiring mind-sets over time. Ten years ago, probably only half of the native wiring aspects were true for me. Now, all of them live in me and form the steadfast core from which I coach agile teams.

As you think about whether you will be a good agile coach, consider the ten abilities and mind-sets prevalent in people who have the native wiring for coaching:

1. They have an uncanny ability to "read a room." As soon as they step into a room, they can tell what basically happened while they were out. They instantaneously read the emotion in the air and know whether all is well.

2. They care about people more than products. Sure, the focus on products is still there, but it's accomplished through caring about people, who, in turn, knowing they are cared for and supported in their growth, create great products.

3. They cultivate curiosity. They know when they don't know. They don't know what people are thinking or feeling, and they don't know why things are as they are. So they ask.

4. They believe that people are basically good. Yes, they know the hard cases exist. But even the most difficult people are good inside, perhaps just a little further back on the road to being a full human being. So, they meet these people where they are and help them take the steps they can.

5. They know that plans fall apart, so they act in the moment with the team, rather than holding on to any one idea or hope about how things should turn out.

6. They have a thirst for learning. They know that they are not done growing yet (ever).

7. They believe that any group of people can do good things in the world, given a growth environment and an audacious goal. They believe excellence exists and is worth pursuing.

8. They have a low tolerance for institutional reasons that hold people back from excellence, the ones that "just are because they have always been." It drives them crazy when someone says, "Yeah, I know it's a waste of time, but that's the way we do it here."

9. They believe that disequilibrium is essential. Chaos and destruction are simply building blocks for something better. Messiness is expected.

10. They risk being wrong. When they are wrong, they own up to it and move on.

Your background doesn't matter. Tester, project manager, business process expert, trainer, or minister—if you have this native wiring running through you or you can adopt it into your life over time, there's a good chance that you will turn into a good coach.

Make Agile Coaching Your Personal Expression

This book offers the provocative and the practical, from alternate ways to think to specific models and tools to use with teams. Amid all this information and many suggestions, you must find your own voice as an agile coach. No one does agile coaching the same way. This book presents an experienced viewpoint of being an agile coach based on one good way—my way—of coaching agile teams.

With practice and attention, you will discover your way, your unique voice as an agile coach. Although written in direct language, nothing in this book should be misconstrued as a directive or a cookbook. Nothing should be faithfully reproduced as a ritual or rigid practice.

Shape everything you learn in this book by your unique way of approaching and coaching the team. You know your context best. You certainly know yourself best. Keep this knowledge in the forefront as you consider the ideas contained in this book and as you encounter many more ideas in your practice with agile teams.

Honor your context and yourself, and make sure you don't stay in your comfort zone. Challenge yourself. Make coaching agile teams an expression of your personal excellence.

A Refresher

Let's lock in the ideas from this chapter:

- Becoming an agile coach entails education, experience, and practice.
- "Being" an agile coach in all you do sets a powerful example for everyone you coach.

- Your constant calling to being the best agile coach you can be means that you recover from attitudes and behaviors that restrict your team's expression of agile done well.

- The paths toward being an agile coach are as many and varied as the places from which individuals start their journey.

- The qualities common to most successful agile coaches reflect openness, people orientation, and a deep and passionate pursuit of personal and professional excellence.

Additional Resources

Adkins, L. 2008. The Road from Project Manager to Agile Coach. YouTube. Use this video to jar yourself from your current modes of thinking and open yourself up to the perspectives and mind-sets that help good agile coaches emerge.

Pink, D. 2006. *A Whole New Mind: Why Right-Brainers Will Rule the Future*. New York: Riverhead. The future of high-touch, high-concept work has arrived. This book offers solid evidence for why this is so and what you can do to flourish in it. Many of the ideas offered in the book can help you develop or solidify your "native wiring" as an agile coach.

Wheatley, M. 2006. *Leadership and the New Science: Discovering Order in a Chaotic World*. San Francisco: Berrett-Koehler. This is essential reading for any agile coach (and all the managers an agile coach encounters) to understand why the machine model of getting work done no longer applies and what the role of "leader" in self-organizing systems, such as agile teams, should be.

Chapter 2

Expect High Performance

Teams often get the basics of agile running within the first few sprints. Agile frameworks, designed to be simple, are just that—simple and easy to get started. And the practices, well-coached, are easy to set in motion, too.

It doesn't take long before the rituals built into agile can leave the team feeling like they are caught in a never-ending hamster wheel—always moving from one ritual to the next and from one sprint to the next and the next and the next. They are making progress on the product they create together but spinning in the hamster wheel nonetheless.

Beyond the company results the team is asked to produce, teams need something else to strive for—something to change the hamster wheel into a journey of their own making. Instead of seeing the same scenery in the hamster wheel again and again, they need to see different signposts and landmarks along the way indicating progress toward something resonant and worthwhile. This "something" is the quest for high performance. It's the daily act of, together, striving to be the best they can be.

We know that motivation in the knowledge age comes when people achieve autonomy, mastery, and a sense of purpose (Pink 2009). Setting high performance as your baseline expectation and giving teams a way to achieve it

---

By the time you finish this chapter, you will be able to answer these questions:

- How can I set my expectation that the team simply will be high-performing?
- What references and images can I use to teach the team a useful definition of high performance?
- How can I help the team create their own path to high performance?

play directly into these powerful motivators. Thus invigorated, everyone wins. The company gets better results. The company gets teams that can do anything. The teams, and the individuals who comprise them, achieve more autonomy, mastery, and purpose in their lives. Everyone tastes the sweet fruits of high performance.

Set the Expectation

Expecting high performance does not mean that you demand it. Expecting high performance means that you simply know achieving it is more than possible; it is normal. Expecting high performance means that you believe the team can attain it, so you hold them, compassionately and firmly, to that expectation. By believing, you urge them to strive for a vision of what they can become together. They get called forth to be more than they are now.

This propels them forward sprint after sprint and release after release. All along the way, they touch moments of greatness together, fueling their desire to continue the journey. They also experience disillusionment and heartache, causing them to fall back. Through it all, you remain steadfast in your belief in high performance—and in them.

You believe in high performance, but what is it? It's a slippery thing; high-performance models, assessments, and descriptions abound, yet a satisfying all-inclusive dictionary-type definition eludes. You will not find that kind of definition of high performance in this book, either. I seek not to pin it down but to free it by acknowledging that high performance is not as much about achieving a certain state as it is a journey toward something better. Teams that "outperform all reasonable expectations" and "even surprise themselves" may be on such a journey (Katzenbach and Smith 2003). So, too, may teams that get fractionally better all the time.

As their agile coach, help them start their journey toward high performance by simply setting your expectation that they will achieve it. Then, give them the raw materials they will use to create their own resonant definition of high performance—a vision that lets them imagine it and reach for it. Coach them to choose the next step on their path (and the next and the next), all the while staying aimed toward their inspirational vision of high performance.

Create a sense of anticipation, expectancy, and excitement for this journey—first in yourself and then let it flow to them. Lead by believing. After all, if you don't believe they can get to high performance, why should they?

Introduce a Metaphor for High Performance

Metaphor is a powerful thing. Professional coaches have known this for a long time. In fact, "metaphor" is a core skill taught in professional coaching courses (Whitworth et al. 2007).

> "I'm the glue that holds this family together."
>
> "I'm the pebble in your shoe, reminding you to tread lightly."
>
> "I am a thousand candles lighting the way."
>
> "I am a bird soaring above it all."
>
> "I am a beacon calling you forth."

Coaches ask questions that help clients create their own metaphor, one that is visceral and resonant. Clients use the metaphor to guide them through the events unfolding in their lives.

If it's keeping one's head above water during a time of rapid and unpredictable change, perhaps the metaphor "I am a bird soaring above it all" serves to help the client stay balanced as waves of change crash all around. Perhaps the client has a calling, something important to share with the world. Maybe then the metaphor "I am a thousand candles lighting the way" helps keep the juiciness of the purpose alive and resonant as it fuels their work.

Teams use metaphors the same way. Through your coaching, a team may create their own metaphor to help guide them through turbulent or exciting times. To get them started and to help them create a vision for high performance, offer images that spark metaphor. One such image features a tree: the High Performance Tree.

The High Performance Tree

The High Performance Tree came into existence when I was coaching several teams that had been together for some time. They were doing fairly well with the basic practices of agile (standard meetings and accomplishing sprint goals), and they were consistently delivering results that mattered, yet their managers knew there was more to get.

As their agile coach, I had no idea how they were going to move toward high performance, and I knew each team would do it their own way no matter what I offered, so creating a highway or even a meandering pathway for them to follow wouldn't work. I had to come up with something evocative that would kindle their desire to pursue high performance on their own terms, something each team could use to come up with their own highway or pathway. Fresh from my own learning about the power of metaphor, I created the High Performance Tree (see Figure 2.1).

Introduce the tree to the team any time. Doing so at the beginning, perhaps in the team start-up, sets them up well, but it also works to introduce the tree as a way to look at a problem or deficiency when one crops up. Once introduced, refer to it as situations arise in the team and use it as material for retrospectives.

To introduce the tree to the team, just draw the tree from the roots up as you teach the meaning of the Scrum values and as you list the characteristics of high performance. You can see from the illustration that you need not be a good artist to do this.

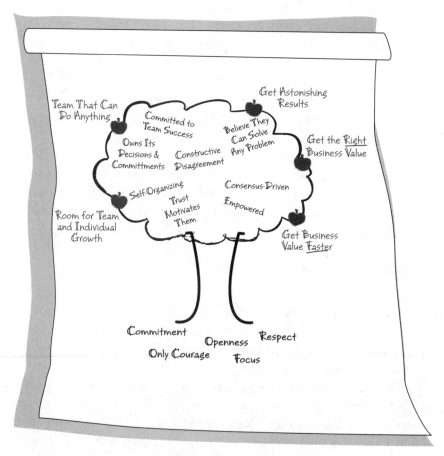

FIGURE 2.1   High Performance Tree

As you write the words for the roots of the tree, teach the Scrum values. Simply stated, they are as follows:

Commitment: Be willing to commit to a goal. Scrum provides people all the authority they need to meet their commitments.

Focus: Do your job. Focus all your efforts and skills on doing the work that you've committed to doing. Don't worry about anything else.

Openness: Scrum keeps everything about a project visible to everyone.

Respect: Individuals are shaped by their background and their experiences. It is important to respect the different people who comprise a team.

Courage: Have the courage to commit, to act, to be open, and to expect respect (Schwaber and Beedle 2001).

If you don't use Scrum but think these values will serve, remove the references to the word *Scrum*. (You don't even need to mention that they come from Scrum.) You can also use Extreme Programming values in place of, or in addition to, the Scrum values if your team develops software. The definitions of these values assume Extreme Programming practices occupy the center of the team's software development repertoire:

Communication: Keep the right communications flowing by employing many practices that can't be done without communicating. Problems with projects can invariably be traced back to somebody not talking to somebody else about something important.

Simplicity: What is the simplest thing that could possibly work? Make a bet that it is better to do a simple thing today and pay a little more tomorrow to change it if necessary than to do a more complicated thing today that may never be used anyway.

Feedback: Concrete feedback about the current state of the system is absolutely priceless. Optimism is an occupational hazard of programming. Feedback is the treatment.

Courage: Have the courage it takes to develop good software, which may mean throwing away code and changing direction, even late in development. What's to say that you won't ever develop yourself into a corner? Courage (Beck and Andres 2004).

If neither of these sets of values fits and your company has established values that will work well, then use those instead. Here's the key: The values you use must be defined so that they are relatable to agile, easily understandable (not full of abstract notions or business jargon), and resonant. Use only those values that evoke a sense of desire in the team members. You know you have a good set when team members consider the definitions and say, "Yes, I want to be more like that. I want us to be more like that. I want our company to be more like that."

As you continue the drawing, go on spinning a vision for them. If the roots are strong, they nourish the tree, and the tree grows up to the sky—straighter and taller. It sprouts leaves that gather in more and more sunlight. As the leaves gather light, they, in turn, nourish the tree. Everything grows stronger, taller, and greener. The tree has become an inviting place, and the team notices they have sprouted some things themselves—the characteristics of high collaboration and, thus, high performance (adapted from Tabaka 2006):

- They are **self-organizing** rather than role- or title-based.
- They are **empowered** to make decisions.
- They truly believe that **as a team they can solve any problem**.
- They are committed to **team success** vs. success at any cost.
- The team **owns its decisions and commitments**.
- **Trust**, vs. fear or anger, motivates them.
- They are **consensus-driven**, with full divergence and then convergence.
- And they live in a world of constant **constructive disagreement**.

These characteristics shape the leaves of the tree. If the roots are strong and the leaves gather in enough light, the tree will bear fruit. These are the fruits of high performance.

The first fruits you may notice are these: You get business value *faster*, and then you get the *right* business value more often. As the roots (values) and leaves (high performance) continue to grow, the team may even bear the fruit of *astonishing* results—the kind that causes a business to leapfrog its competition and the kind agile was meant to create. Through these, two other fruits appear: a team that can *truly do anything* and a team that offers room for team and individual *growth*. These two fruits are the ones that rejuvenate the whole tree and give back again and again. They fuel sustainable growth.

No matter when you introduce the tree, just having the drawing in the team's work room will be enough. It hangs there, a quiet reminder that high performance is normal and your ardent expectation. As in Figure 2.2, it hangs there when they get into trouble or get into a rut and you point to it and say, "Where are our roots weak?" It hangs there when they are showing all the signs of a high-performing team yet their products reek of mediocrity. You sense they can do better, so you say to them, "What fruits do you want to get now?"

- Where are your roots weak?
- What leaves do you want to work on?
- Are you getting any fruits?

Commitment

Courage

Focus

Openness

Respect

FIGURE 2.2 Use the High Performance Tree to spur the team to take their next step toward high performance.

Using the tree this way, your questions become challenges to them, a way to call them forth to a brighter vision of what they can become together. When they take up the challenge, they create the next step in their journey toward high performance. In so doing, they lay down their own path.

For example, perhaps the team feels disappointed in the quality of their work and, through considering the High Performance Tree, concludes that they aren't truly consensus-driven. They recognize that they tend to jump to the first thing possible rather than hearing lots of ideas from all team members. They think that if they entertained a divergence of ideas before converging on the one to use, the quality of their products would increase. So, they might circle "Consensus-Driven" on the High Performance Tree and write themselves a reminder that doing this well means hearing a lot of ideas first. Getting better at being consensus-driven is this team's next step toward high performance.

A second team has been missing their sprint goals lately. Someone notices the word *Commitment* drawn as one of the roots of the High Performance Tree and muses aloud, "I wonder if our problem is that we're not really committed to what we say we are going to do." In the conversation that follows, the team discusses how they have been letting extraneous demands on their time and energy take away from their feeling of commitment. They recognize that as soon as they let one distraction in, a bunch more seem to follow until they are doing everything but what they said they would do. So, they make a pact: "From now on, we will help one another push away distractions so we can truly commit and deliver what we said we would. We will put aside our discomfort and challenge each other when we notice someone has become distracted. We will call distractions out for what they are—impediments." They write these words like a banner across the top of their High Performance Tree. Truly committing is this team's next step toward high performance.

As they address their shortcomings and make plans for getting better, encourage them to make their reflections and choices equal portions of lightness and heaviness. They need not be engaged in self-flagellation to prove to you or anyone else that they are in the act of improving. Hold out to them that the work of becoming high performing can be done with humor, curiosity, and appreciation, too.

> *Over-seriousness is a warning sign for mediocrity and bureaucratic thinking. People who are seriously committed to mastery and high performance are secure enough to lighten up.*
>
> —*Michael J. Gelb*

Approached with amusement or anguish, moving swiftly or sluggishly trundling along, there are no two paths alike, and you cannot even begin to imagine what a team's path might look like in the end. So, it's best that you don't try and, instead, rely on the team to create the path that feels right for them.

You can tell when the tree has taken hold. It's when the team talks about the tree as a metaphor for themselves and their chosen pathway to high performance:

"We can grow if we strengthen our roots."

"We're a tree; we can bend."

"The wind may shake us, but it will not break us."

That's when the power of metaphor shines through and becomes something useful to them, helping them survive turbulent change or reach for that next big goal.

Another Metaphor: Building the Foundation

If the High Performance Tree doesn't grab you, try a different image. Make up your own. It need not be fancy or complicated; straightforward works well, too. Scrum trainer and mentor Tobias Mayer uses the imagery of "building a foundation" in his classes. It's a simple list of five things that make Scrum (and all agile methods) work. He tells people that if you have these five things, then you have everything you need, and the other details will work themselves out (Mayer 2009):

Empiricism: Succeed through a rapid progression of failures. Drive by hindsight, not foresight.

Self-organization: The people closest to the problem know best how to solve the problem.

Collaboration: Foster a "yes, and" mind-set. Re-conceive ideas; do not compromise (Austin and Devin 2003).

Prioritization: Focus! Do the next right thing.

Rhythm: Breathe, and the rest will follow.

About using these, Mayer says, "I see these five principles as the foundation of emergence, which (metaphorically) is Scrum in flower, blooming. Everything emerges in Scrum: ideas, teams, process, design, architecture, products...."

Introducing the imagery of "building a foundation" to the team creates a rich field for metaphor to surface and for them to generate a vision of their journey toward greatness together. See? You need not even call it high performance if that closes people down. Journey toward greatness works well, too. Perhaps you will hear team members use the imagery you offered to create momentum-producing metaphors for themselves:

"Where is our foundation weak?"

"Have we crumbled a bit lately?"

"If we were to lay a new cornerstone today, what would we chisel on it?"

The Destination Never Comes

An agile team's journey toward high performance is just that—a journey. The team may touch high performance now and then, they may even live in a state of high performance for a while, but they have never "arrived" at high performance where the story ends. No, the story continues.

Almost assuredly, as soon as they start living in high performance, something will happen to set them back. A team member will get promoted and start micromanaging his teammates. The company will reorganize, and a new vice president will assert her will over the team's direction. Someone on the team will go on maternity leave, someone will get married and move away, and someone else will simply move on. Every time one of these things happens, team dynamics will change, and the team will take a step back from high performance.

Given this, teach the team to honor their ability to fully and quickly recover from setbacks—even to honor that above the progress they've made so far or where they currently "are" on their journey. For sure, setbacks will occur. Your expectation that they will achieve greatness together, a contagion they catch and then expect of themselves, will sustain them even when the way is rough.

A Refresher

Let's lock in the ideas from this chapter:

- Make sure the team knows that you expect high performance and long for them to reach for it.
- Ignite their journey with imagery and challenges that allow them to create their own path to high performance.
- Support the next step they have chosen by coaching for their greatness and believing they can attain whatever they put their effort and passion into.

Additional Resources

Schwaber, K., and M. Beedle. 2001. *Agile Software Development with Scrum.* Upper Saddle River, NJ: Prentice Hall. Tucked away in the last chapter of this book are the Scrum values. Reading the clear and compelling definitions of these values is mandatory for any agile coach. Reading them several times over a period of time, and considering them carefully, is mandatory for any great agile coach.

Pink, D. 2009. The Surprising Science of Motivation. http://blog.ted.com/2009/08/the_surprising.php. Want to know what matters to people and what this has to do with why they would reach for high performance? Watch this short talk to find out. If you want more, get his book *Drive: The Surprising Truth About What Motivates Us,* which goes deeper.

References

Austin, R., and L. Devin. 2003. *Artful Making: What Managers Need to Know About How Artists Work.* Upper Saddle River, NJ: Prentice Hall.

Beck, K., and C. Andres. 2004. *Extreme Programming Explained: Embrace Change, Second Edition.* Boston: Addison-Wesley.

Katzenbach, J., and D. Smith. 2003. *The Wisdom of Teams: Creating the High-Performance Organization.* New York: HarperCollins.

Mayer, T. 2009. Private communication with Tobias Mayer on September 23, 2009.

Pink, D. 2009. The Surprising Science of Motivation. http://blog.ted.com/2009/08/the_surprising.php.

Schwaber, K., and M. Beedle. 2001. *Agile Software Development with Scrum.* Upper Saddle River, NJ: Prentice Hall.

Tabaka, J. 2006. *Collaboration Explained: Facilitation Skills for Software Project Leaders.* Boston: Addison-Wesley.

Whitworth, L., K. Kimsey-House, H. Kimsey-House, and P. Sandahl. 2007. *Co-Active Coaching: New Skills for Coaching People Toward Success in Work and Life, Second Edition.* Mountain View, CA: Davies-Black.

Chapter 3

Master Yourself

I have a confession to make. I am a recovering command-and-control-aholic. I know I'm recovering because people who meet me now say, "No! You? A command-and-control-aholic? I don't believe it." When I hear this, I smile and thank them, feeling very proud of my hard-won transformation. Still, I know that the command-and-control tendency runs deep, so when I start coaching an agile team, I ask the team members to call me on command-and-control behavior. They can't imagine they will ever have to do this, but then we get into some stressful situation, and I start trying to control what they do and how they do it. They say to me, "Hey! You just morphed into the command-and-control monster. We want our coach back." They have provided me with yet another reminder that my command-and-control monster, although mostly tamed, lurks in the background waiting for the chance to take over.

By the time you finish this chapter, you will be able to answer these questions:

- Where do I stand with my ability to recognize my natural reactions to conflict, my ability to speak without doing harm to others, my willingness to be a servant as leader, and my skill in working with my own emotional responses? Why do these things matter, anyway?

- How much command-and-control-ism is alive in me? What should I do about that?

- What does "master yourself" mean? What are some practical ways to start doing it?

- What can I do in the heat of the moment with teams to improve my ability to respond to their needs?

- What does it mean to listen, speak, and be with teams consciously?

Just as it takes many reminders for me to curb my command-and-control tendencies, mastering yourself so that you can be the kind of coach the team most needs doesn't happen in a single shot, either. It requires constant awareness, practice, and reinforcement from notions such as this: Coaching starts with you, but it is not about you.

Instead, agile coaching is about what you can bring to the team to help them unlock the potential hidden even from themselves. In so doing, they become aware of their competencies and talents and what it means to bring those skills together into a new entity called *the team*.

Yes, you will find many useful and necessary ideas and tools to teach the team along the way. The most useful thing you can bring to the team, however, is simply this: you.

When you coach, bring yourself. Bring yourself completely prepared, ready to coach and to offer the team what it needs in each moment. To do this, you must bring your clear, grounded presence.

In your always-on, busy life it may feel normal to speed through your days scattered and ungrounded. You're simply full. In the context of agile teams, you may find yourself filled up with your ideas and experiences, hopes and fears, plans and agendas, and dreams for them and for you. Being filled up with these things means that you have no room to see the team members for who they are and the given circumstances for what they are. If you could, though, you would see both team members and circumstances clearly and, having truly seen, react clearly for them.

This calls you to master yourself and to come to the team with your uncluttered, unambiguous presence. Empty yourself of personal agendas, emotions, and thoughts. Once emptied, you reflect like a clear mirror in which the team may see themselves anew. Once emptied, you act in *their* best interest rather than from your own needs.

If you feel full now, you may wonder how to begin. Start with yourself. Start with self-awareness.

We see self-awareness as "step 1" in weight-loss programs, abuse-recovery programs, leadership retreats—any endeavor that stimulates recovery and personal growth. The same goes for coaching. This chapter presents you with a host of ideas about good agile coaching that allow you to reflect on yourself and ask some pivotal questions: How does this idea fit with my current world view? How would I have to change to make room for this idea? What practices will I adopt to help me become uncluttered, grounded, open to ideas, and ready to coach?

Start with Self-Awareness

Knowing how you react in certain situations and knowing what "pushes your buttons"—these are important dimensions for knowing yourself and who you are growing into. This self-awareness coupled with your assessment of your current abilities signals your maturity as an agile coach and points you to your next step toward improvement.

Let's call that next step your **growing edge**. As an agile coach, challenged to constantly improve for the sake of your teams, identify your growing edge and do not be afraid to push your limits. You'll know you have found your growing edge when you feel a bit uncomfortable in your own skin. For some coaches, their growing edge requires them to practice seeing each person as a human being rather than an obstacle to getting things done. For me, it's clamping down on the automatic response to take over when things are not proceeding exactly as I would have them. In both cases, you consciously face your shortcomings and choose to practice that which will help teams achieve wild success.

To find your growing edge, let's explore these areas one at a time in the sections to come:

- How you react to conflict
- The words you choose in everyday conversation
- Your position on being a servant leader
- Your comfort with emotional intelligence

I invite you to move slowly through the next few sections, taking the time to reflect on the dimensions so that you can better understand yourself as an agile coach. In so doing, you can recognize your instinctual behaviors and make a conscious choice to follow them or choose something different. As you explore, know that some ideas may feel out of reach for you right now or may not be right for you at all. If so, don't go that far, but do stay on your growing edge.

What Is Your Native Conflict Response Mode?

A number of diagnostics can help you recognize and name your knee-jerk conflict response mode. Many of them are based on the Thomas Kilmann Instrument (TKI), which is a categorization of common conflict response modes: Competing, Collaborating, Compromising, Accommodating, and Avoiding (Kilmann 2007). According to CPP, Inc. (2009), the five modes are described along two dimensions—assertiveness, or the extent to which people try to satisfy their own concerns, and cooperativeness, or the extent to which people try to satisfy the concerns of another person. The modes break down like this:

- **Competing:** Assertive and not cooperative
- **Collaborating:** Assertive and cooperative
- **Compromising:** In the middle on both dimensions
- **Accommodating:** Cooperative and not assertive
- **Avoiding:** Neither assertive nor cooperative (CPP, Inc. 2009)

Think about the last time you were in a conflict. It doesn't have to be about work; any conflict will do. What was your response mode? Were you driven by a desire to assert your own needs or to satisfy another's concerns?

Now, go through that same thought process for a few more conflict scenarios. Context matters, so don't be surprised to find that you react to some scenarios using the Compromising mode and others using the Competing mode.

To really know which of these modes is your "natural tendency," you can take one of many online assessments. Or, you can guess. Or, you can use another method such as asking a friend or family member. The people who know you best and love you dearly have insight that can help you categorize your instinctual reactions to conflict. Ask them.

No matter what you use to learn about your response to conflict, the goal remains the same: to recognize your native conflict response mode so that you take notice when it arises. From this knowledge, you make a conscious choice to go with the response or select something different—whichever you think will serve the people you coach (and the situation) best.

How Violent Is Your Communication?

Probably few of us would say that we bring violence to the people we coach. Most likely our team rooms do not erupt in violence, at least not the physical kind. What about the verbal kind? Although we may not consider the way we talk to be violent, our words can wound people and cause them pain.

To see this in action in your coaching, consider these questions honestly, and count how many "yes" and "no" answers you come up with (adapted from Baran and Center for NonViolent Communication 2004):

- Do you spend some time each day quietly reflecting on how you would like to relate to yourself and others?
- Do you remember that all human beings have the same needs?

- Before every conversation, do you check your intention to see whether you are as interested in others getting their needs met as your own?

- When asking someone to do something, do you check first to see whether you are making a request or a demand?

- Instead of saying what you *don't* want someone to do, do you say what you *do* want the person to do?

- Instead of saying what you want someone to *be*, do you say what action you'd like the person to take that you hope will help the person be that way?

- Before agreeing or disagreeing with anyone's opinions, do you try to tune in to what the person is feeling and needing?

- Instead of saying "no," do you say what need of yours prevents you from saying "yes"?

- If you are feeling upset, do you think about what need of yours is not being met, and what you could do to meet it, instead of thinking about what's wrong with others or yourself?

- Instead of praising someone who did something you like, do you express your gratitude by telling the person what need of yours was met?

If you answered "no" to more than a few of these questions, there is a good chance that your communication has been unintentionally hurtful. It has been violent, and it doesn't matter that you didn't mean it. To have an important impact, the kind of impact a coach needs to have to influence people and help them become good agilists, you must pay attention to your language and take responsibility for your emotional wake (Scott 2007). This means that you own up to your impact whether harm was intended and whether you think the other person should feel hurt or not.

> For a leader, there is no such thing as a trivial comment. Something you might not even remember saying may have had a devastating impact on someone looking to you for guidance and approval (Scott 2007).

As an agile coach, team members look to you for guidance and approval, especially in the beginning when being agile has them at once excited and terrified. The people we coach will not be motivated to change or take a risk when they feel we have hurt them—diagnosed them, judged them, sidestepped

> *When we focus on clarifying what is being observed, felt, and needed rather than on diagnosing and judging, we discover the depth of our own compassion.*
>
> —Dr. Marshall Rosenberg

them, or manipulated them. Go back to the list of questions to see where you answered "no." Consider whether changing those to "yes" answers would increase your ability to influence and reach the people you coach.

Having done that, take a giant step back and consider these questions: How much have you internalized nonviolent communication? How often do you pay attention to the way you interact with people? How often do you take responsibility for your emotional wake?

The answers will provide key bits of information to help you piece together the picture of who you are becoming as an agile coach.

Can You Be Their Servant?

The term *servant leader* gets bandied about frequently when people reach for a model that sums up agile coaching. When I first heard it, I imagined the simple definition of the coach serving the team rather than the team serving the coach. This was certainly different enough from the description of project management leadership I had been working with for many years. In that model, the team certainly served me. All you had to do was attend one of my status meetings to see that in action. So, the simple definition of the coach serving the team was enough of a stretch for me for quite a while.

> *Awareness is not a giver of solace—it is just the opposite. It is a disturber and an awakener.*
>
> —Robert Greenleaf

If you have a history of telling people what to do, perhaps moving toward this simple definition serves as an appropriate amount of change for you. If so, stay here for now.

If you are ready to deepen your understanding of servant leadership and gauge where you stand on some of its main ideas, consider the following from the 1970s essay that coined the term.

On the subject of developing others:

"…Make sure that other people's highest priority needs are being served. The best test, and difficult to administer, is: do those served grow as persons; do they, *while being served*, become healthier, wiser, freer, more autonomous, more likely themselves to become servants?" (Greenleaf 1991)

Ponder these questions: How do you feel about the duty of growing people? How does it fit into your idea of coaching agile teams? Do people leave the teams you coach better than they arrived?

On the subject of listening and giving space for others to respond:

"…Only a true natural servant automatically responds to any problem by listening *first*.

"It is often a devastating question to ask oneself, but it is sometimes important to ask it—'In saying what I have in mind will I really improve on the silence?'" (Greenleaf 1991)

Ponder these questions: What percentage of the time do you listen first? Do people have room to speak when they are around you?

On the subject of accepting one another:

"[People] grow taller when those who lead them empathize and when they are accepted for what they are, even thought their performance may be judged critically in terms of what they are capable of doing." (Greenleaf 1991)

Ponder these questions: How likely are you to accept people as they are and honor where they are on their journey? When you coach, do your judgments create a barrier between you and them?

A powerful model to use for agile coaching, servant leadership builds strength in others (Greenleaf 1991). Strength in others leads to strength in the team, which leads to better, more innovative ideas. As you've considered the core of servant leadership—developing others, listening and giving space, and offering acceptance—where do you stand on your ability to be a servant leader? Know where your growing edge lies. If you're not disturbed and awake, you're not there yet.

Will You Respond Intelligently?

No doubt people characterize you as an intelligent person. You might even have a high IQ, but what about your EQ? EQ, your emotional intelligence quotient, indicates your ability to bring awareness to your emotions as they arise, notice them for what they are, and decide how to best use them (Bradberry and Greaves 2005).

Upping your EQ grows your coaching abilities. There's good news on this front: Unlike other forms of intelligence, emotional intelligence can be learned (Goleman 1998). Books, online assessments, and seminars abound and can help you understand the core skills of the emotionally intelligent. Some of these are listed in the "Additional Resources" section at the end of this chapter. These are skills. You can practice and hone them until you get good at

> *There is a world between stimulus and response. This is where character lives.*
>
> —James Hunter

emotional intelligence. And, as luck would have it, agile teams hand us plenty of opportunities to practice.

How you react to conflict, how you communicate, how well you embrace being the team's servant, and how you bring choice to emotional responses are all facets of who you are becoming as a coach. How and how much you bring these into your coaching is a matter of choice balanced with opportunities lost. The more skilled you become at mastering yourself, the more self-organized and self-monitoring the teams will be. If you cannot or will not do these things well, the consequences will likely not be dire. You just won't be getting as much as you could for the teams or for yourself.

Herein lies the overall pattern in this chapter. With conflict, language, servant leadership, and emotional intelligence, feel your knee-jerk reaction, notice it, and consciously decide what to do with it. Your ability to apply this pattern is a direct measure of your ability to master yourself.

Although you have time to grow into these four aspects of good agile coaching, there's something else that cannot wait, and that's recovering from command-and-control-ism.

Recover from Command-and-Control-ism

Some of you do not have a command-and-control bone in your body. This information still applies to you, so read on. Command-and-control will certainly describe someone you are called to coach—perhaps a product owner, agile manager, or former technical lead finding a new role as an agile team member. Even if you have not personally experienced a command-and-control attitude, you will need to help others recover from it.

For those of you who recognize command-and-control in your own life, read on with yourself in mind. Worry about helping others later. As they say on an airplane, secure your own oxygen mask before assisting others.

When I started recovering from command-and-control-ism, I had to get comfortable with these non-command-and-control thoughts:

> **Be detached from outcomes:** Give the team ample space to come up with the best ideas and build the best product. As an agile coach, you are only one voice on the team when it comes to the specifics of what they will create. Don't linger here; you have a bigger role to play. Stay focused

on *how* the team is working together so you can help them improve the quality and completeness of their work, not only for now but for all the products they will build together. If you stay at the process level and stay away from the details of the team's every decision and plan, you can achieve detachment. Your being detached invites them to attach and to own their results. This helps them achieve those goals asked (and sometimes demanded) of them.

Take it to the team: Believe it or not, you are not the best person to solve the problem, whether the problem lies with the product the team creates or with the way the team works together. Every time you think you need to solve something, stop and raise the observations to the team instead. Let them tell you the root cause and what they will do about it (if anything). If you diagnose the problem and implement a solution, you run the risk of being way off base. Worse, you have subtly undermined the team's ability to solve its own problems.

Be a mirror: Reflect back to them, without judgment, the behavior or symptoms you notice. Let them see themselves through your observation. Simply state what you witness and ask, "Hmmm…what do you think that means?" Then, listen.

Master your words and your face: To do this well, practice nonjudgment and practice nonviolent communication, not only in the tone of your voice and the words you choose but also on your face. If you judge, they will posture around you. You will not get to the core of what is really going on. Instead, you will be told what someone thinks you want to hear. While shedding judgments, retain authenticity. Show your disappointment, sadness, joy, and exuberance when you are sure that you do it for them, not for you.

Let there be silence: Get comfortable with uncomfortable silence. Do not fill it yourself. Let someone else on the team have room to speak. They will.

Model being outrageous: The things that hold teams back will amaze you. These inhibitors center around their beliefs about what they are and are not allowed to do. They may say, "It's just the way things work around here" or "It's normal to wait five days for this type of thing." When you hear these self-limiters, expose them. Ask, "Is this an impediment to getting your work done?" Or ask, "If you had no limitations, what would you do right now?" Be wild, be big, and be bold. You can count on them to tell you when you're being too outrageous. You can't count on them to tell you when you're not being outrageous enough. Let them hear wild ideas from you so that they can question the assumptions that limit them.

Let the team fail: Certainly, don't stand idly by while the team goes careening off a cliff. But do use the dozens of opportunities that arise each sprint to let them fail. Teams that fail together and recover together are much stronger and faster than ones that are protected. And the team may surprise you. The thing you thought was going to harm them may actually work for them. Watch and wait.

Always be their biggest fan, but be careful: Don't offer empty praise, and don't praise them on the "good work they did." The work will flow through the team. It comes and goes. The work itself does not define the team and does not make them great. Getting better as individuals and healthier as a team makes them great. So, notice that. Tell them—and everyone else you encounter—about how much better they are doing *as a team*.

If any of these ideas shock your system, your command-and-control-ism is alive and kicking. It's OK. These things take time. As you recover, recognize that command-and-control can be wielded softly. You need not be a tyrant, or even loud, to be in the grip of command-and-control-ism. So, when you think you have removed it from your life, look a little deeper. It's probably still there.

TRY THIS

To recover from command-and-control-ism, extend trust to the team. This can be a hard pill to swallow because command-and-control behavior creates a vicious cycle that erodes trust. Here's how it works: You don't trust the team, so you tell them what to do. They do what you said, not really what they thought they should do. The results are not what you wanted, so you tell them what to do again, this time more explicitly. And the cycle continues. In this cycle, everyone loses trust.

An agile coach who stays in the world of lost trust is impaired.

To teach yourself to trust again, take yourself on a judgment fast. For one or two sprints, extend trust to the team, and suspend your judgment. Tell them you trust them to know what to do. Do not interfere in their workings. Instead, notice what's happening. This takes incredible self-management.

To help you manage yourself, make use of **control by release**. Control by release works when you "control by turning [the team] loose within well-understood given circumstances…control by trusting the process" (Austin and Devin 2003). Agile provides the well-understood given circumstances and, with that, the all-important safety net. The team can't go too far wrong or do too spectacularly poorly if you and they use agile well. The timeboxed sprint, raising and removing impediments, daily stand-up, and daily commitments to one another—these all represent parts of the agile framework that make control by release possible. As you loosen your grip on the team, you release them into a simple and powerful framework: agile. The built-in checkpoints and inspect-and-adapt loops give you all the control needed while simultaneously releasing the team into their creativity.

To help you during your judgment fast, remember control by release. When you recognize a judgment, instead of speaking it to the team, write it down. Then, look for an agile practice, principle, or value you can reinforce with the team to help them do agile well and address the matter that caused your judgment. Write what you offered down next to the judgment. Keep this "judgment vs. agile" list going while on your judgment fast and see how much trust you can build—trust in them, in yourself, and in agile.

When command-and-control-ism loosens its grip, you may find that its departure leaves a hole. You used to know how to behave; now you don't. What will you do with your day if you are not telling people what to do? You will coach (of course)! When you coach, you nurture an environment that "holds the space" open for the team to create. For the space to be open, you must be open, too.

> You cannot hold space if you are already full. Holding space requires all of your capacity, offered fully and with certainty. Your concerns don't matter to the group, so your preparation is directed at shedding them (Corrigan 2006).

As command-and-control behavior departs, let the hole it leaves behind remain unfilled. Let it be empty, and work to shed your concerns in order to keep it empty. This lets you be ready for what the team brings to you next. Your leverage exists in the present moment, so direct your attention to what has emerged for the team and know that focusing on that is the most important way you can serve them now. Your ability to be with them and help them through the circumstances of each present moment equals your value to them.

Yet, the reality of our way of living crowds in. Our hectic, full lives rail against the idea of being empty to hold space for the team. What to do about that?

Prepare for the Day Ahead

We live in busy times. There are mornings when you run out of the house with your coat half on, a piece of toast in your hand, and the kids climbing into the car as they push and tease each other just as you realize you have misplaced your car keys. Aggravation puts your temper right at the boiling point. After you finally drop the kids off at the sitter's and choke down your toast, you try to catch your breath while you drive, but you can't because your phone chirps every minute, and you know each of those chirps means another e-mail has just arrived. This is a common way to live, but it is no way to start a day of coaching.

To be of service to the team, free yourself from your worries and racing thoughts. Your mind must be still so that you can see, with clarity, what happens with the team. You are likely to witness the best and the worst in people, sometimes just minutes apart. To stand in these storm winds without being blown over, find your center. To do this, master yourself through a daily practice.

Daily Practice

A daily preparation practice helps you clear the "stuff" in your head. This lets you gather yourself together before you start to coach and lets you come to the team free of your own agendas. It also helps you get attuned to yourself so you can pause between stimulus and response and, in the pause, choose what best serves the team in that moment.

Your daily practice can be anything that helps you sweep away the clutter of thoughts and emotions that roll around in your mind and body—anything that tunes up your ability to pay attention so that you can fully observe. For some, the beauty of nature delivers a calming influence, perhaps offered by the tree budding just outside the conference room window. For others, it's reaffirming their "capital T" truth, whatever gives them solace, and restores their faith in human beings.

SERVE WITH GRATITUDE

A colleague of mine has an endearing daily practice of helping his wife get ready for work. She teaches elementary school and must be on time every day. Getting up regularly before the sun rises, she rushes around the house pulling together everything she needs for the day.

As his daily practice, this particular agile coach gets up at the same time to cook breakfast and assist in making her departure to work more comfortable. Maybe he grabs leftovers for her lunch or loads up boxes of equipment for the new project she's kicking off with her students. He listens to her and acts when invited, a calm presence in the middle of her busy activity, helping where he can. He gives this service to her gratefully. This relaxes and grounds him so that he finds his center as she departs. It sets the tone for his day ahead—a day when he will find himself in service to the teams he coaches.

Here are some other ideas for a daily practice:

- Listen to music that calms and restores you.

- Read inspirational books, blogs, daily meditations, and quotations.

- Jog and listen to the sounds of nature around you.

- Write down three things you're grateful for.

- Do yoga or stretching while breathing fully.

- Speak affirmations to yourself to make the life you want vivid in the present moment.

- Let your computer password match something you're working on. Some ideas are L1sten2all, tAkn0spAc, 4giveURself, and 0bsrvA11.

If you don't like any of these, make up your own, or search the words *daily practice* or *mindfulness practice* on the Internet. A lot of people are doing this, not just agile coaches. Many of them have shared their practices.

Stay Connected to What You Care About

Another way to prepare for the day ahead is to stay connected to what you care about. Let's say that an important retrospective happens tomorrow, one that could change the team in big ways. You have prepared well. You are ready. Now, you just wait for the morning to come. You could lie awake all night thinking of the many things they might say and what you might say (or not say) in return. You could drive yourself crazy going over all the permutations of things that could happen, worrying about what you'll do if each one happens. Or, you could get connected to what you care about.

If, for example, what you truly care about is that they find their own voice to speak up about things that impact them, then everything you do will come from this place of helping them find their own voice. Your ability to respond will come from the clarity you have about how you can best serve them. In fact, a good way to discover what you care about arises from your answer to this question: How can I best be of service to the group? Use whatever answer comes to mind. It's probably right or, at least, right enough to be useful.

Staying connected means staying connected to *one* thing you care about. That's the trick to making this work. You probably have a long list of things you care about. That list has its uses but cannot be kept front of mind when you are in the moment and things are happening all around you. So, pick one thing to stay connected to. Just as a product backlog can have only one top priority, you must choose one top thing you care about. Make it the one you feel will best serve the group.

SEE ALSO Staying connected to what you care about is an essential preparation technique for coaching people one-on-one as well. Keep this in mind as you use the ideas in Chapter 5, "Coach as Coach-Mentor," to coach team members, product owners, agile managers, or other outsiders.

Hold what you care about in your mind, and stay connected to it. As team members say and do the things you worried about and the ones you never could have expected, make sure your words and actions come from what you care about. Don't teach any and every lesson that comes along—if you do, you could be there forever, and the few lessons most pertinent for their current situation will be watered down or lost completely. Instead, use the connection to what you care about as your guide and your guardrails. When you interact with the team aligned with what you care about, your words take on the qualities of a guided missile, straight into their hearts and minds.

Practice in the Moment

It's one thing to be a well-grounded sage in the comfort of your home or in the quiet moments of solitude you give yourself at work. It's another proposition entirely to keep your balance and listen to your wisdom in the heat of the moment with a team. We practice mastering ourselves in the moment so that we can better open ourselves to being a servant leader and to harness our emotions and choose what to do with our reactions. Yet we're human. We react.

Sometimes, the team needs you to remain unfiltered—to see your reaction as a reflection of what just happened. More often, though, your reaction is about you and has no place in the coaching. Notice your reaction, and consciously choose whether to act on it. This is the practiced skill.

Along with wielding the skills we've been exploring comes the important theme of noticing how you regard the people you coach. Do you see them as obstacles to overcome or as people with hopes, dreams, fears, and aspirations just like you? If you don't know, rest assured, they certainly do.

> "…We can sense how others are feeling toward us. Given a little time, we can always tell when we're being coped with, manipulated, or outsmarted. We can always detect the hypocrisy. We can always feel the blame concealed beneath veneers of niceness. And we typically resent it. It won't matter if the other person tries managing by walking around, sitting on the edge

of the chair to practice active listening, inquiring about family members to show interest, or using any other skill learned in order to be more effective. What we'll know and respond to is how that person is regarding us when doing those things" (Arbinger Institute 2000).

Get in touch with how you regard the people you encounter. Know whether you are thinking about them as objects or people. To amplify your impact, move toward thinking about people as people more of the time.

TRY THIS

As you go through your day, imagine that everyone you meet has a letter on their forehead. That letter reflects how you view them in this moment. If you view the person as standing in the way or being a problem to solve, then imagine a big *O* on their forehead. You view them as an object, someone to overcome. If you view them as a person who is trying to attain their hopes and dreams the best way they can, then imagine a big *P* on their forehead. You view them in a straightforward manner, as a person, just like you.

When you visualize a big *O* on someone's forehead, then turn down your judgment and turn up the curiosity. Get curious about how you obtained such a view. What has this person done to "earn" your view of them as an object? What stories have you made up to explain their behavior (and to cling to your judgments)? After doing this for a while and getting curious when the *O*'s happen, you may see patterns in the way you view people. With this new awareness, perhaps you start to see more *P*'s on people's foreheads.

Then, from there, acquire the skill of detecting any automatic response as it pops up and deciding what to do about it. Some practices for honing this are special ways of listening, speaking, and being with the team. These are covered in the sections that follow. Regarding people as people, together with these practices, makes for a winning formula for mastering yourself in the moment.

Are You Listening?

What a rare gift to be truly listened to. An agile coach knows this and capitalizes on it for the sake of each person's full contribution to the team and, by extension, the quality of the products the team creates. Once again, we're talking about skills, not talents. You can develop the ability to fully listen through applying frameworks that help you bring attention to the matter—that, plus lots and lots of practice. One good framework that helps coaches is Levels of Listening from the school of coactive coaching (Whitworth et al. 2007).

Level I—internal listening: When the coach listens at Level I, the coach hears the speaker's words and may be very attentive, but the words get interpreted through the coach's own lens. Everything the speaker says is met with some version of this thought in the coach's head: How does this affect me? Imagine that the speaker starts talking about the potentially negative impacts of having a new team member join the team, an idea the team had been kicking around lately. In response, the coach may say, "We've added team members before between sprints. As long as we're not doing it during a sprint, we're OK." The coach's focus stayed self-centered on "How does this affect me?" In this case, the coach's desire to be seen as a "good coach" by upholding the rule about adding team members only between sprints undermined the coach's ability to listen to the speaker. As a result, the coach completely missed the chance to learn what the speaker really wanted to say.

Level II—focused listening: When listening at Level II, a hardwired connection gets established between the coach and the speaker. The coach is "over there" in the speaker's chair—intently focused on what the speaker says. Freed from the personal lens, the coach listens and responds in the moment with the questions and silences that help the speaker move through whatever they are expressing. In our example, as the speaker starts talking about the changes that may happen when a new team member joins the team, the coach stays focused solely on the speaker and notices a lot of emotion coming up. The coach isn't sure what's really happening, but instead of making assumptions or filtering the speaker through a personal lens, the coach goes with curiosity and says, "I can't tell what's happening as you're talking about this. Excitement? Fear? Nervousness? What's going on over there?" And then the coach listens.

Level III—global listening: The coach uses everything in the environment when listening at Level III. The speaker's tone of voice, posture, changes in room temperature, what noises are happening around them—all of these things are noticed and used by the coach. The Level II hardwired connection remains strong, joined by the coach's antennae that pick up everything. When the antennae function, intuitions emerge. As the speaker goes on about how good a new team member will be for the team, the coach notices that the air suddenly feels stifling and says, "I hear you talking about how good you think this will be, and yet there is a sense of being stifled. What does that mean to you?" The speaker may say, "Stifled? No, that's not it at all. It's more like excited but nervous about adding a new personality to the team." Or, perhaps the speaker says, "Stifled? (silence) I didn't realize it until now, but it's true. I always feel stifled when I work with people who have more experience than me." In either case, the coach and speaker have gained a deeper understanding.

TRY THIS

Pay attention to your levels of listening, and give yourself a score after each interaction. How much did you listen to people through your own concerns (Level I), hardwired to them (Level II), or hardwired with your antennae up (Level III)? What do you notice about people's ability to be creative and solve their own problems when you listen at Level I? Does that change when you listen at Level II and Level III? How?

To increase the amount of time you spend in Level II and Level III listening, enter each conversation with a fresh mind. Remind yourself that you truly don't know what the person will say next. So, stay on the edge of your seat.

Are You Speaking?

When you have the urge to speak, check yourself first. What is your "come from" place? Ask yourself, "Why do I want to offer this thought now?" If you feel compelled to speak because you want the team to see how smart you are or you want them to know that you are adding value, then don't even bother offering it. Presumably, you have a whole team of people being smart and providing value. That's *their* job. As the guardian of quality and performance, your job provides value on an entirely different level.

SEE ALSO There often comes a time for the coach to speak, usually at the beginning of a team's life together or when they're first learning agile. At these times, the coach works for the team in a teaching style. See Chapter 4, "Let Your Style Change," for more information.

Every time you want to speak, make sure your "come from" place is all about them. Ensure that your words are aimed at helping them get better as a team. The following are some practices to help.

Don't Speak First

Instead of speaking, count to 10 (or 100). Use this classic exercise with a twist: While you count, pay keen attention to see whether someone else in the group will speak your thought. If you wait several minutes, you will likely hear your thought, or the core of your thought, expressed by someone else. If you wait several minutes and no one expresses your thought, wait a few more and then see whether it is still relevant or helpful. If so, speak it with clarity and simplicity. You've been thinking about it for a while now, so you should be able to express it in an incredibly short, precise, and impactful manner. Aim for the type of statement that will send the group into a whole new realm of discovery or action.

Sometimes, after you wait for a few minutes and then wait for a few more, you find that your thought has become irrelevant. The group has moved on. So be it. Keep your thought to yourself, and trust that they are going where they need to go. If you detect they are straying too far from fertile ground, resist the urge to jump in and steer them back to course (because it's your course, not necessarily theirs). Instead, consider a well-placed powerful question such as "Are you getting what is most useful in this moment?"

> *It is interesting to note that the words* silent *and* listen *contain all of the same letters, just rearranged.*
>
> —*Suzanne Marsh*

Don't Speak at All

Sometimes in conversation, questions are asked and silence follows. This can be especially true with new teams but can happen anytime. Coach the team to see that sitting with silence creates enough space for the really big ideas to emerge. To coach the team to do this, you must first do it yourself.

Whenever a team member asks a question, do not be the first to answer it. In fact, using the "don't speak first" technique, perhaps you won't answer at all. This can be especially difficult when you are the question poser. "So, team, looking back at how we worked together this last sprint, what sticks out as something we want to keep?" The room gets so quiet you can hear crickets in the background. Uncomfortable silence pervades the room. Team members are not even looking at one other. In this moment, your greatest gift to them is showing that you are comfortable with uncomfortable silence. So, just stand or sit there, not doing anything, not demanding anything from them, but staying connected to them. Gaze at them, each one, gently. Give each person the silent invitation to step in and speak. Someone will.

I once stood in silence for five minutes—but only once. After that, the team realized that speaking and silence were both welcome, and uncomfortable silences became comfortable, fruitful, and shorter.

Are You with Them?

Simply *be* with the team. To practice this, cultivate presence and reground yourself.

Cultivate Presence

As you read this book, do you truly take in the words, letting them come into your mind and your body? Letting them change who you are and what you think? If so, you are probably fully present in this moment. Your full attention and intention remains on the book, these words, *this* moment. If, while you read these words, your mind goes to the grocery list or worries about a misunderstanding that happened yesterday, then you are not fully present. Presence means being here now—not in the future, mentally adding items to the grocery list, and not in the past, worrying about a misunderstanding. Here.

Our minds move away from the present and escape into the past or future constantly. It happens all day long quite normally. My mind gets noisy. The noise may be anxiety about what the team will do next, judgment about the product owner being too directive, aggravation about a team member not truly participating, elation that the team just released a new product, and so many other thoughts. All in there, thoughts get jumbled up and try to elbow their way to the front of the attention line. Loud and distracting, they lead me away from what I need to do as the coach—to tune in to what's going on with the team right *now*.

When I "get present," I notice what is really happening with the team, and from that clear place, I help them move forward in a constructive and positive way. Looking back, I often see that the path they took was perfect for them and very different from I would have suggested if I allowed myself to be driven by worry, judgment, aggravation, elation, and more.

Practicing mindfulness helps you "get present." Through mindfulness, you learn to be fully present more of the time, and your self-awareness increases. Being present and being self-aware are two sides of the same coin and the very things you need to help you notice when your mind has become noisy again.

MY DAILY PRACTICE

I have a host of mindfulness books in my library. To get present before I coach, I choose one and flip it open randomly. Nine times out of ten, I am astounded that the book "just opened" in the perfect place for me and gave me the message I needed that day. (Through my experience, I have come to believe that usually the other one book in ten also holds a message I need but one that I am just not ready for yet.)

Just now, I randomly opened the book *Wherever You Go There You Are: Mindfulness Meditation in Everyday Life* and received these words:

"Trust. Trust is a feeling of confidence or conviction that things can unfold within a dependable framework that embodies order and integrity. We may not always understand what is happening to us, or to another, or what is occurring in a particular situation; but if we trust ourselves, or another, or we place our trust in a process or ideal, we can find a powerful stabilizing element embracing security, balance, and openness within the trusting which, in some way, if not based on naiveté, intuitively guides us and protects us from harm or self-destruction" (Kabat-Zinn 1994).

The text goes on and offers more to ponder and then a practice the reader can do to take a step toward trust.

As I think about these words, I reflect on the connection between this and the idea of trusting the agile framework that I have been writing about in the "control by release" text of this chapter. The "coincidence" astounds me and signals to me that there are more and deeper messages for me in this passage about trust. So, I'll keep these words with me as I go through my day and see how they can reveal themselves relevant to my desire to be present so I can best write this book and help the people I coach.

Consider expanding your library by one or two "get here, get present" books so you can allow their wisdom to help you cultivate your presence. Such titles on my bookshelf, other than the one I just mentioned, are

The Tao of Holding Space by Chris Corrigan

The Parent's Tao Te Ching by William Martin

The Seven Spiritual Laws of Success by Deepak Chopra

Comfortable with Uncertainty by Pema Chodron

The Compassionate Life by the Dalai Lama

Why is this "getting present" so important? Here's the deal: When you "get present," the ground beneath you stays solid. With presence (and using all the other skills we've talked about), you coach people from a place of certainty, you speak with clarity, and your words impact the team. Your intervention makes a difference, far more than yet another person throwing in another idea.

Presence is also a crucial skill for each team member to develop. If we were all truly in this moment together—not multitasking, not with our minds in the future or the past, but right here, right now, giving our attention to one another and our intention to the work at hand—what do you think might happen? I think nothing could stop a team like that from creating astounding products that make a difference for the world and for each of them.

Reground Yourself

Let's say you have decided to intervene for all the right reasons. You waited to see whether your thought would be spoken by someone else. You waited some more and decided it would still be useful. You delivered a succinct and insightful statement. And it fell flat. Or the team started to run with it, but you notice it's not serving them. You could keep the conversation going to avoid embarrassment (but this may be a waste of their time), or you could reground.

To reground, reconsider whether the intervention was useful to the team. If not, withdraw it with transparency. "Something about this is not working right now, so feel free to ignore it and move on." If you want them to really pay attention when you speak, then you must honor their time and their creative process above your embarrassment.

Be a Model for Them

Going for the astonishing results that agile promises will take a lot of open-minded and open-hearted conversation between the team members. If the team practices many of the things you're practicing, they can help themselves have the quality conversations they need. Imagine their interaction with one another free from personal agendas, aware of how they react to conflict, applying nonviolent communication, and approaching each conversation with an uncluttered presence. Most people have never heard of these things, let alone consciously practiced them. So, as their coach, act as their model, and know that they can (and will) change.

Support Yourself

Everything about mastering yourself is a learned skill that requires practice. You won't be perfect as you try these things and incorporate them into your coaching. Can you extend the same compassion to yourself that you extend to others? Can you chuckle at "failures" and forgive yourself so that you can get back to practicing? Will you balance your needs with your team's needs so that you remain true to what you want from the relationships? To make a contribution? To be of service? To make a difference in people's lives? To help the team create something great?

Discover the answers to these questions, and let them be your touchstone as you practice mastering yourself. Also, use a crutch. One such "crutch" is a structure—any device that reminds you to be in action with the thing you are practicing (Whitworth et al. 2007).

One structure I use (yes, I am still working hard at mastering myself) is to pick a practice that I will keep in mind all week. More than once, my practice has been to remain silent after I've asked a question so that others have the chance to speak. To remind myself of this, I might scribble "pause...breathe... give space" on a note and let it stick out of my notebook. I write in my notebook a dozen times a day, so I have at least 12 reminders that I am in practice with that specific skill.

Another coach wears a "busy-bee pin" on her clothes to remind herself that her need to be busy all the time should not spill over into the team and create unnecessary stress for them. You can set your watch and let it chime on the hour to signal you to count the times you have caught yourself listening at Level I in the past hour. You can ask a co-worker to call you on your command-and-control behavior. The possibilities for using structures are endless. Get creative.

Always Work on Yourself

I never realized how much being a coach of agile teams was going to require me to work on myself. It does, and the journey has been rich and fruitful as a result.

You can spend thousands on coaching classes. That will certainly expand your skills and help you master yourself to be a better coach. Or, you can spend far less on a helpful book or two. Or, you can spend 30 minutes checking out inspirational blogs. Working on yourself need not be expensive or time-consuming, but it needs to be constant. Do what you can do and, above all, keep moving.

Keep learning and applying new ideas. Try them. If you hate an idea after you try it, throw it away, but keep trying. We teach teams to inspect and adapt. This goes for us coaches, too.

A Refresher

Let's lock in the ideas from this chapter:

- As an agile coach, you serve as a model for what a good agilist is and does. What you say, what you do, how you manage yourself—all these things matter. They're watching.

- Become aware of your abilities, and identify your growing edge. Then, go to that edge, improve your abilities, and find the next growing edge.

- Recover from command-and-control-ism.

- Discover practices that help you cultivate presence to prepare for the coaching day ahead and keep your footing as the day progresses. Do them.

- Learn to listen, speak, and be with the team consciously.

- Extend to yourself the same compassion and support you offer the people you coach.

Additional Resources

Arbinger Institute. 2002. *Leadership and Self Deception: Getting Out of the Box*. San Francisco: Berrett-Koehler. This book helped me understand why I had so many "people problems" on my teams and what I could change to make that not so.

Corrigan, C. 2006. The Tao of Holding Space. www.archive.org/details/TheTaoOfHoldingSpace. One of my daily preparation practices is to flip this booklet open to a random page and read the wisdom that unfolds before me. It's uncanny how many times I get exactly what I need to serve my team. Note that I said I get what I need. It's often not what I want. That's how I know it's what will serve the team, rather than serving me.

The Consortium for Research on Emotional Intelligence in Organizations. Emotional Competence Framework. www.eiconsortium.org/reports/emotional_competence_framework.html.

Greenleaf, R. 1991. *The Servant as Leader*. Westfield, IN: The Robert K. Greenleaf Center. This booklet is the source of the term *servant as leader* and gives a complete treatment of what that phrase really means.

Kornfield, J. 2000. *Meditation for Beginners.* Louisville, CO: Sounds True. Ultra-practical, this audiobook of short meditation sessions led by the author will help you step into the world of uncluttering your mind and cultivating presence. Between meditations, the author explains the practical aspects of meditation: What happens when my thoughts run away with me? What if my legs go to sleep? What if I have an itch on my nose? I find this audio-book pertinent to experienced meditators, as well. I certainly learned a thing or two that improved my meditation practice.

Queendom: The Land of Tests. One of many online EQ assessments. www.queendom.com/tests/access_page/index.htm?idRegTest=1121.

References

Arbinger Institute. 2000. *Leadership and Self-Deception.* San Francisco: Berrett-Koehler.

Austin, R., and L. Devin. 2003. *Artful Making: What Managers Need to Know About How Artists Work.* Upper Saddle River, NJ: Prentice Hall.

Baran, G., and Center for NonViolent Communication. 2004. 10 Things We Can Do to Contribute to Internal, Interpersonal and Organizational Peace. www.cnvc.org/en/what-nvc/10-steps-peace/10-things-we-can-do-contribute-internal-interpersonal-and-organizational-peace.

Bradberry, T., and J. Greaves. 2005. *The Emotional Intelligence Quick Book.* New York: Simon and Schuster.

Corrigan, C. 2009. The Tao of Holding Space. www.archive.org/details/TheTaoOfHoldingSpace.

CPP, Inc. 2009. History and Validity of the Thomas-Kilmann Conflict Mode Instrument (TKI). https://www.cpp.com/Products/tki/tki_info.aspx.

Goleman, D. 1998. *Working with Emotional Intelligence.* New York: Bantam Books.

Greenleaf, R. 1991. *The Servant as Leader.* Westfield, IN: The Robert K. Greenleaf Center.

Kabat-Zinn, J. 1994. *Wherever You Go There You Are: Mindfulness Meditation in Everyday Life.* New York: Hyperion.

Kilmann, R. 2007. Conflict and Conflict Management. www.kilmann.com/conflict.html.

Scott, S. 2007. *Fierce Conversations: Achieving Success at Work and in Life One Conversation at a Time*. New York: Berkley.

Whitworth, L., K. Kimsey-House, H. Kimsey-House, and P. Sandahl. 2007. *Co-Active Coaching: New Skills for Coaching People Toward Success in Work and Life, Second Edition*. Mountain View, CA: Davies-Black.

Chapter 4

Let Your Style Change

Dozens of kids in neat rows, all practicing the same simple movement, over and over again. Each of them concentrating like you didn't know little kids could concentrate. This is my daughter's preschool tae kwan do class.

Old people in the park in the early morning hours. Tracing the air with graceful movements, the forms of tai chi. Swooping and bending and doing something else besides—stilling their minds. This sight greets me as I take my morning walk.

If you ask someone in the group what they are doing, they would say, "We are practicing."

My limited experience with tai chi over the past 15 years has taught me this, too. I first took a tai chi class as an up-and-coming businesswoman when it was recommended to me as a way to help me chill out. Later, I took it again as a pregnant lady who spent the first ten minutes of every class rediscovering her center of gravity. Later still, I practiced by myself, just those few movements I remembered from the lessons of the past. Again and again, the same movements and my instructors' voices coming back to me, "Each of these is perfect exercise for body and mind. Do them over and over again; that's all there is."

By the time you finish this chapter, you will be able to answer these questions:

- What stages do teams go through as they learn agile and begin to apply it?
- How can I tell the overall stage of a team at a given time?
- What are possible coaching styles, and how do I match them to the team's current stage?

One exceptionally hot, sticky Houston night made worse by the lack of air conditioning in the martial arts studio (because air conditioning was for wimps), I practiced the forms. Dripping with sweat and frustrated by my glacial progress, I asked my instructor, "How long has it taken you to master tai chi?" Judging from the trophies lining the walls, he was accomplished in several forms of martial arts, so I expected that he would have a step 1-2-3 answer. He certainly couldn't have mastered all of those forms in one lifetime otherwise, I reasoned. He looked at me and said, "I don't know yet. I am still practicing." They must teach this line in martial arts instructor school because I have heard tell of other instructors saying something remarkably similar. Or, maybe it's true.

Years later still, when I coached agile teams, I passed on the same answer to one of my coach apprentices when, in frustration with her progress, she asked me, "How long did it take you to become a master coach?" I paused and said, "I don't know yet. I am still practicing." Today, tomorrow, next year, and who knows how many years after that, I'll be practicing still.

In my coaching, however, I have noticed that I've traveled through stages over time. Many things felt like someone else's skin when I first tried them on. They felt weird, uncomfortable. After a while, I didn't notice them as much, and then after more time and practice, I didn't notice them at all—they had become my own skin. People go through these stages. You will. Teams will, too.

Agile Team Stages

One good model for mastering anything (if that's possible) comes from martial arts. A martial arts student progresses through three stages of proficiency called Shu Ha Ri. Shu: Follow the rule. Ha: Break the rule. Ri: Be the rule. These stages also describe agile teams as they first practice and then get good at agile.

When in Shu, the student copies "the techniques as taught without modification and without yet attempting to understand the rationale" behind them (Cockburn 1994). Follow the rule, again and again and again. "Shu stresses [the] basics in an uncompromising fashion so the student has a solid foundation for future learning" (Shuhari Dojo Martial Arts). This "foundation can be built most efficiently by following only a single route" (Cockburn 2008). One way. The rule's way.

Rules abound in agile. In Scrum, for example, the stand-up is 15 minutes long, it starts and ends on time regardless, and each person answers three questions. Certainly, a deeper meaning to the stand-up exists and can be discovered when one applies these rules. However, if the rules were applied mechanically throughout a team's life, the stand-up might likely become an empty ritual. If these rules are not applied mechanically in the beginning of a team's life, the stand-up will certainly become as empty as the status meeting ritual they already know well. The rules break people out of their well-worn patterns. They teach new patterns through perfect mimicry and repetition. Shu: Follow the rule.

After Shu comes Ha. Having reached Ha, one has attained the basics and now spends time "reflecting on the truth of everything" (Sensei's Library). The student comes "to a deeper understanding of the art than pure repetitive practice can allow" (Cockburn 2008). The student can now instruct others as an additional way to advance their own practices. In the quest to advance, "individuality will begin to emerge" as the student begins to "break free of the rigid instruction of the teacher and begins to question and discover more through personal experience" (Shuhari Dojo Martial Arts). While breaking free, the student carefully upholds the principles underlying the practice. For example, once a team reliably demonstrates their ability to do stand-up well following the rules and then once they see the deeper principle of stand-up as a commitment meeting rather than a status meeting, they may be ready to break the rules. They have the practices entrained in their muscle memory. They understand the principle underlying the practices. They can break the rules. And then let the inspect-and-adapt mechanism of agile tell them whether it was positive and useful. Ha: Break the rule.

After Ha comes Ri. When in Ri, the moves become part of the student. Although the student still follows well-worn rules, including those broken and renewed, "There are no techniques...all moves are natural" (Sensei's Library). "The student is now learning and progressing more through self-discovery than by instruction" while "treasur[ing] the wisdom and patient council of the teacher" (Shuhari Dojo Martial Arts). When in Ri, the team may decide to replace stand-up with something else entirely. The replacement practice still achieves the principle of stand-up and takes it even deeper. The coach offers advice to the team. The team considers it well and then does what it will. Ri: Be the rule.

In Ri, student and teacher are peers, and if done well, the student becomes as skilled as the master and beyond.

> Ultimately, Shu Ha Ri should result in the student surpassing the master, both in knowledge and skill. This is the source of improvement for the art as a whole. If the student never surpasses his master, then the art will stagnate, at best. If the student never achieves the master's ability, the art will deteriorate. But, if the student can assimilate all that the master can impart and then progress to even higher levels of advancement, the art will continually improve and flourish (Shuhari Dojo Martial Arts).

To surpass one's master, one must first master the rules—fully. Then break the rules safely. Then create new rules that allow a deeper expression of the principles behind the rules. The progression rarely follows this three-step straight path, however. As shown in Figure 4.1, it's not a linear progression.

> It is more akin to concentric circles, so that there is Shu within Ha and both Shu and Ha within Ri. Thus, the fundamentals remain constant; only the application of them and the subtleties of their execution change as the student progresses and his or her own personality begins to flavor the techniques performed (Shuhari Dojo Martial Arts).

A team can be in one or all of these stages simultaneously. Perhaps they inhabit Ha for their stand-up mastery while they learn the rules of release planning in Shu. Perhaps, overall, their skill level pegs them at Ha, yet some practices advance the state of the art and, thus, are worthy of Ri. Each person on the team inhabits one or more of these stages simultaneously, too. Even though each person can be pegged at different levels for various skills and the team as a whole can also be at different levels simultaneously, still a sense of the team being "mostly" at a given level stands out.

If the team holds the fundamentals constant even as they experiment with new ways of doing things, they will progress through the stages safely. If the fundamentals get lost, take that as a sign that they have moved too fast or skipped a stage. To help you know what's going on, ask the team for their opinion.

Ask their opinion when you teach this model to them, and let them assess where they think they are at given points in time. As a retrospective backdrop, for example, this model really gets the conversation about

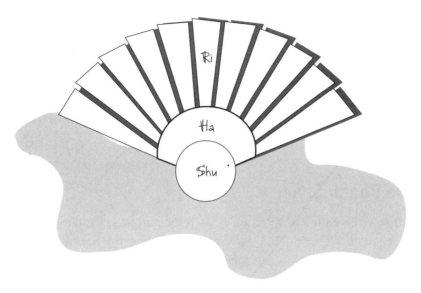

FIGURE 4.1 Shu Ha Ri stages of mastery

improvement going. So, bring it up in a retrospective or whenever it seems useful to the team.

TRY THIS

Play with ways to use the Shu Ha Ri model in a retrospective. Perhaps you draw it big on a whiteboard and team members can play a version of "pin the tail on the donkey" (without the blindfold). Instead of "tails" of the donkey, they place sticky notes with agile practices, principles, values, and roles written on them in the Shu, Ha, or Ri level where they think they are currently operating. Once the sticky notes are placed, the whole team steps back and discusses what they see. Where do they agree? Where do they disagree, perhaps revealing that different people see the team at different levels for the same thing? What seems to be the next thing to practice more or investigate more deeply?

Get creative with this model. It can be fun as well as useful.

As the team travels their own paths through Su Ha Ri, remember that these stages apply to you, too. Your mastery of agile coaching moves through Shu Ha Ri in total and in part. In total, you move from Shu to Ha to Ri as your overall coaching skill develops. Once in Ha, you are ready to teach others and to become an agile coach. The concentric circles are at work, though. Although you are at Ha for most practices and principles, certain aspects may be at Ri and others at Shu. Some rules are artfully expressed in your coaching and advance the art of agile as a whole. You are at Ri for these. Others require you to hang about a little longer in repetitive practice at Shu. For these, get your own teacher. The student is the teacher, and the teacher is the student. Always.

Agile Coach Styles

Over time, I have noticed three agile coach styles in myself and in the coaches I have apprenticed: Teaching, Coaching, and Advising. For best results, employ these three styles using a "coach approach," which means saving some attention for Modeling and Reaching as well. Figure 4.2 depicts these styles. Modeling allows you to show desired behaviors that lead to team delivery and success. Reaching allows you to get to the core of each person on the team to help them become the best agilist they can be. The "coach approach" of Modeling and Reaching calls upon you, through your example, to transfer tools, techniques, values, and mind-sets to the team so they can improve as individual team members and as a whole team. With Modeling and Reaching in play, you are ready to try the three coaching styles.

> **Teaching:** When you teach, you lay down the law and teach the rules. This can be done gently or forcefully, that matters not, but it must be done with a steel rod in your back—that matters. You know a better way to work, so feel the steel rod as you teach agile. Convey the rules strongly, along with your belief that agile gives us a better way to work. Back this up with your experiences illustrating why this is so. In so doing, you teach both the practices and the principles. Both are rules. The practices are the basic moves. The principles tell the "why" for each practice. When in the Teaching style, embody these sentiments:
>
> "Follow these rules. I have followed them before, and I know they will give you what you want. So, for now, just follow."
>
> "The rules work. Anything else is an impediment."
>
> "Everything you could need is right here, in this simple framework, so look here for your answers first."
>
> "Here's how this works…."

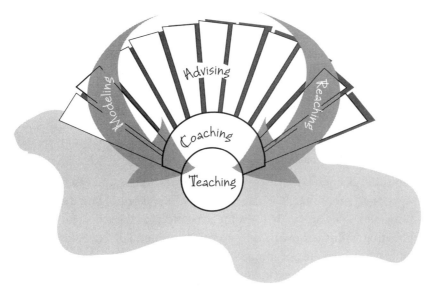

FIGURE 4.2 Agile coach styles

| **SEE ALSO** | See Chapter 7, "Coach as Teacher," for ideas on teaching agile when a team starts up and during teachable moments as they work together. Chapter 6, "Coach as Facilitator," tells you the "why" behind each of the major agile meetings. |

Encourage the team to relax their incessant need to know everything right now. Instead, ask them to follow you and get agile practices working well as their first job because doing so leads to their initial successes. These successes hold the organization at bay (long enough) while the team practices agile, makes the inevitable mistakes, recovers from them, and then strengthens their practice. With the lions thus held at bay, it becomes possible for the team to truly master Shu and move on to Ha as a natural outgrowth of their success with the practices at Shu.

Coaching: The Coaching style requires the foundation laid by the Teaching style. With agile practices working well, the team starts transforming from compliance to rules to internalization of values from their range of experiences with agile. You need not prod them to go here; they will do so on their own, often too early, so feel free to kick in the Teaching style when they need more practice with the rules. Otherwise, stay in the Coaching style when you notice that they have started to see the intricate simplicity of agile done well and have discerned some reasons why agile works. As they move beyond muscle memory to consider a little more deeply what underlies the practices, help the team along by peppering the group with questions such as these:

"How do the values and principles of agile relate to your life?"

"Why does this way of working work?"

"What kills it? What renews it? What feeds it?"

From this deeper exploration, team members' minds open to multiple ways of accomplishing the same thing while still upholding the values and principles. They are ready for some exceptions to the rules and for experimenting with their own expressions of the rules. The exceptions will be different for each team; you need not bring your favorite ones from past teams to them. Some exceptions will not be acceptable because they violate the underlying principles. Call this out, and then let them do as they will. But don't save them from the consequences of their decisions. They need direct experience and feedback to be able to truly inspect what happened so they can assess whether the change was helpful or hurtful.

Advising: The Advising style comes when the team has fully internalized the practices, values, and principles of agile and radiates good health. Things are running like a well-oiled ecosystem. As they push the edges, some altered expressions of the rules run their course and die off, and others spring up. Both outcomes get handled gracefully by team members as part of the natural course of life in an agile team. Self-organized, self-monitoring, and self-correcting, the team runs without you, but they may not realize it yet. To let the realization dawn, stay out of their way, knowing that they will ask for help from their trusted advisor (you) when they need it. When asked, the coach replies with advisor-like answers:

"I don't know. What do you think?"

"May I offer an observation?"

"That could work. Try it."

When Advising, rest assured that you have done your job well and now the team members know as much (sometimes more) than you. They are free to find their own ways. Allow the students to surpass the master so that the art of agile can continually improve and flourish.

The whole time, as you move from Teaching to Coaching to Advising, ensure that you also pay attention to Modeling and Reaching. Regardless of the coaching style you choose at any given moment, be actively Modeling. Constantly model the behaviors that lead to success: listening to one another, building on each other's ideas, courageously facing impediments, and tending toward the simplest thing possible. Everything you do transfers a mind-set or tool the team can incorporate into their way of being to enhance their success. And, yes, this diminishes their reliance on you.

> *When you need me but do not want me, then I must stay. When you want me but no longer need me, then I have to go.*
>
> —*Emma Thompson as Nanny McPhee*

SEE ALSO See Chapter 5, "Coach as Coach-Mentor" for guidance on Reaching each person on the team, as well as the team as a whole.

Reaching means reaching out to each team member and the team as a whole to help them achieve the best expression of agile possible. Be aware of each team member's beliefs, aspirations, and approach to agile, and coach them to take their next step toward becoming an excellent agilist. In so doing, you influence the whole. As you move from one style to the next, carry with you the intention to reach each person. Find out what they want, and help them see how to get it through agile.

Feel Free to Let Your Style Change

In the beginning, with a new team, the choice of style is easy. It's Teaching. You teach constantly as the team picks up the basics of agile and gets going producing real value. From here, your style flows naturally from Teaching to Coaching as the team moves from Shu to Ha.

If you are not sure where the team is on the Shu Ha Ri scale, look for these things to help you decide:

- Is the team new to agile or to one another? If so, they are at Shu.
- Has the team changed or dropped agile practices and lost the intention behind them? Have they mashed up agile with something else so that their practices are not clear even to them? Do they look at you cockeyed when you bring up the agile manifesto? If any of these are

true, the team may have progressed to Ha too early. They are truly at Shu and need you to guide them to practice at Shu.

- Does the team live by the ideals in the agile manifesto? In all they do, do they stand on the side of individuals and interactions, working software (really, any product), customer collaboration, and responding to change (Beck et al. 2001)? Do they have the basic practices working well and producing new insights that let them improve each sprint? Do they pause—really pause—to consider the ramifications before they alter, drop, or add an agile practice? Do they face the consequences of these changes squarely? If these are true, your team is at Ha and needs you to coach them to a deeper expression of agile.

- Has the team altered their practice of agile and done so consciously, keeping the values and principles of agile alive? Have they broken through walls of dysfunction in their company so that their practice of agile leads to progressively better and faster delivery and higher satisfaction? Have they imbibed the skills and mind-sets necessary to be truly self-monitoring and self-correcting? If these are true, the team is at Ri and needs you to let them go.

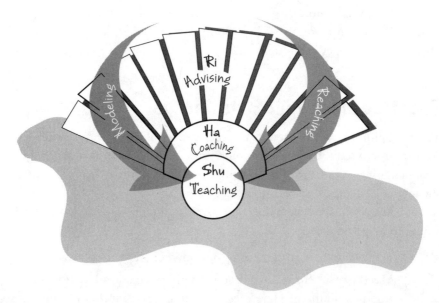

FIGURE 4.3 An agile coach's style changes with the team as they move between Shu, Ha, and Ri.

You'll know it's time to allow the team to move to Ha when the practices are done well and fully and when their conversations about changing the practices keep the underlying principle whole. Until then, when they want to change a practice, perhaps to avoid a dysfunction they'd rather not face, remind them that they are in Shu and, at this stage, they play by the rules. They must face the dysfunction, at least long enough to name it and explicitly decide whether to pursue changing it.

When a team shows signs of being ready to move to Ha, change your style from Teaching to Coaching right away. This calls them forth to Ha. Teaching has its place, but it has an unintended consequence: It creates a reliance on you. Loosen this reliance, and give them permission to move to Ha by relaxing the teacher and inviting in the coach. Using the Coaching style, stand in Ha waiting for them to arrive while illuminating the way.

When a team has arrived at Ri, they will want to stretch their wings. Usually, they tell you it's time to let them go. Do so and advise them as they like.

Perhaps you notice a team is inching toward Ri, but you're not sure. In this case, test the situation by changing your style from Coaching to Advising. Advise them and then notice your impact. Does their expression of the art of agile blossom in new and exciting directions? If so, they are ready for Ri. Do they fall back into more strict expressions of the practices and principles? If so, perhaps a little more time at Ha is useful.

Remember that the stages are like concentric circles; each successive stage contains the others. If the team resides at Ha, use a Coaching style, but bring in a Teaching style when you introduce a new practice or idea to them, for example. Match them and then call them forth to the next stage as soon as you see an inkling of it.

Once a team is up and running and has experienced all the agile practices and done them well, you will likely find yourself interacting with them using all three styles for various topics or skills or at various times. No one needs to know which style you use for what situation except you. All this switching back and forth is your burden to bear.

Remember that you, too, are going through your own Shu Ha Ri stages with regard to your agile coaching abilities. You may be Ri at agile while being Shu at coaching skills. Honor your current level of skill and stay there to master it. Constantly interrogate your use of styles: Are you holding the team back from progressing to the next stage of mastery because you are not ready? Are you holding on to Coaching longer than needed because it feels so good to be valued and wanted? Are you moving to Advising too fast to avoid going deep in some area that is hampering the team's expression of agile? In all these cases, inspect and adapt. Adjust your style as your skill and experience allows. If you can't adjust, as in the situation where the team has grown past your abilities, involve a more experienced coach as your mentor to help the team (and you) grow.

A Refresher

Let's lock in the ideas from this chapter:

- Teams (and you) master agile through stages called Shu Ha Ri. You master agile coaching in much the same way.
- Let your style flow from Teaching to Coaching to Advising to match the team's Shu Ha Ri stage.
- Always model successful team behaviors, and reach each person on the team to help them become a great agilist.
- Let it be fluid. None of these stages or styles moves cleanly from A to B to C. That would be too easy.

Additional Resources

Hunt, A. 2008. *Pragmatic Thinking and Learning: Refactor Your Wetware*. Raleigh: Pragmatic Programmers. Use this book to take your brain on a tour of different ways to approach your work and view the progression from newbie to master.

References

Beck et al. 2001. Manifesto for Agile Software Development. www.agilemanifesto.org.

Cockburn, A. 1994. Private conversation between Alistair Cockburn and L. Sensei Nakamura as documented in Alistair Cockburn's compilation of

his Shu Ha Ri writings applied to software engineering. http://alistair.
cockburn.us/Shu+Ha+Ri.

————. 2008. Compilation of Shu Ha Ri writings applied to software
engineering. http://alistair.cockburn.us/Shu+Ha+Ri.

Sensei's Library. http://senseis.xmp.net/?ShuHaRi.

Shuhari Dojo Martial Arts. www.shuhari.com/site/view/ShuharisMeaning.pml.

PART II

Helping the Team Get More for Themselves

Chapter 5

Coach as Coach-Mentor

I had been working as an agile coach for a few years when a colleague said to me, "You know, there's a whole world of professional coaching out there. Maybe you should check it out." This was his diplomatic way of saying, "You call yourself a coach, but you're really not one." He was right.

My practice of agile coaching up to that point was useful for starting up teams and getting the basics working, but it stopped well short of tapping into each person's potential to improve the team's overall performance. For that, I was using the tried-and-true (but not very effective) management techniques I had picked up during my years as a project manager.

So, I went to coaching school and discovered that the world of professional work/life coaching applies 100% to agile coaching. Everything I learned there

---

By the time you finish this chapter, you will be able to answer these questions:

- What is agile coaching, and what are we aiming for when we coach?
- How do I know when to coach people one-on-one vs. when to coach the whole team?
- What coaching tone can I use to urge the team to reach for high performance?
- How do I coach people one-on-one? How do I get started? What should I expect?
- How can I make one-on-one coaching conversations more than friendly chit-chat?
- What coaching do product owners and agile managers need so that they can be of high value to teams?
- How do I coach new agile coaches to function on their own?

could be directly applied to the agile teams I coached in the business world. Imagine my delight!

It was then that I discerned the difference between coaching and mentoring and realized that I had been working with only one side of the equation, the mentoring side. Once I added coaching to the mentoring I was already doing, I understood what a powerful combination the two could be. The teams I coached realized it, too. Now I am a professional work/life coach, and I mix those skills with agile mentorship quite fluidly to guide other coaches, team members, whole teams, and the people who surround them.

In this chapter, we explore much of what I have learned about applying coaching skills to an agile context. We start by defining agile coaching more clearly, and then we introduce the levels of coaching that go on all the time— the individual level and whole-team level—diving deeper into how to coach individuals, with special treatment for coaching other agile coaches, product owners, and managers.

What Is Agile Coaching?

To understand agile coaching, let's look at the world of professional coaching first. In this world, coaching happens through a series of artful conversations in which the coach helps the coachee see new perspectives and possibilities. From here, the coachee can imagine the next step in their personal and professional growth and move into action to take that step.

In the context of agile teams, coaching takes on the dual flavor of coaching and mentoring. Yes, you are coaching to help someone reach for the next goal in their life, just as a professional work/life coach does. You are also sharing your agile experiences and ideas as you mentor them, guiding them to use agile well. In this way, coaching and mentoring are entwined for the sake of developing talented agilists so that more and better business results arise through agile.

The pattern repeats at the whole-team level. Coaching helps the team's performance get better, in a series of steps coached by you and chosen by them. Mentoring transfers your agile knowledge and experience to the team as that specific knowledge becomes relevant to what's happening with them.

Each side—coaching and mentoring—is useful and can be powerful on its own. Together, they are a winning combination for helping people adopt agile and use it well. The context of agile makes you a mentor; the focus on team performance makes you a coach. Both parts of the equation come together to make agile come alive and bring it within their grasp.

In the agile world, coaching and mentoring have been wrapped up in the cumulative term *coaching*. It's no big deal; just know that the phrase *agile coach* involves both coaching and mentoring. Also, know that we are using skills from the world of professional coaching, but we are not truly professional coaches. A serious point of ethics for professional coaches holds that the coachee's agenda must be the single guiding light of the coaching relationship. The coach exists solely for the coachee, not so for us. We can't let the coachee's agenda rule completely because we must also mix in our agenda: to influence the coachee to use agile well.

Again, it's no big deal; just know that we are coach-like, using tools from professional coaching, and we are mentors with an expertise in agile. We educate from this expertise and use coaching skills to help each person make the transition to using agile well. I have this dynamic duo in mind when I proudly say, "I am an agile coach."

What Are We Coaching For?

Agile coaches champion the brilliant use of agile so that businesses achieve their goals faster and better. If we want to stretch to the full capacity of agile, we'll amend that statement to be faster and better with innovations marvelous and yet undreamed. That's what agile was built to do.

To these ends, you coach to

- Help the organization achieve astonishing results, the kind that will matter to the business and the team members in a fundamental way

- Help the team develop and get healthier together (or recover more completely when not healthy)

- Help each person take the next step on their agile journey so they can be more successful agilists and contribute in a way that feeds team improvement and their own growth

Increasing the joy and accomplishment people feel in their work may be a separate, perhaps side, goal for you. It is for me, because I hold strong the belief that people should be fulfilled in their work, where they spend most of their waking hours. And, I notice that teams that pay attention to creating joy and feeling accomplished have many accomplishments to feel joyful about. This virtuous circle feeds itself.

Coaching at Two Levels

When you coach an agile team, you simultaneously coach them at two levels: the individual level and the whole-team level. There is a time for each. Also, coaching happens as a layer on top of your agile framework of choice rather than as a replacement for any of it. First and foremost, we uphold agile. Second, we coach.

Coaching interventions have their strongest effect at the beginning and end of a project (Hackman 2002). Project boundaries become blurred with agile because we value creating products that meet the business needs rather than finishing projects on a predetermined end date. Since agile harnesses change for good, the beginning and end of the whole project becomes less useful to us as a way to mark time than the built-in boundaries of sprint and release. The advice about coaching interventions still applies, though. For agile teams, it means that coaching at the beginning and end of a sprint or a release has the most impact.

Even though you channel your coaching intentions at the beginning and end, coaching doesn't go on vacation in the middle of a sprint. You still help the team remove impediments, fulfill their roles fully, and, in general, keep moving. When in midsprint, though, you pause and think hard before bringing a major observation or improvement opportunity to the whole team. Instead, you let them work, and you make plans to bring it up at the end, when whole-team coaching comes to the fore again.

As Figure 5.1 shows, your coaching switches from team to individual and back to team again over the life of the sprint. An ill-timed coaching intervention can do more harm than good (Hackman 2002), especially in an agile framework where we give teams the necessary gift of focus during a sprint. Switching your coaching intentions from team to individual and back again prevents the harm and increases the good.

The whole time, be their ground crew. Help them when they get stuck, remind them of the goals they set out to achieve when they have delved so far into the details that they can no longer recall the purpose, advocate for them to uphold the way they said they wanted to treat one another as they work together, and encourage them constantly.

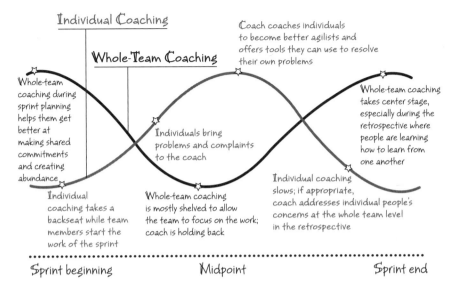

Individual Coaching

Whole-Team Coaching

Coach coaches individuals to become better agilists and offers tools they can use to resolve their own problems

Whole-team coaching during sprint planning helps them get better at making shared commitments and creating abundance

Individuals bring problems and complaints to the coach

Whole-team coaching takes center stage, especially during the retrospective where people are learning how to learn from one another

Individual coaching takes a backseat while team members start the work of the sprint

Whole-team coaching is mostly shelved to allow the team to focus on the work; coach is holding back

Individual coaching slows; if appropriate, coach addresses individual people's concerns at the whole team level in the retrospective

Sprint beginning   Midpoint   Sprint end

FIGURE 5.1   Whole-team and individual coaching interventions during the sprint

Coaching at the Beginning

As one sprint ends and another begins, the time for coaching the whole team is ripe. Educational coaching takes center stage, such as helping the team get agile practices working well or teaching them to really embody their agile role. Through this kind of coaching, keep your eye on the goal: to help the whole team see how agile works beautifully when simply done. Conduct this coaching "out loud" in the team room as the perfect moment to teach a particular concept just happens to arise. Or, plan a teaching intervention to introduce or reinforce something about agile that the team needs now. If they need to learn how to use their velocity information better to plan sprints while maintaining focus and creating abundance, for example, then prepare to teach them about this when they are in the middle of sprint planning. Educational coaching interventions have their greatest impact when they are delivered in the midst of the activity they are meant to improve.

SEE ALSO	Helping the team maintain focus and create a sense of abundance so that they commit to just the right amount of work is discussed in Chapter 6, "Coach as Facilitator."

Coaching at the Very Beginning

The coaching intervention at the beginning of the team's first sprint together sets the tone for much of what follows. The coach aims to "breathe life into the team's structural shell [in our case, agile] and thereby help the team start functioning on its own" (Hackman 2002). To breathe life into the team, plan an educational coaching intervention as the team start-up, teaching the team about the agile framework to be used, teaching them about each other and themselves together as a team, and teaching them about the vision of the project and the work ahead.

SEE ALSO	What and how to teach during the team start-up is the subject of Chapter 7, "Coach as Teacher."

Coaching in the Middle

In the middle of a sprint, coaching at the whole-team level quiets down. The coach becomes physically quieter, too, as the team works. If any whole-team coaching happens, it will be only for the biggest-impact insights that the coach consciously decides to insert.

Since performance strategy conversations are appropriate for midpoint coaching interventions (Hackman 2002), you may ask the team whether a mid-sprint check would prove useful (especially if the burndown chart looks like a ski jump). As a simple, lightweight conversation between the team members, a midsprint check yields renewed ideas and plans about how they are going to get the rest of the work done. It stops short of stirring up a midsprint retrospective, and the coach guards against this.

Since agile coaches protect the team's ability to focus by leaving them alone to work, midsprint is the perfect time for individual coaching. Coincidentally, this happens to be the time that team members often bring problems to the coach.

With individual coaching, agile coaches address a person's issues while keeping in mind the natural rhythms of agile so as not to disturb the team at work. If the problem is between two team members, encourage the problem-presenting person to resolve it one-on-one with the other person. If the problem is not earth-shattering, suggest the retrospective be geared to bring it forth. You can suggest the retrospective option any time, but especially as you near the end of the sprint.

Midsprint is also a great time to recognize and reinforce competent team behaviors that spontaneously occur (Hackman 2002) by coaching "out loud" in the team room. When someone does something particularly helpful or powerful, talk to them about it in front of the rest of the team. You need not make a big scene. A regular, respectful conversation the rest of the team will overhear works well. This means you must be present and observant to "catch" someone doing well.

Coaching at the End

At the end of a sprint comes the final coaching intervention. The end signals a natural time for the team to look back at how they worked together and decide what they will do to make the next sprint even better. Agile frameworks support this intervention through the formal pause at the end of each sprint—the retrospective. During this intervention, facilitate the team's conversation so that they come up with a few things they agree to change in the next sprint. Over time, ensure that your coaching during the retrospective helps them do more than generate a to-do list of improvements. Coach the team to develop "to the point that members learn *how* best to learn from one another" (Hackman 2002).

The end of one sprint and the beginning of another happen in such rapid succession that the beginning and ending coaching interventions can be pushed together as one event with two pieces: looking back and educating for the future.

Coaching at the Release Level

The coaching interventions cycle is repeated at the release level. The most useful interventions are the same here—education at the beginning of a release cycle and learning through looking back at the end of a release cycle, with a whole-team check during the middle of a release cycle along with individual coaching.

Pay attention to where the team is in the sprint or release cycle to make whole-team and individual coaching useful and powerful. Strike this balance: Coach individuals and teams at the same time, and choose the type of coaching that will be the most impactful and least disruptive.

Coaching Tone

No matter whether you are coaching at the whole-team or individual level, set your coaching tone to these frequencies: loving, compassionate, and uncompromising. At first glance, those three words don't seem to go together. Am I really saying that you should let your coaching be loving and compassionate *and* uncompromising? Oh, yeah.

Love each person just because they are human, like you, and give them the gift of acceptance so that they know they are supported as they strive to become a better team member (and person). Have compassion for each person's journey so they know you honor where they *are* as you help them become what they *want to be*. When they know—and feel—that you are loving and compassionate toward them, they can shed the all-too-common posturing and preening and get real with you. With these shed, the coaching can begin.

To bring love and compassion to your coaching, you don't have to get all lovey-dovey in the workplace. Hugs and exclaiming "I just love this guy!" are insincere substitutes for the deep expression required of you. Embody the type of love and compassion that rings so true that they can see it in your eyes, in the way you really listen to them, and in the way you honor them as the experts on their own lives.

You don't ever need to say the words *love* or *compassion* for them to know they are supported and valued. In fact, it's better if you don't. Instead, you just *are* loving and compassionate. And here's where the power lies: Being loving and compassionate allows you to be uncompromising.

Gift them with your willingness to be uncompromising, because having seen their great self, you expect the best from them and simply believe that they will become the person they wish to become and achieve the things they wish to achieve. Coaching has nothing to do with stroking their vanity and making them feel good about themselves. Instead, the coach takes the strong stand needed to get to the next level of agility possible for each person and, in so doing, raises the level of agility all around. Coaching helps each person get to that next level of professional growth that makes their work relevant to their whole life. Through effective coaching, individuals emerge who can contribute fully to agile teams so that we reap astonishing results, not just mediocre results delivered a little faster.

There's a trite, but true, saying in coaching: A friend loves you just the way you are. A coach loves you too much to let you stay that way.

Love them too much to let them stay as they are, and let this be the seed of your uncompromising stance. Loving, yes. Compassionate, yes. And 100% uncompromising.

If team members want to "tailor agile" so that they don't have to address dysfunctions in their company, that's their choice, and you can't make them choose differently. But don't buy into it, either. Remember the mentor side of your job—you know what an excellent agilist looks like, talks like, and acts like. Don't demand the team members immediately meet your high bar of agility, but don't ever let them pretend that their compromise has changed the definition of good agile and that now they've "arrived" so they can stop working at it.

I've coached plenty of teams whose definition of agile has been twisted around the dysfunctions of the people in and around the team and the organization itself. As their coach, I hold out a clear picture of what agile done well looks like, and I do not ever compromise that vision. If they don't want to get there, OK, but they will never hear me say that where they are is "agile enough." I hold fast to the vision of agile done well for their sake—for the sake of their greatness as an agile team member, as an agile team, and even as an agile organization.

Holding fast to your knowledge of agile done well can be a significant challenge, especially in one-on-one coaching conversations when team members' stories of woe suck you in until the woes start sounding like reasonable excuses for why they can't be good agilists. That's when you hold the line even stronger. This next section prepares you to do just that.

Coaching People One-on-One

There comes a time to coach people one-on-one. Perhaps a team member comes to you with a problem, or perhaps you decide to proactively have a conversation about something you see happening. Sooner or later, the one-on-one coaching conversation knocks on your door. This section gets you ready to open that door. First we lay four pieces of groundwork for one-on-one coaching, and then we tease apart the arc of the coaching conversation so that you can know what to look for as you coach people one-on-one.

Lay the Groundwork for One-on-One Coaching

The four pieces of groundwork to set in place before one-on-one coaching commences are as follows:

- Meet them a half-step ahead.
- Guarantee safety.
- Partner with managers.
- Create a positive regard.

These four together create a basis from which to coach people, a place for you to start.

Meet Them a Half-Step Ahead

A basic principle in professional coaching states that we meet our coaching clients "where they are," not where *we* are or where we think they *should* be or where we *know* they have the ability to go, but where they *are*—right now. Because agile coaching carries agile mentorship with it, we modify this rule to say we first recognize where our one-on-one coachees are, and then we meet them just a *half-step ahead* of where they are. Because we are mentoring them using the agile tool kit—practices, principles, values, mind-sets—as coaches, we are already ahead of them on the agile path.

Just because we know what agile done well looks like doesn't mean that we coach from that far-distant place. This is why we meet them a half-step ahead, not ten steps ahead of where they are or even two steps ahead. We don't ask them to run a four-minute mile if they've never gotten off the couch, for example.

A half-step ahead is a fine place to stand. From here, we offer agile knowledge and experience that may help them take their next step. Although we care about the individual as a work/life coach would care about them, we aren't coaching them in general. Our purpose stays on target when we remember we are coaching them in agile. Having said that, we coach the whole person who shows up in front of us, not just the work side and not just the life side but whatever combination they bring. We do this because work done well cannot be separated from personhood done well. And agile done well cannot be separated from values lived well.

To detect where they *are*, listen to them. Listen to their beliefs about how the working world works and should work. Let them talk about the high points and low points in their past. Let them tell you about their current struggles. Ask them what they think about agile and whether they think it will change what they already know and how they have learned to behave in the workplace.

Then, imagine an "agile journey" path, and fix a point on that path where you think they are. Maybe they're very young in their understanding of agile, and they are open-hearted, so you think of them as being just a few steps along the path. Maybe they have been exposed to agile for some time but staunchly refuse to change, so you see them near the start of the path. Maybe they have the basics down and want to understand the deeper principles behind agile, so you imagine they are somewhere near the middle of the path.

Don't fret. You don't have to get this right the first time or every time. Just imagine the coachee on an agile journey path, and coach them as if you were standing just a half-step ahead of them. Then, notice what happens as you coach. Maybe the person is further along than you first thought and they're ready for more; maybe they talked a good game, and you now realize that they are far behind where you first thought and you need to scale your agile ambitions for them back. No problem. Just adjust. Remember inspect and adapt? It works for coaches, too.

Guarantee Safety

Agile coaches uphold an environment of experimentation and risk taking because we know that only in such a place will brilliance emerge. Agile teams need to be free to act silly, bumble around, say extreme things out loud, and make mistakes—all without the specter of the performance review process hanging over their heads.

Team members don't need their coach blabbing about something cute they said in the team room or bumping into a manager in the coffee area and letting loose with, "Wow, Judy really does have quite the temper." Such utterances do not slip from the coach's mouth, not even informally or even in jest. What happens in the team stays in the team.

Even if the team does not yet enjoy an open and creative atmosphere, people still need space to be human, make mistakes, and recover from mistakes together, as a team. Otherwise, they never will.

When you coach individuals and teams, they need to know they have the space to be human and that you are holding what happens between you two and what happens in the team room as confidential. To do this, simply declare confidentiality and safety, and stick to it.

Of course, don't check your common sense at the door. Some situations, luckily rare, should not be handled within the confines of the team alone. Situations such as harassment, discrimination, and violence in any form are reasons to break the confidentiality rule. As the coach, you protect their physical and emotional safety and hold that as more important than their license to blunder.

> **SEE ALSO**   Conflict is inevitable on any team, but especially on an agile team because we expect agile teams to collaborate, which means being vulnerable with one another. For ways to coach teams to work constructively with conflict, see Chapter 9, "Coach as Conflict Navigator."

Barring these infrequent situations, trust that the team can and will—with your coaching—handle what happens. Coach them to work together to resolve problems within the team. Coach them to recognize when the problem extends beyond the team and they need to ask for help. Guide them through a few situations, and notice what happens to their ability to be self-reliant and self-correcting. I'll bet it grows each time.

Partner with Managers

If we honor "What happens in the team stays in the team," then partnering with team members' managers may seem a violation of this rule. If your intentions are not in the right place, it very well could be a violation, so check those first. Positive intentions revolve around your desire to help each person reach their full agile potential. As long as this is at the center of your partnership relationship with a person's manager, you will be able to uphold your guarantee of confidentiality and safety.

Team members' functional managers are the ones they "report" to and who administer their performance review results. At the very least, they influence each team members' ability to participate in the team. At the worst, they are blockers to teamwork through the way they motivate individualistic behavior. For these reasons, you need to coach the managers, too.

Each team member's manager affects the whole team overtly and covertly. Overtly, the manager's performance review expectations drive certain behaviors. Covertly, the manager's support or derision of agile comes through in conversations with team members. If the manager does not support agile, it's hard for the team member to invest fully in the team.

Create a partnership with the manager so that you know their "plan" for the team member you are coaching. What performance measures are the team member expected to achieve this year? How much does the team member need to be able to clearly identify their solo contribution to meet those performance measures? Basically, you need to know how the team member will be rewarded so you can see whether it supports or thwarts working in a shared-commitment environment. You may also find you need to educate the manager about how agile works if the manager's approach and direction to the team member stands in the way of the team having a healthy shared commitment.

PARTNER WITH MANAGERS TO UNRAVEL TEAM PROBLEMS

The tension was so thick that the team was choking on it, yet no one could name the cause. It was affecting everyone, especially a small group of team members who were working on a new area of the product together. If you looked in on a typical conversation, you would think that these three hated each another. Raised voices, talking over one another, doing things "my way" regardless of what the others were doing—this was common. They were running (fast!) in three different directions at once. It wasn't just the way they were working together; what they were producing was a problem, too. The product owner thought their work was uninspired, too deep in some areas and too light in others. Worse, their attitudes were infecting the rest of the team.

When we got to the core of the problem, we discovered that each of them had just received their yearly performance review, and each of them had been told something like this by their functional manager: "To get the rating you want next year, you have to grab something and make it your own. We need to see results and see you driving those results." Each of them took that to heart. They were grabbing work, they were grabbing air time, and they were grabbing each other by the throat.

This only came to light through one-on-one coaching conversations with each team member. Each of them wanted to know why it was so hard to get along with the other two. About the second time I heard the latest performance management edict, I started to piece the story together.

Often, an innocent move by someone's functional manager can have unintended consequences for the whole team. In this case, it torpedoed teamwork and made the idea of shared commitment impossible.

These three turned out fine. Once we realized what was going on, each shared their performance review plan for the coming year with the others, and they realized why they had been working at cross-purposes. I spoke with the functional managers to let them know the impact on these three and the larger team. I made no bones about it. I let them know the team would not meet its commitments if each person were incented to stake their own territory.

The managers were resistant because the "stake your territory" message was what their manager told them to deliver. So, I went to talk to that manager. Through our conversation, he realized how detrimental the message would be to his main goal, which was to get more and better products from the agile teams. The edict was relaxed, the team understood one another better, past sins were forgiven, and the team got back on track.

Partnering with managers can often be helpful and, in this case, essential. Without the manager-coach conversations, the problem would have continued to fester.

You also need to let the manager know that you will be coaching their direct report. The two of you may work together to support the team member's next step whether that be a desired behavior change or an opportunity to stretch into a new area. To do this, you need not violate the "What happens in the team stays in the team" rule. You need not give details to the manager to be able to partner with them.

If you sense some intense coaching coming up soon with a team member, let the team member's manager in on the action. At the very least, the manager needs to know the team member may be experiencing some changes and, perhaps, some not-too-fun times. This is a good time to reinforce the guarantee of confidentiality and safety, especially if the manager sees this as an opportunity to get your help with a needed behavior change. Make it clear to the manager that you will share the person's actions and impacts but that you will not get into details, blow-by-blow analysis, or "he said/she said" reenactments.

Oftentimes, the behavior that gets in the way of an agile team is the very behavior that the manager has been telling a direct report they should improve for some time, but without a good way to make it happen. Agile gives managers great help in this regard. Because agile demands full participation, which often means facing one's shortcomings, agile teams are fertile environments for growth and change.

Create Positive Regard

You don't have to like the people you coach, but you do have to help them. When you coach someone you dislike, your feelings can easily show through. The dislike leaks out. People know when they're being "handled." They know when you view them as a problem to solve rather than as a human being with hopes, dreams, and desires.

The book *Leadership and Self-Deception* describes it this way: Imagine a box. Imagine that when you view people as objects, as problems to be solved, you are in the box. The box is a place of blaming, justification, and perceptions so distorted that the truth of the situation can no longer be seen. In the box, we inflate other's faults and inflate our own virtues (Arbinger Institute 2002) so that we can maintain our view of others as the problem. When we're in the box, all the management, coaching, facilitating, and cat-herding tools and techniques in the world don't matter:

> Helpful skills and techniques aren't helpful if they're done in the box. They just provide people [you, the coach] with more sophisticated ways to blame (Arbinger Institute 2002).

Our job as coaches is to stay out of the box. To do this, we must view people "straightforwardly as they are—as people like [ourselves] who have needs and desires as legitimate as [our] own" (Arbinger Institute 2002).

One way to do this is to believe that everyone is doing the best they can with the skills they have and the cards they were dealt. This helps you keep in touch with the humanity the two of you share so that you can see them straightforwardly and, in so doing, see the truth of the situation clearly.

SEE ALSO For practical ways to stay out of the box and see people as people rather than as problems, check out Chapter 3, "Master Yourself."

As you prepare to coach someone, check yourself. If you view the coachee as a problem to solve, you are in a barren place for coaching. All the coaching skills and agile experience in the world will fall flat if you coach from this perspective.

This becomes even more challenging when you dislike someone or maybe just dislike the impact of their actions on themselves or others. Even in this situation, your job as agile coach calls you to create a positive regard for them. Do this by changing your view of them. Regard the person as a human being with hopes, dreams, and desires (like your own) so that you can approach them with love and compassion, two essential ingredients for good coaching. The Dali Lama has this to say about compassion:

> True compassion is not just an emotional response but a firm commitment founded on reason. Because of this firm foundation, a truly compassionate attitude toward others does not change even if they behave negatively. Genuine compassion is based not on our own projections and expectations, but rather on the needs of the other: irrespective of whether another person is a close friend or an enemy, as long as that person wishes for peace and happiness and wishes to overcome suffering, then on that basis we develop genuine concern for their problem. This is genuine compassion (The Dalai Lama 2003).

Following this lead, feel genuine compassion for where this person is in life and work. Feel genuine compassion for the impact they have on themselves and others through their actions. Then, reaffirm your belief that no one would knowingly negatively impact themselves, and believe, again, that everyone is doing the best they can.

Now, with love and compassion on board, you are ready to be uncompromising in your knowledge of what it means to be a good agile team member and to help the person move toward that vision, as they are willing and able.

How to Coach People One-on-One

You've laid the groundwork for coaching by detecting where the coachee is on their agile journey and meeting them a half-step ahead, guaranteeing confidentiality and safety, partnering with managers, and managing yourself so that you create a positive regard for the person to be coached. Now it's time to coach.

Getting started with the coaching conversation and knowing what to do while in it are the next bits to learn. Once you have experience with these, then the job becomes knowing when you are out of your depth as a coach. Let's take them one at a time.

Starting the Coaching Conversation

Getting started with a coaching conversation can be one of the hardest bits. The conversation may feel uncomfortable for both coach and coachee, especially if the coach is new to addressing people's lives and "being real" with them. It is almost certain that the coachee will not be accustomed to real conversations in the workplace, so they will likely be uncomfortable at first. Real conversations are fierce.

> But a "fierce" conversation? Doesn't "fierce" suggest menacing, cruel, barbarous, threatening? Sounds like raised voices, frowns, blood on the floor, no fun at all. In *Roget's Thesaurus*, however, the word *fierce* has these synonyms: robust, intense, strong, powerful, passionate, eager, unbridled, uncurbed, untamed. In its simplest form, a fierce conversation is one in which we come out from behind ourselves into the conversation and make it real (Scott 2007).

Real conversations are fierce. Fierce conversations are real. You don't see this often in most business environments, yet…

> While many fear "real," it is the unreal conversation that should scare us to death. Unreal conversations are expensive, for the individual and the organization. No one has to change, but everyone has to have the conversation. When the conversation is real, the change occurs before the conversation is over (Scott 2007).

As you approach the coaching conversation, be ready to be real and to invite the coachee to be real, too. If the two of you can do this, you may see the change occur before the conversation ends. A shift in the coachee signals the change—perhaps a shift into action, perhaps a shift in perspective, or perhaps a shift in emotional viewpoint. That's what you're going for.

Getting started is easy when the coachee initiates the conversation. It just happens to you! As the conversation starts, relax and go with it. Do your best to check yourself on the four pieces of groundwork as you begin. Say to yourself, "I am looking for where the coachee is right now so that I can meet her a half-step ahead. I will ensure there is room for being real, knowing that I have an ally in her manager so we can best help her take the next step, whatever she decides that is. I view her positively, bringing compassion to the conversation so that she is supported in taking that next step."

Other times, it's up to the coach to start the conversation. When this is the case, make the conversation informal. Just "happen" to run into the person of your intentions in the break room or when you get up to take a stretch. Open with an observation or an invitation.

An observation opening states your perspective: "I noticed that you seemed frustrated during the stand-up today. Did I make that up?" An invitation opening leaves the field of possibility wide: "What did you notice during the stand-up this morning?" Regardless of which you choose, after you open the conversation, be silent and wait for a response. Wait as long as it takes. If you do, the coachee will talk and then probably talk and talk and talk.

Table 5.1 offers a few more examples to show you the difference between observation and invitation openings.

TABLE 5.1   Observation and invitation openings

Observation opening	Invitation opening
"It seems like you have been distracted lately. When people engage you in conversation, you seem a million miles away. What's really happening?"	"What are the ways we're getting distracted lately?"
"Wow! We are full of conflict all of a sudden. What's your take on this?"	"What did you notice about the feel of the team's conversation this morning?"
"Something's up. You are not your usual positive self. What's going on?"	"I can make up a thousand reasons why I think something is going on with you. Instead I'll just offer you this: I am here."

TRY THIS

In the next week, start four coaching conversations. Notice anything that seems off with the team or a particular person. Then, plan your opening. Will it be an observation or an invitation opening? Will you stand in silent invitation (as long as it takes) for the coachee to talk?

Then, notice the impact. What has shifted in the person? On the team? Real changes are often hard to detect; they are deep within, so watch for small miracles.

As soon as you start coaching a team, open the one-on-one conversations immediately when there's nothing wrong and there's every chance for a wide-ranging open dialogue. Remember your job: to help each team member take the next step in their agile journey. To do this, you need to know where they are today. If you haven't already done so, today is a great day to find that out.

On a new team, have one-on-one conversations that let you get to know each person and what you can do to help each next. Feel free to ask the question directly, "What can I do to help you take the next step in your use of agile to deliver for the company (and yourself)?" You will be doing good for the team overall, and when you need to address an issue, you already have a history of such conversations to use as a springboard.

Watch for the Arc of the Conversation

When coaching one-on-one, look for the arc of the conversation. You'll notice the conversation itself goes through a few stages as you listen and respond. Attending to the arc and moving the coachee through the conversation produces far greater results than months of friendly chit-chat.

As shown in Figure 5.2, the coaching conversation has a beginning, middle, and end—it's an arc of activity. The arc of the conversation need not be long. In fact, some of the most productive coaching conversations can happen in the span of ten minutes, once you get good at it.

> *While the coachee vents, remember this: The opposite of talking is not listening. The opposite of talking is waiting.*
>
> —*Fran Lebowitz*

Conversation Beginning Whether the coach or the coachee opens the conversation, the beginning is much the same. In the beginning, venting happens. The coachee needs to get something (or many things) off his chest, and he needs to be heard. During venting, the coach practices listening fully and being totally present.

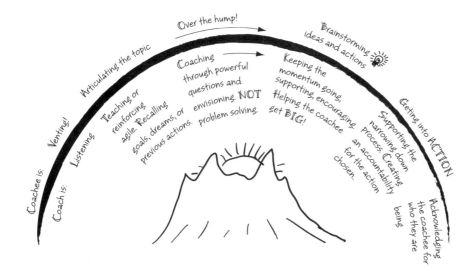

Figures labeled on arc: "Over the hump!", "Brainstorming ideas and actions", "Articulating the topic", "Coaching through powerful questions and envisioning. NOT problem solving.", "Keeping the momentum going, supporting, encouraging. Helping the coachee get BIG!", "Teaching or reinforcing agile. Recalling goals, dreams, or previous actions.", "Getting into ACTION", "Listening", "Venting!", "Supporting the narrowing down process. Creating an accountability for the action chosen.", "Acknowledging the coachee for who they are being", "Coachee is:", "Coach is:"

FIGURE 5.2   The arc of the coaching conversation

The venting wears itself out (or the coach offers a timebox to finish it up if it seems that it may go on forever). Then, the real reason the coachee has started talking begins to emerge. The coach checks in with the coachee about the topic ("I think this is about feeling ignored by the team. Did I hear that right?") as they move into conversation centered on the topic. Reinforcing something about agile may be useful at this point. Perhaps recalling a practice, value, or role characteristic will help address the topic. If so, bring it up. You may also help the coachee call to mind a personal goal or action they have previously expressed as it relates to the topic.

Conversation Middle   You are getting close to the midpoint and getting over the "hump" of the conversation when the coachee starts to climb out of the dead-endedness of the topic.

This happens because the coach asks powerful questions that invite introspection. Perhaps the coach has taken the coachee on an imaginary trip into the future where the topic has already been resolved perfectly. From this place of possibility, the coachee can see his own solutions. He arrives at the midpoint of the conversation with a resounding "It's not hopeless after all!"

SEE ALSO   Powerful questions, including what they are and how they can be used, are covered in Chapter 6, "Coach as Facilitator."

Perhaps he sees new ways to address the topic, perhaps he sees something within himself that holds him back, or perhaps he feels renewed just having shared something deep and bothersome.

Next, the coachee starts looking for specific solutions. Coach and coachee may brainstorm together while the coach encourages and supports the process. Oftentimes, supporting the process means giving the coachee room to be big, wild, and unbridled in brainstorming possible actions. This means the coach may also need to get big, wild, and unbridled. Note something the coach purposefully avoids during the conversation: problem solving. If you do offer solution options, it's only to keep the coachee's juices flowing. You couldn't care less whether the coachee chooses "your" option because you know that for it to be meaningful the action must be freely chosen by him.

Conversation End   You can feel the conversation coming to a close when the coachee starts narrowing down to a few specific actions to take. Let it close at this time. Even if a new topic arises, don't pursue it. Let the coachee move forward on what he has already decided to do. Rest assured, if important enough, the other topic will come back. The two of you can deal with it then.

Once the coachee has chosen the action to take, the coach supports the coachee by setting up an accountability for that action (Whitworth et al. 2007). The accountability can be either explicit or soft. An explicit accountability is an agreement the coachee makes about when the action will be done and how he will let the coach know. It's the coachee's job to move forward with the action, not the coach's job to "make" him do it, so the coachee should not be pressured into making an explicit accountability. Put all the responsibility where it belongs, squarely in the coachee's court.

The accountability can also be soft, such as the coach asking, "May I check in with you in five days to see what has happened?" This is often more comfortable in a business context because people aren't accustomed to being "pinned down." (That's quite a commentary on the weak state of personal accountability in the workplace, isn't it?)

As you repeatedly coach someone, without forcing, move from soft accountabilities to explicit accountabilities. This ratchets up the coachee's ability to be accountable, an essential agile skill.

The conversation ends with the coach acknowledging the coachee for who he is being. For example, "I want to let you know that, in this moment, I see courage in you that is palpable." An acknowledgment is not "Thank you for being courageous in the way you are addressing this issue." The "thank-you," although polite, raises the coach above the coachee and saps the coachee's power. A well-delivered acknowledgment, in contrast, honors who the person had to be in order for you to feel their courage. Receiving such an acknowledgment magnifies the coachee's power.

Throughout the conversation, the coach and coachee remain on the same peer level. Certainly, the coach has a few skills, such as all the things you are learning in this book, but that doesn't make the coach superior. For this to work well, the coachee needs to remain the honored expert on his life.

Being aware of the arc of an agile coaching conversation can help you keep it positive and forward moving. Reading the signs as you move from the beginning to the middle to the end will help the conversation flow smoothly. Remember, though, that the person is more important than the formula. So, if the coachee needs something different, give them what they need. You can experiment with this, as with all things, to make it your own.

Subject-Matter Expertise and Coaching

In the pursuit of a thriving agile team, you will coach all kinds of people one-on-one, such as team members, product owners, managers, and other coaches. All of these people may have far more subject-matter expertise in their specific area than you have. That's OK. In fact, in many cases, it's a benefit. You need not be an expert in any of their domains to coach them well, as long as you stick to coaching and veer away from solving their problem for them. Certainly, learn about the latest software refactoring technique or peruse the cool trend data for the product's target market if that interests you, but don't let that knowledge move you into solution mode. Instead, offer insights as their agile mentor, and coach them to come up with their own solutions.

If you have a tendency to take on other people's problems as your own, check your actions to ensure you have not unintentionally burdened yourself with responsibility for the coachee's situation. The problem and the action rest with them. You cannot make the problem go away by solving it for them. Your solution can be only a temporary fix at best, so don't solve. Instead, coach.

Coaching from a Distance

Once the coaching relationship has been established, you can take it to the phone or to a videoconference. When you coach at a distance, though, you will not witness the events as they unfold on the team firsthand. You only get vignettes of what's going on through the retelling of events as various team members convey snippets of conversations colored by their individual perspectives. To avoid the "he said/she said" trap, focus solely on the coachee and what the coachee wants next in their agile life. You can still offer your solid mix of coaching and agile mentorship, but the relationship shifts to be more with team members one-on-one rather than coaching the whole team in the moment. If you miss the moment, you miss the coaching.

Know Your Limits

Your main job as agile coach revolves around enabling people to use agile well. Sometimes, this means reinforcing a practice or helping someone see how agile solves something they struggle with. Oftentimes, this means getting into how people feel about their work or their role on the team. In other words, this means addressing the whole human being in front of you.

Agile itself blurs the line between work and life because, to do agile well, we ask people to bring their whole selves to the endeavor at hand. We don't ask people to check their courage at the door. In fact, coaches create an environment that invites people to be courageous. We don't tell people to shut up and go along because we need the diversity of ideas that come from every voice being heard.

A set of strong value statements in the agile manifesto and a fundamental belief that, given a simple framework, small groups of people can achieve great things together are what form the core of agile. Human relationships are, very simply, the center of the agile manifesto. Expect that as you coach people well, they will start to open up and tell you about their whole selves—their work and their life.

Professional work/life coaches know when they're out of their depth, and you should, too. When the coachee brings up a hurtful event or issue in their home life, you may feel ill-equipped to "go there" with them. If so, don't. Suggest they find a professional work/life coach. Refer them to the International Coach Federation website (coachfederation.org) where they can learn about professional coaches and find one. Or, become one yourself.

You may also catch yourself being the "expert opinion" in the conversation—the person who knows what the coachee should do next, how the coachee should go about doing it, and maybe even how the coachee should feel about it.

When you catch yourself doing this, know that you have violated a coaching rule, specifically, the rule that the coachee is an expert on her own life. Feel free to offer expertise about agile (after all, you are her agile mentor), but stop short of offering her your expert opinion on what's right for her in her own life. Only she knows that.

If you cross the line, just as in other situations, transparently recognize the gaffe and apologize for it. Then, get back to territory you are able to handle, and give yourself a break. You have just bumped against an important border. Having found it, you will not cross it lightly again because you know that it is no exaggeration to say that people's lives are at stake.

Coaching Product Owners

Working with product owners means teaching them their role and then showing them how to work agile to their best advantage. This is the mentoring part of the agile coach's job. The coaching part entails helping them make the transition to being a good product owner. Their journey toward agile may be similar to yours if they came from a management role where command-and-control behavior was prized and maybe even essential for climbing the ladder.

Like you, they will need to recover from command-and-control-ism. Like you, they will need to focus on business value delivery rather than micromanaging the next move of every team member. Like you, they will learn to trust the team. You have a lot to help each other through as you both learn to do agile well together.

As you discover new ways to appreciate the joy and power of agile done well, share your discoveries with the product owners in your life to help them see new ways for it to benefit their company and their careers.

To be able to coach product owners, you need a common language. That common language comes from the short list of things a team needs a product owner to be: business value driver, vision keeper, daily decision maker, heat shield, and the one ultimately responsible.

Once the product owner understands their role, you can start coaching. This means giving them feedback in the moment when something they've just done either undermined the team or supported the team brilliantly. Just as we tell our teams they are empowered, we coaches must also assume we are empowered to give feedback to the product owner. After all, we're aimed at improving team performance, and the product owner's work and behavior heavily influences the team's performance. Of course, we need to coach them!

The idea of having such open conversations with a product owner and providing direct and sometimes unpleasant feedback may seem like a daunting task, especially if the product owner sits a few organizational rungs above the coach. This can put the coach in an awkward position.

To alleviate the awkwardness, claim the authority and influence that comes with the agile coach role, and use it to start direct conversations with the product owner regardless of the product owner's organizational position. As the bulldozer, shepherd, servant leader, and guardian of quality and performance, you must address anything that affects the team's ability to deliver and continuously improve. By fully stepping into the agile coach role, your focus on team improvement makes it clear that the coach/product owner conversation is about team health rather than personal opinion or politics. Such a clarity of role and intention yields positional authority. Use it.

SEE ALSO	For clarification of the aspects of the product owner role as business value driver, vision keeper, daily decision maker, heat shield, and the one ultimately responsible or of the aspects of the coach role as bulldozer, shepherd, servant leader, and guardian of quality and performance, see Chapter 7, "Coach as Teacher."

To coach the product owner, first view the product owner as you view any other team member. All of the things you do to coach team members pertain to coaching the product owner, as well. This includes establishing a coaching relationship from the beginning, getting to know where the product owner is on their agile journey, and partnering with the product owner's manager. It all applies.

Coaching product owners falls into three broad areas: running their business, being a product owner for the team, and getting good at the product owner role. Coaching in some or all of these areas will be needed based on the maturity, business expertise, and agile experience of the product owner.

Coaching Product Owners on Running Their Business

Agile frameworks teach us to harp on business value delivered; we hold business value delivered as the one and only measure of progress and value. We ask product owners to sort the product backlog based on business value and to let nothing but business value guide their decision making. So, what is business value?

This critical question must be answered deeper than a return on investment (ROI) or profit number. Yes, one (or both) of those measures form part of the equation that makes up business value, but they are joined by other, non-numeric considerations such as risk and knowledge to be gained (Cohn 2006).

While balancing all those aspects of business value and moving toward the complete end vision, which may be months away, product owners need short-term goals to act as stepping-stones toward total business value. Let's call these stepping-stones *business value microdefinitions*. They are the goals at the ground level that determine where the product owner points the team, sprint after sprint.

Business Value Microdefinitions

In the throes of building a product, the product owner will make many trade-off decisions, several to dozens a day. On what basis does the product owner make these decisions? They make trade-off decisions according to the business value microdefinition, which conveys the next critical business objective.

Perhaps increasing the volume of users on the current product is a must-do to ramp up profit now while the team also performs the work necessary to ready new channel partners. If so, those two objectives are the current micro-definition. Think of it this way: The microdefinition expresses the next critical business objective we must achieve on the way to creating the whole product.

Given this clarity, every decision the product owner makes filters through the microdefinition: Does [the thing we're considering] ramp up users or get channel partners ready?

For example, when prioritizing the product backlog, the items that support the microdefinition rise to the top of the list. Even decisions such as whether to accept a meeting request get filtered this way: Will this meeting help us ramp up users or get channel partners ready? If not, the meeting should be delayed.

Require product owners to know the business value microdefinition at all times. If necessary, help them discover the value microdefinition through coaching. Using powerful questions and your insights, help them unearth the next microdefinition. Once it's unearthed, help the product owner walk the fine line between achieving short-term and long-term goals for the product. Help them recognize when they are about to make a short-term trade-off decision that compromises their ability to get what they want in the long term, and vice versa.

You may run into product owners who very plainly do not possess the business acumen to do the job of steering the product (and the team). They may not know how to frame up releases, how to find out what the real customers need, or how to work the corporate politics. Even if they have these skills, they might not be subject-matter experts in the product domain.

DOING DONUTS IN THE PARKING LOT

Agile expert Rich Sheridan recounts this story illustrating the incredible power product owners have at their disposal with agile teams (Sheridan 2010).

People who come to Menlo Innovations or take our classes are often fascinated with the power and simplicity of our paper-based planning game. When we first introduced this planning game process at my old company, Interface Systems, my boss/CEO Bob Nero was thrilled to see us planning and revisiting our plan every two weeks. He saw a level of productive interaction between the business and technology teams that he had previously only dreamed of. This had gone on for several months when one day Bob came in and expressed a grave concern about this process. I believe Bob uttered words that no business executive had ever spoken to the head of a technical team:

"Rich, I have a great concern about this system you've created. It's too flexible."

"What do you mean, Bob?" I asked.

He said, "Rich, every two weeks we gather together for this planning activity, we lay out the stories we want you to work on, and you follow exactly the plan we lay out."

I said, "Yes. That's how it works."

He said, "We could come back two weeks later and completely change the plan going forward, and you would once again follow that plan."

I assured him that was true.

He said, "Rich, we could use this tool to do the planning equivalent of 'donuts in the parking lot,' and your team would follow our lead." I saw where Bob was heading.

I tried to coach him through a metaphor. I said, "Bob, tonight when you drive home in your Lexus, down I-94, do you realize you are holding in your hand a steering wheel and, should you so choose, you could jam the steering wheel to the right or to the left, tumbling your car and killing yourself and probably several others?" He responded, "Yeah, but I would never do that!"

I said, "Precisely! So don't do that with this process. This process requires a responsible driver at the steering wheel. If major changes are necessary for the business, we will follow. But if only minor tweaks are needed, then that should be the order of the day."

The planning game is a powerful tool and a dangerous tool. If the business chooses to do "donuts in the parking lot" and loses sight of the vision and direction for a project, nothing will be accomplished. However, having a simple tool that allows the business to steer, married to a process where the team will actually follow, we create an opportunity for a powerful collaboration between two teams that far too often have never learned to communicate in an effective manner.

Simple tools can provide profound results.

When you encounter such a product owner, get help. Just as we cultivate relationships with each team member's manager, do so with the product owner's manager and the sponsor (if not one and the same). Rely on these people to plug the holes in the product owner's business acumen or replace the product owner if the holes are too big to plug.

This can work only if you use the practices of agile to raise impediments and face them squarely. Remember that you don't have to do the product owner's job or sugarcoat their shortcomings; you just need to use your impediment-resolving responsibility to get them the help they need.

Gaming the Business Value System

If you ask a product owner to prioritize the product backlog, what you may get is a muddled ordering. It's muddled because the product owner weighs many things to figure out the priority, only one of which is business value to the company (a combination of value, cost, risk, and knowledge gained).

If you don't believe this, just have a conversation with the product owner after the product backlog has been sorted. Get curious about why a particular user story has been judged higher priority than another one. Ask open (and powerful) questions about what's behind the ranking of one vs. another. When you get down to it, you will likely find the backlog has been prioritized based on many extraneous things. Among these may be

- Who the product owner promised a particular feature to and whether he would be embarrassed to go back and change the delivery expectation
- The product owner's personal performance evaluation criteria
- Which features the product owner has become attached to
- Which external groups are "ready" for the team
- Which external groups are resistant to working with the team
- "Hard" dependencies the product owner assumes are immovable

Somewhere lurking at the bottom of this definition (if we're lucky) is the notion of which feature returns the highest business value. When coaching product owners, your job is to help them get that one combination criterion—business value—to the top of their definition of *priority*.

To achieve this, the next time the product owner sorts the product backlog, ask that it be done in two passes. Instruct the product owner to let the first pass be based on business value alone. Coach the product owner to be unreasonable in this first pass. Tell him to take the position that this product is the single most important initiative for the whole company. Ask him to imagine that he has just stepped into a world where he can get anything he needs to deliver the highest impact for the company *now*.

Then, with the product backlog sorted in this "unreasonable" way, the highest business value things are at the top. Anything that stands in the way of delivering them, starting with the most valuable one first, are impediments. Treat them that way.

In the second pass, the product owner lets the impediments in, one at a time. For this pass, invite the team to join the party. Together, they may find that some impediments are truly hard technical dependencies and cannot be moved. If so, perhaps a lesser-value story needs to get done before the higher-value one. Almost anything else, though, falls into the category of "We'd like to help you, but…," which signals that the company simply doesn't value the product highly enough to remove the impediment or that the cost of removing the impediment outweighs the benefit. In either case, don't sweep it under the rug. Make decisions transparent, and make the impact on the team known. If it's true that the company chooses to allow the team to deliver less value than they can, then let that reality stand in full view.

When faced with a value-restricting impediment, coach the product owner to take a stance such as this one: "The team can create the final piece we need to capture the teen market segment. To do so, we need a client relations expert to work full-time with our team for two weeks starting next week. We know the client relations team has a two-week lead time to get someone assigned to our team. That will be too late. Ms. Client Relations Vice-President, will you clear this impediment for us?" Otherwise, the product owner may just assume the company won't clear the impediment so he decides to accept the status quo as the final answer. In this case, his stance may be something like this: "Well, I guess we just have to deprioritize capturing the teen segment because the client relations group is just too busy to help us get new partners ready." If you were the CEO of the product owner's company, which stance would you rather he take?

Coaching Product Owners on Being a Good Product Owner for the Team

When I am asked to help agile teams figure out what's wrong with them, I often notice that the agile coach and product owner roles are jumbled up. I see these two people stomping on each other or filling in when one of them is not living up to their role.

This happens most frequently when the agile coach fills the void left by an absent product owner. Perhaps the coach accepts the rationalization that the product owner is too busy to be with the team, too busy to groom the product backlog, or too busy to be a product owner!

As human beings, we tend to cover for one another and try to keep things going even under strained circumstances. Hear this clearly: An agile coach cannot make up for an absent or poor product owner by filling in the gaps. It catches up with the coach and the team in unpleasant ways.

If the agile coach remains "on the hot seat" for schedule and budget information, you know that the coach's tendency to fill in for the product owner has already become a problem. This can be an easy trap to fall into, especially if the coach's pre-agile role was project manager. Many project managers grew accustomed to the hot seat. If this describes you, then don't take the hot seat with you into the agile world. If you do, all types of outsiders—managers, other teams, stakeholders—will come to you and want to know why the team will not deliver a certain feature, what's coming next, and how and where the money is being spent. These are not agile coach questions. They are product owner questions.

Everything related to the direction, schedule, and budget of the product falls into the product owner's job because the product owner makes the business decisions that impact these aspects of the product. In a healthy relationship, with a fully functional coach and a fully functional product owner, when asked about direction, schedule, and budget, the agile coach simply replies, "That's a good question for the product owner. She has all the details."

A whole host of team problems can usually be remedied by teaching (or reteaching) the roles of agile coach and product owner. When you do this, include the team by asking them to hold both agile coach and product owner up to these role definitions and expect that they will fill them completely. Consider anything less an impediment.

Once the product owner has received education on the role and you have provided coaching as appropriate, that's the end of your responsibility. Let's use the product backlog as an example. As the agile coach, make sure the product owner knows how to prioritize the backlog and when to have it done. Offer to coach him through the thinking needed to prioritize it, but if he declines your offer and shows up to sprint planning with the backlog unprepared, then let the consequences be what they will be. In other words, let the product owner fail.

No one on the team gets to fail for very long or with spectacularly bad results because short iterations keep the extent of failure in check. If you let the failure happen, then the poor results should come up in the retrospective and boil down to the root cause—the product owner did not prepare for sprint planning. The team and the product owner can move forward, together, to correct the situation because they have seen it clearly.

If you step in to "cover" for the product owner by preparing the backlog yourself, the results will likely be disastrous. When you step in, you assume a proxy role, and you have no choice but to guess at how to prioritize the product backlog. It will be wrong. Worse than that, the learning will be lost. The team will not be able to see the situation clearly because you have muddled it for them with your well-intentioned help. They will not confront the product owner with their needs. The product owner will not learn, and you will have cemented your role as the proxy.

When you coach product owners to be good for the team, remember this: Teach the role, coach the role, and ask the team to expect the product owner to uphold the role. Beyond this, let the role fail. Then, help the team and the product owner learn from the failure, recover from it together, and become stronger.

Coaching Product Owners on Getting Good at the Role

Being a good product owner means more than fulfilling the role definition, grooming the backlog, working with the team, and working with everyone else to create a compelling and profitable vision of the product. That's a lot, but it's not enough. Good product owners pay attention to the *way* in which they do each of these things. Style matters. Intentions matter.

Product owners may be under pressure from their organization to get something done (fast!). In the best case, the product owner will collaborate with the team and agile coach to determine how to deal with the pressure and deliver the right stuff at the right time. When pressure rises and expectations become unrealistic, the team must recognize it and raise the situation as an impediment. Together, the agile coach and product owner must determine the source of the pressure and neutralize it, or at least reduce it.

If the product owner implicitly accepts the pressure, though, you may see their stress-induced behaviors come out. Some of the more common ones are bullying the team into taking on more work than they should or misrepresenting the complexity of features and then pouring on the pressure when the complexity becomes evident. When under pressure, some product owners freeze up and avoid all decisions. Still others become "too busy" to work with the team. Trust that product owners aren't devious and they don't have malicious intentions toward the team. Know, instead, that the pressure they are under yields stress, which often provokes harmful behavior.

As the coach, be prepared to clash with a product owner when his stress behaviors kick into gear. Do this only as necessary, and err on the side of education more often than clashing as you help him learn new responses to pressure:

- **Move from schedule-driven to business-value-driven thinking:** Most product owners have probably been conditioned to demand dates and features and then manipulate everything else in a futile attempt to hold dates and features constant. This was never a realistic approach. To accommodate reality, the product owner must make the transition from schedule-driven thinking to business-value-driven thinking. Teach the product owner to slice product features into thin slivers of value that can be delivered frequently, each returning real results to the company. This requires that the product owner become proficient at managing the business, the one the product is intended to impact, and the changes that occur constantly in the business. Work with the product owner to see change as a catalyst that causes a better product to emerge rather than a force to be neutralized or ignored. Help the product owner embrace change and tame it through a business-value-driven mind-set rather than holding on rigidly to his original ideas and schedules.

- **Cultivate business-value-driven thinking in all interactions:** The business-value-driven mind-set works not just for prioritizing the product backlog and slicing it into profitable releases. It influences everything: deciding which meetings to take now vs. later, letting go of schedule demands that don't make the business value cut, and even setting the order in which the product owner addresses particular topics during a conversation. These are all useful business-value-driven thinking practices for the product owner. The final one, conducting conversations in business value order, can be especially useful for working inside the team. Agile frameworks put teams under significant pressure to build something of value and quality in a matter of weeks. Time feels precious to a healthy agile team. One way the product owner honors this is to talk with the team about the most valuable topics first and let some things of lesser value (at the moment) drop off the conversation list.

- **Be of one mind with the sponsor:** The product owner and product sponsor must be so completely synchronized on the current and future direction of the product that if they were standing side by side there would be no daylight between them. Feel free to ask the product owner about the last time she and the sponsor talked about the product and what the results were. Check in with the sponsor every so often to gauge the level of one-mindedness with the product owner. When these two get off track with one another, the team and the product often suffer.

- **Ask for more (or less) rather than micromanaging:** Let a silent alarm go off in your head when the product owner thinks she needs to get into the details of how team members are performing the work. This often happens when the product owner has not challenged the team with enough work or has pressured them into taking too much. The product owner's best control comes from *how much* she asks the team to do, not how they are doing it. Coach her to use this as a lever as she prepares the product backlog items for the next sprint. Insist she stay out of the details in the meantime.

- **Hold the team to their commitments:** No one ever said an agile team should be let off easy. No one ever said a product owner should "make nice" all the time. In fact, it's just the contrary. When the team members fail to meet the commitments they set for the team and the product owner feels disappointed, let the product owner know that showing disappointment is acceptable. Also, ask the product owner to be open to reasons. Reasons are not excuses; they are circumstances that can be changed so they do not interfere with future commitments. Showing emotion should never be staged or dramatized. Instead, coach the product owner to show disappointment when it is real and to guard against using it as a manipulation tactic. When it's real, though, let the product owner know that it's OK for them to be real, too.

- **Leverage critical moments:** The product owner's leverage with the team lies between sprints for direction setting and during the sprint for momentum flow. Having a vision of the product and a well-groomed backlog helps the product owner convey the direction. The secret to keeping the team's momentum going lies simply in being present. Coach the product owner to be with the team to answer questions or make trade-off decisions in the moment. This keeps the team's forward momentum going strong. Any time a conversation or decision waits for the product owner, a dam gets created, and the waiting conversations pool up like water behind the dam, swirling around waiting to flow downriver. Ask the product owner, "How is the team's momentum today?" and then let this lead into a conversation about the product owner's considerable leverage that either promotes or inhibits the flow of work on the team.

To do all this, spend time with the product owner, talking about how the product is going, how the team is doing, how each of you are fulfilling your roles, and how you can help one another. Create no-nonsense communication, and prize honesty. Become allies in the cause of helping the team create astonishing results.

Coaching Agile Coaches

As time passes, you may be presented with the opportunity to train an agile coach. Perhaps you are moving on to a new place or a new team. Or perhaps your job is to train new agile coaches. Whatever the situation, once you feel confident enough in your own skills (or, perhaps just slightly before), taking on an agile coach apprentice can be a marvelous opportunity for your own growth. No better way exists to deepen your coaching skills than to teach them to someone else. You may be amazed at the brilliant ideas that come from your mouth as you explain how to coach agile teams. I often found myself thinking, "Wow, that was good. I gotta write that down." In many ways, that's how this book was born.

A useful framework for coaching other coaches and ScrumMasters to deepen their skills consists of three parts: exploratory, apprentice, coach. If someone thinks they want to be an agile coach, let them first explore the role by watching you perform it. It may be exactly what they thought it was, or they may fall in love with the idea all over again. Or, they may see that it doesn't match with their career or personal aspirations. Letting them shadow you for a short time will help them decide for themselves and will ensure no one wastes precious time and energy.

If they want to be a coach after the exploratory period, invite them to be your apprentice. I have found three months to be a useful time frame for apprenticing new coaches to independence. The first month, you perform the role and debrief your actions (or lack of action) with the apprentice. Get the apprentice good at observation and choice making by watching you do the job. See what they notice about what's happening with the team, and ask what choice they would have made in a given situation. Explain the choice you made and what you were aiming for as you interacted with the team or a team member. Let them learn the whole job by watching you do it: coaching the whole team, coaching individuals, teaching agile, facilitating agile meetings, and mastering yourself by carefully choosing your interventions.

You may think it strange to have a "third wheel" in a one-on-one coaching conversation. It is, a bit, but you can make it work by explaining that the apprentice has joined the conversation so that she can learn to do the one-on-one coaching job. Also, perhaps, in a few months she may be that person's agile coach, so having her in one-on-one conversations now smooths that transition later.

As you move toward the second month, start turning over agile events to the apprentice coach. Perhaps you fade into the background during sprint planning, and the apprentice moves toward the foreground, for example. As soon as this transition begins, let the team know that the apprentice coach has started to step into the coaching role, and you are stepping out. Before each event in which the apprentice takes the lead, work with the apprentice to plan it. Remember, though, that the apprentice bears the responsibility for the planning; you are there to assist. After each event, give the apprentice notes. You probably noticed things the apprentice could have done differently. Perhaps there are things you were curious about. Where did you see that they were dead-on in their description of agile, and where were they off in the weeds? Offer these useful personal notes. At this point, you are the apprentice's personal coach.

As the month progresses, so does the transition of agile events. By the end of the second month, the apprentice has become the team's primary coach, and you have moved into an advisory role.

In the third month, you are the coach of the new coach. You no longer intervene with the team directly. Your recently "graduated" apprentice does that. Instead, you work with the new coach to provide helpful tips or insights so that their unique voice as a coach can come through. The unique voice, the one that feels natural to the new coach and powerful to those being coached, often emerges during this final month. Listen for it.

At this point in your relationship, your interaction changes to be at the peer level. The new coach has experienced your guidance for two months and has enough experience to do the job well enough for a newbie. As you debrief an agile event, for example, you may offer a way you would have handled something but hold the belief that the new coach's way was valid, too. The interaction between you takes on the flavor of comparing notes rather than giving notes. As the third month progresses, you fade away, and by the end of the month, you are not present with the team at all. The new coach has taken your place.

Coaching Agile Managers

There are so many people to bring along as your team moves along its agile journey! Some of these people are managers of all types: managers of the team members, managers who are responsible for a program or a platform within which the team is organized, managers of allied (or not-so-friendly) teams, or stakeholders (who are managers) from all over the company.

They are all agile managers, but they probably don't know it yet.

They probably still work in their old ways: telling team members what to do; reorganizing people, groups, and whole companies without consulting teams; making crucial technology decisions solo. When teams "beneath" them are self-organized and producing real results frequently, much of what managers used to do becomes no longer useful and can be harmful. They need a new job, one that works with the power of the team (and agile) to benefit the company. By the time I joined him, agile coach and organizational change expert Michael Spayd had thought long and hard about the role of agile manager. He had become convinced that teaching managers their responsibilities in the agile world would be instrumental to a successful agile transition. I had to agree. I had seen more than one attempt at agile falter when managers applied their traditional techniques to empowered, self-organized, committed agile teams.

To put it in sharp focus, we coach agile managers to make changes in three fundamental areas to adopt agile mind-sets and behaviors:

- **Managing teams** now happens at the intersection between a team's self-organization and the manager's leadership intelligence. For the agile manager, teams become a fundamental object of study, including how they work and develop over time; how to form them and nurture their growth; and how to measure, reward, and sustain them for the long term. The agile manager's domain is as "intimate outsider" and champion of the team, not inside micromanager or "chum."

- **Managing investments** becomes less focused on schedules and the "next big deadline" and more focused on what is the best investment *now*. In the pursuit of delivering the most business value possible to gain competitive advantage, the agile mind-set regarding managing investments is "What is the best investment *now*?" rather than "Are we on schedule and on budget?" Getting the most from agile means moving from the "conformance to plan" paradigm to "conformance to value" thinking.

- **Managing the environment** is about helping the organization think "lean." Agile teams operate within an overall organizational environment that includes support processes and suppliers. When agile teams begin operating with newfound speed and agility, the rest of the organization tends to slow them down. The agile manager is in the position of bringing a lean perspective to focus on flow and the elimination of waste (Spayd and Adkins 2008).

These three areas are not new. Managers have always worked in the realm of managing teams, investments, and the surrounding environment. An agile manager, though, approaches each of these areas with an agile mind-set. Becoming adept in these new, agile ways is what we coach agile managers to do.

An overarching skill set helps the agile manager achieve the agile mind-set and enhances their ability to manage organizational change. It takes finesse and savvy—real artistry—to help the organization move through agile adoption (and re-adoption). As organizational change artist, agile managers are called to influence a range of situations and circumstances, chief among them are…

> Affecting existing performance management systems, working with peer managers to lean-out business processes, saying "no" to starting more work—these are typical examples of thorny organizational impediments that an Agile manager will likely face. When Agile is introduced into an organization, a tremendous amount of organizational change must occur to empower and enable Agile teams in their pursuit of delivering business value. An Agile manager needs to develop keen skills in organizational change and an ability to shepherd an organization through the adoption change curve (Spayd and Adkins, 2008).

How Do You Coach Agile Managers?

The act of coaching agile managers looks much like coaching any person one-on-one. First, train them on their role, and let them know which behaviors will be useful and hurtful to the team. Then, coach them on it by catching them doing well and helping them see when their actions have a positive impact. Also catch them unintentionally harming the team, and bring that specific behavior into clear view for them. Always, coach them on their agile journey. Find out what they need in their careers and lives next, and help them see how agile helps them achieve it.

| **SEE ALSO** | Teaching the agile manager role is covered in Chapter 7, "Coach as Teacher." |

Coaching opportunities naturally arise when you see managers "armchair quarterbacking" the team. Most managers got where they are because they are good at solving problems, which often means doing things *for* the team or *to* the team. Through their interactions with individual team members or through what they see in sprint reviews or stand-ups, they may come to conclusions about what's happening with the team. Often, these conclusions are erroneous, and if left to themselves, managers may jump into action to "fix the problem."

Imagine that a manager approaches you in the hall and says, "I think the team is getting burned out. I noticed they had low energy in the stand-up yesterday. We should do something about that. Maybe take them on a fun day to help them recharge?" As the team's agile coach, you accept the insight but do nothing about it except to say that you will bring it up with the team. Reinforce the fact that agile enacts a natural cycle in which the team plans, works hard, produces real product, and then looks back to improve the way they work. In agile, the natural time for problems to come up and get resolved is built in. Outsiders need not interfere to make something happen.

Maybe the manager has concluded correctly. Maybe the team is getting burned out. If so, the coach can look for it. The coach can reinforce sustainable pace, the idea that each person needs to work at a pace sustainable for them and their current life situation. The coach can create a retrospective agenda that allows the burnout topic to emerge, get talked about, and resolved. A manager need not plan a fun day to help relieve perceived burnout.

The wisdom you teach agile managers, because you are learning it yourself, is to "take it to the team." Take any perceived problem to the team. They know what's really happening and what to do about it. Everyone can rely on the cadence agile gives them to consider such problems. It's called the retrospective.

Above all, do not let managers "fix" team problems from the outside. Their insights and observations are welcome, valued, and essential. Their solo actions are not.

Sometimes you'll catch their actions in time, and sometimes you won't. When a manager intervenes and causes damage or just confusion, let the consequences roll. If a team member is hopping mad that the agile manager "fixed" something on their behalf, then encourage the team member to speak with the manager about it. If the whole team is up in arms because they feel manipulated by a manager's actions, then help them have a team-manager conversation. Protect no one from the natural consequences of the situation because therein lies the learning. Coach the manager one-on-one to take the lesson further. In this way, you accomplish damage control that addresses the current situation and may compel the agile manager to take the next important step in their agile journey.

Oftentimes, a special kind of outsider plays a more specific role and has a greater impact on the team. This person is the team's sponsor, also called the **customer** in some organizations (not to be confused with the real customers, the ones who will use the team's products). No matter what role name this person goes by, you know you have the special one—the sponsor—because they pay the team's bill.

The Sponsor Is a Special Kind of Manager

The sponsor has the same role as any other agile manager and can be coached just like any other manager. The sponsor also has a special power—the power of the purse strings. In general, let the sponsor know that she can get the results she wants by working with the product owner on all things and remaining aligned with the product owner at all times.

Coach the sponsor to serve the team so the team can get the work done brilliantly:

- **Articulate the vision from their point of view:** Although the product owner gets top billing for being the vision keeper, something magical happens when a sponsor articulates that same vision to the team. When the sponsor tells the team why the product is important to the company and the outside world, the magic really gets going. Even more amazing magic happens when the sponsor tells the team why the product is important to them personally. Knowing these "whys" can be strong motivators for the team.

- **Be present and attentive in sprint reviews:** For certain, the sponsor should be present and attentive in the sprint review. The team wants to know how well they did (or not). Hearing this from "higher-up" every once in a while helps them know that their efforts were worth it and that they are valuable to the company. This can be especially impactful if the product owner sits fairly low on the corporate ladder. Especially in this case, sponsors can speak for the company in ways the product owner cannot. Hearing feedback directly from the sponsor closes these questions: Do we matter to the company? Does the product we're building matter? Having received this feedback, the team can move on to the next sprint cleanly.

- **Talk about business trade-offs and managing expectations:** Coach the sponsor to know that almost everything they bring up with the team falls into one of two categories: business trade-offs or managing expectations.

  During a sprint review, for example, it is acceptable for a sponsor to tell the team and the product owner how much effort the company is willing to invest in a certain direction, technology, or idea. That's a business trade-off, and it's an important and useful constraint for the team as they get ready to plan their next sprint.

  Similarly, much of the sponsor's talk to the team revolves around how he and the product owner, together, are managing people's expectations outside the team. The team needs to know that the two of them have this well in hand and are providing "air cover" so they can focus on their piece of the endeavor—building great stuff. The sponsor should provide just enough information to let the team know what's happening but not so much that the team worries about the politics constantly in play at that level.

- **Hold the team accountable:** With the product owner, the sponsor should hold the team accountable to what the team said they would do. Coach the sponsor to hold the bar high, and expect (and truly believe) the team can reach it.

The best time to coach sponsors occurs just prior to a sprint review. Go over the bullets you just read with them. Talk with them about the behaviors you are teaching the product owner and other agile managers because these are the same behaviors you expect from them.

Remember that you are teaching them their role in the agile world, so preparing them for the sprint review is a normal part of your job. It doesn't matter that they are "above your pay grade." You are their coach, too, and doing agile well means that everyone learns new ways to behave—even them.

Set the expectation that you will have another conversation with them after the sprint review. In this conversation, give the sponsor notes just as you would an apprentice coach. Let them know what they specifically did that was supportive or corrosive to the team. Do this so that the sponsor learns to interact in ways that assist the team as they strive to perform at top levels. In so doing, the team can produce the results the sponsor hopes for. The sponsor learns to support the team, the team produces more and better, and the sponsor gets more. Everyone wins.

A Refresher

Let's lock in the ideas from this chapter:

- Coaching happens at the individual level and the whole-team level all the time. A good agile coach pays attention to where the team is in the sprint and release cycle to make whole-team and individual coaching useful, powerful, and nondisruptive.
- Coaching in the agile context = coaching + agile mentoring. We are interested in people's whole lives as we coach them to become excellent agilists.
- Start coaching conversations with people immediately. This way, when a problem arises, you have established the coaching relationship, and you already know where the person is on the agile journey.
- A good product owner makes for a healthy agile team. Coach this person well.
- Teach someone else how to coach to strengthen your own skills and knowledge. Take on an agile coach apprentice as soon as you are able.
- Managers impact team performance. This puts them in your purview as agile coachees.
- Sponsors are a special kind of manager and require coaching so that they learn how to get more than they imagined they could from self-organized teams.

Additional Resources

Hackman, J. R. 2002. *Leading Teams: Setting the Stage for Great Performances*. Boston: Harvard Business School. This book is useful from cover to cover, especially the section entitled "Expert Coaching."

Scott, S. 2007. *Fierce Conversations: Achieving Success at Work and in Life One Conversation at a Time.* New York: Berkley. Not just a good read, this book contains exercises for individuals and groups in each chapter. Many of these are appropriate for retrospective activities.

Whitworth, L., K. Kimsey-House, H. Kimsey-House, and P. Sandahl. 2007. *Co-Active Coaching: New Skills for Coaching People Toward Success in Work and Life, Second Edition.* Mountain View, CA: Davies-Black. This book formalized the world of professional coaching and remains the seminal work on the subject of coaching.

References

The Arbinger Institute. 2002. *Leadership and Self-Deception.* San Francisco: Berrett-Koehler.

Cohn, M. 2006. *Agile Estimating and Planning.* Upper Saddle River, NJ: Prentice Hall.

The Dalai Lama. 2003. *The Compassionate Life.* Somerville, MA: Wisdom Publications.

Hackman, J. R. 2002. *Leading Teams: Setting the Stage for Great Performances.* Boston: Harvard Business School.

Scott, S. 2007. *Fierce Conversations: Achieving Success at Work and in Life One Conversation at a Time.* New York: Berkley.

Sheridan, R. 2010. Doing Donuts in the Parking Lot. http://menloinnovations.com/blog/?p=449.

Spayd, M. K, and L. Adkins. 2008. The Manager's Role in Agile. www.scrumalliance.org/articles/103-the-managers-role-in-agile.

Whitworth, L., K. Kimsey-House, H. Kimsey-House, and P. Sandahl. 2007. *Co-Active Coaching: New Skills for Coaching People Toward Success in Work and Life, Second Edition.* Mountain View, CA: Davies-Black.

Chapter 6

Coach as Facilitator

I can hold an intelligent conversation about healthcare delivery, natural gas distribution, municipal water systems, credit card recoveries, oil well production, website content management, and streamlining national defense systems. I know something (in fact, quite a lot) about all of these, just to name a few topics. Although I am curious by nature, I haven't gained this eclectic mix of expertise to satisfy my thirst for knowledge. I gained it because I had to do so. Becoming an expert in these various topics was a key to success, and sometimes survival, when I was a project manager.

As a project manager, I understood the rationale behind every decision and often spoke on the team's behalf, even on complicated technical topics. As the linchpin between team members who didn't work together face-to-face, I carried knowledge from one team member to another so that the "parts of the whole" could eventually come together. I held all the pieces of the project in my head (or on my project schedule) and made sure they got done. Often, I was the only one with the "whole picture" of the project, so developing domain expertise was imperative.

By the time you finish this chapter, you will be able to answer these questions:

- What are the purposes of the standard agile meetings? How do I coach the team to help them achieve these purposes?
- When should I intervene in the team's conversation, and when should I hold back?
- What else am I doing if I'm not taking part in the details of the conversation?
- How can I use powerful observations, powerful questions, and powerful challenges to help the team improve their formal and informal conversations?

I felt proud of my contributions to the team and wore my expertise like a badge of honor. Once, long ago, I remember a co-worker exclaiming, "The way she talks about cathodic protection, you would think she has worked gas pipelines her whole life!" I basked in the glory of being considered a knowledgeable insider.

I had a rude awakening when I coached my first agile team. Not only did they not need me to tell them what to do, but they didn't really need me to participate in their conversations, either. A healthy agile team works together in high-bandwidth, high-quality communication. They know "the plan" on a release-by-release basis and on a daily basis. It was completely opposite of my previous experience as a project manager, and I saw clearly that the team didn't need me to coordinate their work, speak on their behalf, or act as the hub of communication between them. It dawned on me that the reasons for being a subject-matter expert no longer existed. This left a gaping hole that caused me to doubt my value.

It was hard for me to move from being a project manager with subject-matter expertise to being an agile coach until I had this realization: I can be just another voice on the team discussing today's problem, or I can step fully into this role of agile coach, helping them get better and better. This is important and something no one else is doing yet.

Helping the team get better and better meant that I had to drastically improve my facilitation skills. I quickly learned that helping the team achieve great results in standard agile meetings and their everyday conversations was valuable to them.

The agile coach facilitates by creating a "container" for the team to fill up with their astounding ideas and innovations. The container, often a set of agenda questions or some other lightweight (and flexible) structure, gives the team just enough of a frame to stay on their purpose and promotes an environment for richer interaction, a place where fantastic ideas can be heard. The coach creates the container; the team creates the content.

In this chapter, we explore the agile coach's job as a facilitator serving the team in both standing meetings and informal conversations. We'll take it meeting by meeting: stand-up, sprint planning, sprint review, and retrospective. Keeping the "Why do we do this meeting, anyway?" purpose in mind, we explore methods the coach uses to teach the team "the ropes" of the meeting and then let them get to it.

With informal conversations, the coach stays focused on working within the team to increase the quality of their interactions so that they can increase the quality of their products. This is so much more expansive and valuable than being yet another subject-matter expert!

Wield a Light Touch

With both standing meetings and informal conversations, this basic facilitation intention endures: Support the team's self-organization, and enhance their ability to deliver real business value all the time. You will know when this happens because the products they create will astonish them and delight their customers.

Astonishment and delight emerges from the work of a self-organized group creating products that make them proud. This is why I recommend a light touch when serving the team. Light-touch facilitation means that the coach always remembers that "This is their meeting, not mine." Repeat it to yourself as many times a day as it takes. Let it soak in.

The amount and type of facilitation varies depending on the specific meeting, but the coach stays aimed at the goal of the team eventually conducting the meetings themselves. Self-sufficiency does not happen overnight and may not ever happen for some teams, but if the coach holds this intention, it will ensure that the coach does not become the center point, undermining the team's self-organization.

Facilitate the Stand-Up

To organize themselves for the day's work ahead, team members answer three direct questions:

What did I get done since the last stand-up?

What will I do before the next stand-up?

What are the impediments blocking me or slowing me down?

This simple and powerful formula invites each team member to devise a daily work plan, get help clearing barriers, and make a commitment to the team. Here are some things the team achieves when they do the stand-up well:

Peer pressure: Healthy agile teams experience peer pressure. On these teams, all team members have committed to complete the work of the sprint together. This makes the work (and the people) interdependent and accountable to one another. If a team member says she is going to do the same thing three days in a row, her lack of forward momentum becomes obvious and eventually impossible to ignore. Her undone work becomes someone else's impediment.

Fine-grain coordination: Team members should have quick, focused interchanges during the stand-up. "Oh, I didn't know you were planning to do that this afternoon. That means I need to change the order of things I was going to do to get you what you need. OK, I can do that. I'm glad you said something, though." This fine-grain coordination lets team members know how and when to count on each other. An agile team should expect zero wait time because waiting is waste. Getting to this level of coordination boosts their chances of experiencing zero wait time.

TWO-PIZZA TEAMS

In his book *Succeeding with Agile,* Mike Cohn offers an easy way to tell whether you have the perfect team size. If you can feed the whole team on two pizzas, you're there.

The purpose of stand-up can be more easily achieved on a two-pizza team because these teams are family-sized. We humans are wired to easily keep track, in our heads, of what's happening in a group that's family-sized. We readily remember each person's daily commitment and can better hold one another accountable for individual and team results.

Focusing on the few: Through the use of the story/task board during the stand-up, everyone readily sees what's sitting in progress and what's really getting done. Healthy agile teams focus on getting things done, which means that tasks don't stay in progress all sprint long. Each day, during the stand-up, the team affirms which *few* tasks receive their focus so that they can get done expeditiously. Having 30 things done yields more value than having 50 things in progress.

Daily commitment: Each team member makes a daily commitment to the team. This allows the team to know what to expect from one another and how to hold each other accountable.

Raising impediments: Impediments can be brought up in the team anytime, but the stand-up offers a golden moment to pause and reconsider "Is there anything blocking me or slowing me down?"

Facilitate During the Stand-Up

On a new team or anytime you use a Teaching style in your coaching, reinforce the general cadence of stand-up: fifteen minutes, three questions, no long conversations, plus whatever rules your team has come up with. Teach this and then step back. The team does not need you standing with them or being the emcee who cues each team member to speak. They can do this just fine on their own. So, move to the back, preferably out of direct eyesight of the team.

SEE ALSO   Find tips on when and how to use the Teaching style in Chapter 4, "Let Your Style Change."

As a guiding principle, do not intervene during the stand-up unless you are teaching or reaffirming how stand-up works. You'll intervene more with a new team at the beginning, while they're learning to adhere to the stand-up rules. Pretty soon, though, stop intervening. Instead, offer observations afterward. Ask the team, "May I offer you some stand-up observations?" If they say, "No," then let it drop. If they say, "Yes," then deliver your observations succinctly, without judgment and with a sense of curiosity to invite their introspection. If conversation happens and they figure out how to do stand-up better next time, that's great. If conversation doesn't happen, that's acceptable, too.

During the sprint, the team's job is to sprint. Therefore, if they don't incorporate a change from having heard your observation, don't force it. Doing so may create additional inspect-and-adapt cycles. These cycles could be beneficial if completed in a few minutes' time but could also be detrimental if they drag on or raise so much dust that the team can't see their way clear to continue the work of the sprint, so leave minor infractions for the retrospective.

TRY THIS

Let the team start the stand-up by themselves. When the "magic time" arrives, don't be their rooster, crowing out "Stand-up time!" Instead, just stand.

As they notice the stand-up time has come (or come and gone if they miss it totally), they will sheepishly stand. Remain silent and let someone (anyone) start the stand-up. If you don't announce the stand-up and kick it off, they will do it.

No matter when they started, hold the timebox. When 15 minutes after the scheduled start comes, announce, "That's 15. Stand-up is over." You'll only have to do this a few times. Pretty quickly they get good at starting the stand-up on their own and finishing it within 15 minutes.

Fixing the Stand-Up

Sometimes, horrible stand-up behavior can best be addressed in the moment. Perhaps a few team members have developed the habit of missing the stand-up.

Perhaps team members talk over one another, do e-mail, or otherwise ignore one another during the stand-up. These situations go beyond a minor infraction and call for immediate intervention.

It can be hard to decide when to "fix it" and when to leave it alone. On a new team, when you teach them how stand-up works, err on the side of fixing it. Intervene to model positive stand-up behavior, and nip negative stand-up behavior. On an established team, consciously choose whether to address stand-up ills or not. If the lesson they may learn from living with an ineffective stand-up could be more instructive to them than getting the stand-up "perfect," then let the behavior go, even if you judge it as horrible. Make this judgment call based on the intervention's potential value vs. its disruption and the chance of subtly undermining the team's self-organization. Indeed, it's a fine line to tread.

Let's assume that you have carefully considered whether you should intervene and have decided to do so. Here are two things that work well as interventions and address a range of stand-up ills:

> **Reinforce the purpose of the stand-up:** Teach the team what we are trying to achieve using the stand-up: Create peer pressure, use fine-grain coordination, focus on the few, make daily commitments, and raise impediments. Then ask, "How is stand-up working for you? Are you getting these things?" Through the conversation that follows, the team may choose to use the purpose statements as a daily meter and, after stand-up, rate themselves on how well they just did. This can be a powerful self-management tool for them.

> **Ask for eyes and support:** This can be introduced as a game to the team. The game works like this: When one person talks during stand-up, everyone else looks at that person and makes eye contact. Don't let the person speaking catch you looking away! This technique typically helps the person speaking be brief and increases the overall understanding of what each person is saying. This, in turn, helps speed a team toward a more robust daily plan (adapted from Devin).

Remember that one-on-one coaching is always an option available to you. If the behavior seems localized and the whole team would not benefit from addressing it openly, try the one-on-one approach.

SEE ALSO Although most detrimental stand-up behavior can be addressed in the group, coaching team members one-on-one is an option, too. Chapter 5, "Coach as Coach-Mentor," offers guidance about when and how to coach one-on-one.

What happens if you intervene and they still don't fix the stand-up? Remember, the accomplishments and bumps are theirs, not yours. Agile works when they learn how to rely on one another. It has nothing to do with you looking good as a coach. So, if they do not improve, accept it for now, and instead gear up for ways to create the space for them to bring it up in the retrospective.

In the meantime, they will certainly pay the consequences of ineffective stand-ups. Don't let those moments slip by. People often cannot see the relationship between cause and effect, so draw their attention to it. Capitalize on the moments when they feel a consequence to help them see the connection. You might reinforce the purpose of stand-up and ask anew, without bitterness, "Do you think this could have been avoided if the stand-up were different?"

Behavior change happens, but it happens slowly. It may take several tries from different angles before a team changes their stand-up behavior. Be patient. Keep trying. They will change when they need to, but only if you don't shield them from the natural consequences that follow from poor stand-ups.

Facilitate Sprint Planning

Sprint planning requires very light-touch facilitation, even in the beginning. If you offer teams a structure they can use to conduct the mechanics of sprint planning, they can typically do it on their own. A set of agenda questions or the list of things we are trying to achieve with sprint planning works well as a structure.

Whatever structure you use to guide the team, ensure that it supports the purpose of sprint planning:

Know the work: For the team to get going on the work ahead, they must understand, choose, task, and volunteer. They must first *understand* the scope and size of highest business value product backlog items, the ones the product owner asks them to bring into the sprint. With this understanding, they *choose* which of these can fit in the sprint. They create *tasks* for the chosen product backlog items. With this full understanding, team members are able to *volunteer* for tasks as the sprint progresses.

Get a fresh start: No matter how the last sprint ended, this sprint is new. The team comes to sprint planning with a renewed sense of commitment resulting from the agreements they made with one another during the retrospective. The past is gone. The future is uncertain. This sprint is the only thing the team can control.

Commit to shared goals: All team members understand *all* the work in the sprint and jointly agree to achieve the sprint goal. They commit to completing the product backlog items they have chosen to take into the sprint.

Create focus and abundance: By choosing the right amount of work for the sprint based on the team's previous achievements, the team has created focus for themselves. They are able to give the work their focused effort because they are excused from worrying about everything. That mental load has been lifted. Instead, they worry only about what they have committed to do. This gives them a sense of abundance: "Ahhhh, there is enough." Enough time, enough people, enough creativity. They have what they need to get the work of the sprint done.

SPRINT PLANNING STRUCTURE

Create a flip chart with these words, and let that be the structure the team uses to guide themselves through sprint planning:

Sprint planning is done when we can answer these questions:

- If the goal of this sprint were a newspaper headline, what would it be?
- What is the team composition for this sprint?
- What is the total team capacity for this sprint?
- What are the highest business value product backlog items?
- What are the concerns (technical, political, cultural) about these product backlog items?
- What other concerns does the team have?
- Given all this, what are the stories, conditions of satisfaction, tasks, and estimates for the items that will form the sprint backlog?
- Given all this, is there any change to the stories or conditions of satisfaction for this sprint? Do items need to move from the sprint backlog back to the product backlog?
- What is the team's final commitment for this sprint?

(Adapted from Tabaka 2006.)

Sprint planning is done when we have achieved these purposes. Did we get these things from it?

- Know the work—understand it, choose it, task it, volunteer for it.
- Get a fresh start.
- Commit to shared goals.
- Create focus and abundance.

Prepare for Sprint Planning

The coach has two jobs when preparing for sprint planning: get a structure (the meeting "container") together and ensure the product owner has prepared the product backlog. The structure can be any list of guiding questions or agenda items that helps the team achieve the purpose of sprint planning, such as the ones just discussed.

The second job requires the product owner's engagement and hard work. The coach makes sure the product owner knows the importance of having the product backlog groomed and ready for sprint planning. You'll know the product backlog has been made ready because the highest value product backlog items are marked as such, the product owner has done the work necessary to represent to the team the business aspects of the items they are asked to create, and those items are broken down into "sprint-sized" slivers of value.

SEE ALSO	How to coach product owners is included in Chapter 5, "Coach as Coach-Mentor." For now, recognize that there is a time to teach the product owner the expectations of their role, there is a time to coach the product owner to fully embody that role, and there is a time to let the product owner fail (or wildly succeed) in performing that role.

Often, the product owner works with the team to groom the backlog, which includes the team's estimate of effort for every item. This can happen throughout the sprint or in a meeting a few days prior to sprint planning. In his book *Agile Product Management: Creating Products That Customers Love*, Roman Pichler offers direct advice to product owners on how and when to prepare the product backlog and get ready for sprint planning, as well as ways to make the work happen in collaboration with the team. The acronym DEEP acts as a memory-jogger that a well-groomed "product backlog has four qualities: detailed appropriately, estimated, emergent, and prioritized, making it DEEP" (Pichler 2010).

Facilitate During Sprint Planning

To facilitate sprint planning, introduce the structure, and ensure all team members understand it and agree to use it (or change it with them in the moment). With this done, let them know you will hold the timebox and leave the rest up to them.

To hold the timebox, first ask the team how long the timebox should be to complete sprint planning. When the time runs out, sprint planning has ended. The pressure of a timebox gives the team exquisite focus and permission to think only about the immediate work ahead—planning. Note that the timebox should be measured in hours, not days, and that the team should become more efficient and effective with this meeting over time.

Once the timebox has started, step back and let them fill the void with their own initiative. This doesn't mean you go have a long chat with your friend down the hall. Stay with them, listen to their conversation, and pay attention to their progress. To an outsider, you probably look as if you're just sitting there, doing nothing. You are actually doing something very active, though. You intently listen for teachable moments—those moments when a few well-placed words will cause lightbulbs of understanding to light up in their heads. The lightbulbs light up because the teaching happens at the most opportune time, pertinent to what they struggle with in that moment.

As the team moves through sprint planning, check in a few times. Ask, "Which of these agenda questions do you know the answers to now?" Asking this question helps them keep track of their progress while clearly reinforcing that the responsibility for sprint planning resides with them. Throughout it all, hold their timebox. Give them time checks: "You have 2 hours left…you have 1 hour left…you have 15 minutes left…OK, sprint planning has ended. Let's roll."

Teachable Moments During Sprint Planning

In sprint planning, teachable moments are often about the product backlog items the team has just taken into the sprint. So, teachable moments about user stories will certainly come up: What makes a user story good? How do we create them? Why are they so long-winded? Who is a real user? These questions, and many more like them, are common. Mike Cohn has written two must-have books on the subject: *User Stories Applied: For Agile Software Development* (Cohn 2004) and *Agile Estimating and Planning* (Cohn 2005). Both are useful well beyond software projects, so don't let the software-centric subtitle of the *User Stories* book make you shy away.

Other common teachable moments during sprint planning give the coach opportunities to

Harp on business value delivered: Challenge the team to keep the goal of delivering real business value in the forefront. You may say, "Great user story, but so what? What real value gets delivered in this story?" Or, "Why would we do this work at all? What real user gets anything from it?" Notice the repeated use of the word *real*. That's intentional.

Promote strong product ownership: Reinforcing the product owner's role as the vision keeper for the team helps the product owner stay at the product level. As the vision keeper, the product owner says "what" needs to get done and stays out of the team's domain, which is "how" it will get done and "how much" effort it will take. When the team asks you a question about the product, refer them to the product owner. Reinforce the product owner's role by letting the product owner be the one voice for product vision and decisions.

SEE ALSO	A full description of the product owner's role, as well as how the product owner's role interlocks with other agile leadership roles, is contained in Chapter 7, "Coach as Teacher."

Uphold healthy role boundaries: Sooner or later, roles will get blurry. The product owner may bully the team or get pushed around by the team. The agile coach (you) may get too involved in the task-level detail of sprint planning and forget to coach. When these things happen, step in to uphold healthy boundaries between the product owner and the team as well as between your role, the agile coach, and the product owner. Give the team permission to help you stay true to your role, as well. We don't do this for the sake of upholding a rule. We uphold healthy boundaries to allow the three roles—product owner, agile coach, and team member—to work together for maximum propulsion.

Improve tasking: Teams often get stuck when they move into tasking, so any method that increases the momentum of tasking will be welcome. In a desire to increase momentum, however, ensure the team does not sacrifice understanding. Since the whole team commits to all the work in the sprint, each team member must understand every story. Use mind mapping and silent tasking to increase both momentum and shared understanding. "A mind map is a diagram used to represent words, ideas, tasks, or other items linked to and arranged around a central key word or idea," according to Wikipedia. With mind mapping, team members simultaneously draw a chart of all the tasks needed to complete a story. The story itself occupies the center of the mind map. They do this with minimal talking, each adding to what others have drawn in the mind map. The other method, silent tasking, is just that—silent. Each team member creates tasks for all the user stories, working silently together, and puts the tasks on the story board. At the end, everyone goes through the tasks and makes sure they all understand them. Duplicates naturally arise and are collapsed. Missing tasks also become apparent and are added.

Facilitate the Sprint Review

The agile coach plays a background role when it comes to the sprint review. Leading up to the sprint review, remind the team that they need to "pull it together" to show the real products developed during the sprint. Pulling it together does not mean creating big presentations or tuning up one's public speaking skills. It means doing the minimum amount needed to show stakeholders the products the team actually created. Time spent polishing the presentation equals time lost for creating products, so keep this in mind while helping the team be comfortable with the trade-off: You want more time for real work, less time for making things look better than they really are.

As the time for the sprint review draws near, remember its purpose:

True-up: The team made a commitment at the beginning of the sprint. Now, they clearly call out what was and was not accomplished during the sprint and formally ask for acceptance of the work from the product owner.

Show and tell: Show what was accomplished, not with fancy slides or polished oratory but with real product.

Get direct feedback: Hear from the stakeholders, customers, and users of the products just created. How useful are the products? Do they serve their intended purpose? What other genius ideas do they spark?

Offer insights: Give the stakeholders a window into how the team has been working together and with the larger context of their organization. If the team held the retrospective before the sprint review, there may even be fresh insights for the team to share, if the insights are helpful to the sprint review audience or the team and if the team feels comfortable sharing them.

Ask for help: The team raises the big impediments that they need help eradicating. These are the ones they and their agile coach and product owner cannot resolve. Use the sprint review to make those gnarly impediments heard by all and to ask for specific help from outside stakeholders to clear them.

With this purpose firmly in mind, you may coach the team to speak in value-first order. Imagine this: Ray has agreed to show the new "remember me" functionality of the website in the sprint review. Instead of telling the attendees everything he did to create the function, including all the dead ends he went down and the hurdles he had to jump, Ray simply states, "Here is the new 'remember me' feature that will save our customers about three minutes when filling out online application forms." He starts with value first, the "why do I care" that encapsulates all the effort he put into the product. This allows sprint review attendees to see what they came to see: real products yielding real value. Perhaps, then, Ray will share just the essence of what he learned from the dead ends and hurdles if he thinks that it will be instructive to the attendees.

During the sprint review, the coach is insignificant (or, at least, seems so from an outsider's point of view). The coach sits in the back, away from the main action. This advice may be hard for you to swallow, especially when the team is just forming or is formed but is falling apart. Maybe it's hard for you even when the team is doing well. You may feel a strong temptation to step in and play an emcee role during the sprint review. You have good intentions. In so doing, you try to ensure that the sprint review flows well, the team gets to show off how brilliant they (and you) are, and no one gets embarrassed in front of the stakeholders. Know that the team does not need you to play emcee or save them from themselves. If you give them the room to handle the sprint review by themselves, they will. You have other things to do that offer more value, so sit in the back, be silent, and watch.

Just because you sit away from the main action does not mean you lie dormant, however. All during the sprint review, draw your attention to what is happening *for* and *to* the team. Make observations, and take notes.

While you are observing the team, call to mind the purpose of the sprint review: true-up, show and tell, get direct feedback, offer insights, and ask for help. With the purpose in mind, keep your antennae up as you consider questions such as these:

- How are the team members interacting with one another? When one is speaking, do the other team members give their attention, their energy, and their support to that person? Do they look at the speaker? What is the effect? Are they paying half-attention to the speaker and half-attention to something else? What is the effect?

- What is the nature of the interaction between the team members and the product owner? Customer? Other stakeholders? Did any of these people make requests of the team that the team implicitly accepted or ignored?

- Did the product owner use the product backlog as a way to manage requests that came up? Was there a clear acceptance of the new request and a reaffirmation that its business value would be understood and considered in comparison to the other requests in the backlog?

- Was anyone bullied or mollified?

- Did the team members hand off attention to one another smoothly? Did every team member who wanted to speak get to speak?

- What misconceptions or misuses of agile came up in the conversation?

Jot down anything that grabs your attention. Agile coaches Rachel Davies and Liz Sedley recommend capturing a "mini-quote—taking note of the exact words used" especially when you have heard someone voice a misconception or misuse of agile (Davies and Sedley 2009).

After the sprint review, offer to share your notes with the team. Whatever you have written down is just fine; your notes don't need to be polished or even conclusive. Your notes may be things you are curious about, things that just don't add up, or things you haven't fully figured out. Trust that speaking these will allow the team to add them up. They know what's going on. Your greatest good comes from helping them see that they know.

Expect that the team may strike up a conversation about these observations. Also expect that they may hear them and not respond. They may be too tired or too wound up to take more in right now. Both outcomes are acceptable. Having just offered the observations is enough.

Observation Types

As you start to observe the sprint review in this way, you may find that your observations tend to fall into two classes: reinforcing and deepening.

The reinforcing ones uphold agile. They call to mind something about agile, perhaps a practice, principle, role, or value. These are the "good for you" or "oops, missed that one" statements. For example:

Good for you: "Good use of the product backlog as a way to handle new requests."

Oops, missed that one: "The customer pointed to the burndown chart and beat you guys up over that big spike in the middle. You missed a chance to tell her how the burndown works and that the big (meaningless) spike in the middle means nothing. "

Deepening observations tend to be ones that reveal the inner working of the group to themselves. When they are delivered, they follow this pattern: "Here's what I thought I saw. What did you see?"

As the coach, know that your deepening observations may be accurate or inaccurate. What you think you saw may not be what's really going on. Accuracy of these observations doesn't matter as long as you deliver them in a way that causes the team to inquire—that's the observations' real purpose. So, offer your observations without being attached to whether they are "right" or not. Then, ask a question that invites the team members to use your observations as raw material for their own reflection.

If the team has no mental or emotional bandwidth to respond to your observations just after the sprint review, then honor that by not requiring an on-the-spot conversation about them. Perhaps you speak them and let it end there. Perhaps you write them on a flip chart and post them somewhere in the room. More than likely, they will spark a conversation later.

Observation Examples

Here is a list of observations one might make during a sprint review. See whether you can tell which are reinforcing observations and which are deepening observations.

- "The sponsor is all in! She is here, engaged, and supportive. That is fantastic!"

- "I noticed that there was a big silence after the sponsor asked, 'How has agile been working?' So, think back and remember…what was happening for each of you in that moment?"

- "We had a challenge from a stakeholder about getting more data. What do you think lies at the root of that question? What is he worried about?"

- "Did anyone feel like someone else spoke for them?"

- "I noticed that no one was sending text messages or e-mails during the sprint review. Bravo! I can only imagine that this helped the stakeholders see how much you actively support one another."

- "I saw proactive management of requests! Good for you, product owner, for catching new requests and reaffirming how we use the backlog to manage them based on highest business value."

- "Did anyone go unconscious during the meeting? Did you find that your mind wandered when someone else was speaking? What did you do when you noticed the wandering?"

- "I heard an offer to add someone to the team. I want to make sure that you know the team has a say about who is on the team. Having a say requires you to say something. Otherwise, someone else will make the decision for you."

- "There seemed to be a loss of momentum when we started talking about the steps for the upcoming release. Did I make that up?"

- "A couple of stakeholders seemed to talk and talk about the same topic. I thought that was curious. What did you make of that?"

- "I noticed your sponsor was pushing a few messages today. I think I heard things like 'Get close to your customer' and 'Take your time to do it right.' What did you hear?"

Facilitate the Retrospective

The agile coach plays a starring (facilitator) role in the retrospective, especially for a new team. Since the coach focuses on being the guardian of quality and performance for the team, the coach pays keen attention throughout the sprint. While observing, the coach keeps the purpose of the retrospective in mind:

Inspect and adapt: The retrospective calls for a stop in the action, allowing the team to take a breather and get curious about what happened during the sprint.

Look back at how, not what: The team considers how the work got done—not only what they produced and how good it is but how they worked together to produce it.

Do (even) better next time: The team commits to a handful of things they will do differently next sprint to become even better. Becoming better can be anything that has meaning for the team: getting faster, producing higher-quality products, or truly feeling a whole-team commitment. Strengthening any of these things helps them improve their velocity or improve something else that is as important as velocity, such as quality.

Prepare for the Retrospective

As the sprint goes on, the agile coach jots down observations about how the team works together—what goes well, what seems sticky, or what feels strange. The coach could choose to reveal any of these as they arise, but unless they are devastating problems, the coach holds back knowing that the retrospective offers the best time for the team to consider them. While in a sprint, the team focuses on their commitment. So, the coach honors this by letting the team sprint without worrying them about how they are sprinting. Remember, though, that new teams may need a little more support as they learn the basics of agile, so you may choose to reveal more of your observations in this case.

While the team sprints, the coach pays attention, noticing how things are going. Some things the coach may ponder while watching are

- Is the team using the structures of agile to stay coordinated?
- What is the team tolerating?
- How well does the work flow?
- Where are the breakdowns in communication, coordination, attendance, attention to one another, and collaboration?
- Where are the brilliant moments?
- Where does it feel slow, like molasses on a cold day?
- How does the team's level of anxiety change throughout the sprint?
- Are people present physically, mentally, and emotionally?
- When and how does the level of excitement change?

As the retrospective draws near, peruse your list of observations. Perhaps a theme or two jumps out at you. You may choose one of these to be the main topic of the retrospective. Also, check in with a couple of team members and the product owner to get their perspectives. What have they seen this sprint? What are they curious about? What is bothering them? A note of caution: Be careful not to start a mini-retrospective during this check-in. Let the conversation stop at surfacing what's on a person's mind as an input to the retrospective, not halt their progress as they agonize over a sprint they're still in.

With these observations and inputs, prepare the retrospective agenda. The best book I have found for helping agile coaches do this is *Agile Retrospectives: Making Good Teams Great* because it offers activities teams use to obtain a new view on the past sprint so they can see new ways to improve and so all voices—even the quiet ones—get heard (Larsen and Derby 2006). That's so much more effective than sitting around a conference table talking.

Design the retrospective agenda to address the "biggest bang for the buck" theme that emerged during the sprint. Or, let it be a learning agenda where you introduce a new framework or way of thinking about something, and then ask, "How does this apply to us?"

Mixing these two, you can also design a learning agenda specific to a theme that emerged. This allows you to address the theme without assessing blame or shutting people down. For example, if unproductive or subsurface conflict has occurred frequently during the sprint, you may choose to teach the team about a useful conflict framework and then ask reflective questions: Where have we seen conflict this past sprint? Have we used conflict to our advantage? How can this framework be helpful to us?

SEE ALSO	A conflict framework used with agile teams is offered in Chapter 9, "Coach as Conflict Navigator."

Regardless of the agenda you create, the things that bother people tend to surface. So, don't be too concerned that the agenda will hold them back. If they are bothered enough, they'll find a way to bring it up no matter what you have planned.

Facilitate During the Retrospective

An agile coach always makes clear the firm belief that the team knows the right thing to do. So, too, with the retrospective. Modeling this belief, present the agenda, tell the team what activities have been designed to go along with the agenda items, and ask permission for the agenda (Tabaka 2006). Ask, "Does this agenda sound like it will get us to the key things this retrospective should focus on today?"

When you ask this question, be ready to "give it all away" should the team decide to take the meeting in a different direction. If they say, "The agenda is good, but the thing we really need to explore is what changing the product owner has cost us." In this case, you keep the agenda and change the subject. Perhaps they say, "The overall topic is exactly what we need to talk about, even though we really don't want to. So, maybe a less-engineered agenda would work. Can we just talk?" You say OK to this. In the worst case, they flub up the retrospective and get nothing out of it. This, too, leads to learning. Take the gamble because, in the best case, the gamble pays off, and they get exactly what they need.

Regardless of what does or does not get done during the retrospective, the coach keeps the timebox. If the retrospective was expected to run for an hour, the coach holds that timing for the team. With 15 minutes to go, the coach says, "The retrospective ends in 15 minutes. Should we wrap this up into a few things that you all agree to do next time?" When one hour has elapsed, the coach says, "The retrospective is over." If team members want to continue, they may as long as all of them agree and as long as that, too, takes place inside a short timebox. This keeps people from being held hostage in a meeting that seems to have no end. As the extra time expires, anyone can speak up and ask that the meeting end. Throughout the retrospective, the coach works toward a constructive outcome, using the agenda to bring the team back to their purpose when they need a reminder.

Once the team has come to a handful of agreements they pledge they will put into effect, the coach invites them to write the agreements and post them in a conspicuous place. The agreements hold much more weight when written by a team member, so whenever possible, have someone on the team do this.

Facilitate After the Retrospective

Throughout the next sprint, observe and gather ideas for the next retrospective. Also, pay attention to whether the current retrospective agreements get incorporated or forgotten. In either case, bring this to the team's attention several times during the sprint. Perhaps give a fantastic example of someone changing their behavior to honor a retrospective agreement. Give public acknowledgment to this person. Perhaps the retrospective agreements have gotten buried under other flip charts and have become a distant memory. Pretty soon, someone will violate one of the agreements, and the team will feel (but may not acknowledge) the impact. Don't let this pass. Call it out. "Hey, guys, what happened to the agreement you made where you said you weren't going to do that to each other anymore?" This will likely cause someone on the team to unearth the flip chart listing the agreements and make their presence felt again.

Throughout the sprint, look for situations that allow you to hold the team's agreements up to them. If you model this, they will likely start to hold them for each other. When they do this, you can step back.

As time goes on, the team may be able to facilitate the retrospective themselves. Perhaps a team member comes forth and says, "Let me design the next retrospective agenda." You can help this person or not, as it feels right to both of you. Maybe facilitating the retrospective rotates on the team. As long as the team achieves the purpose of the retrospective, let it happen. When they are ready, you step back. They will call on you when they need to do so. And, you are not going anywhere. You will still attend and observe the retrospective, stepping back in if the purpose of the retrospective gets twisted or forgotten.

Facilitate During Team Conversations

Much of the time, the team engages in formal and informal conversations. You will see them naturally converse in small groups, as a whole group, and one-on-one. All of these conversations serve up opportunities to observe and coach. What are you coaching for? You're looking for the quality of the conversation, not the content. The subject matter of the conversation matters not. The quality does.

When the team converses, don't join in and act as a team member. There are already enough team members. Be a coach instead. Help them improve their conversations so that they can come up with higher-quality ideas that translate directly to the products they build.

You will recognize a quality conversation because the team will be in a rich discussion, where lots of ideas emerge and are built upon to come up with something new, something none of them could have created themselves. They generate insights and envision an amazing product—the one they will build. They disagree with one another as they tussle with the hard problems. They do all this while managing the art of the conversation themselves, making sure everyone gets to speak, truly listening to one another, viewing each new idea as a gift, and moving forward...always moving forward.

Three main tools you can use, right now, to help the team have quality conversations are powerful observations, powerful questions, and powerful challenges.

Powerful Observations

Keep a running list of questions in your head as you observe a team in conversation. You can use these questions when it's the whole team talking, just a few talking, or only two team members talking. Questions such as these let you hone in on the quality of the conversation:

- Is everyone who wants to talk getting airtime? Are there dominant people in the room who need to listen more? Are there quiet voices that want to be heard?

- Are the ideas high quality?

- Is the team moving toward the simplest thing possible?

- Is the team getting tired?

- Is it tense? Do they need comic relief?

- Is the team being audacious enough? Do they come up with great ideas or break through barriers?

- Are they taking on as much as they could, or are they letting "accepted" barriers get in the way?

- Is the team couching everything in terms of customer value?

- Are they stuck? Do they need a new perspective, one that brings them more possibilities?

In all cases, as you make an observation about the quality of the conversation, first pause to consider whether you should share it. As a general rule, keep your observation to yourself for a few minutes to see whether one of the team members picks up on the same thing and calls it out or to see whether the team moves on to more fertile ground, which makes your observation irrelevant.

TRY THIS

Keep this list of observation questions handy, somewhere that you can quickly access when a conversation just happens around you.

Over time, you will probably come up with your own observation questions. They will naturally arise from what you observe (that's how this list was initially created). Add your questions to the list and share them with fellow agile coaches. See whether you can help build up an agile coach storehouse of great observation questions.

If you decide to share the observation, consider your words carefully. Remember that the team really does know what's best, so they will know the right direction to point themselves. You offer another view into the situation, possibly opening up some new avenues of inquiry for them or moving them toward action. When you share your observations, consider using powerful questions.

Powerful Questions

Powerful questions work because they are truly open. They are not asked with a "correct" answer in mind. Because of this, they invite introspection. They may present additional solutions or lead to greater creativity and insight. A powerful question sends people into the realm of discovery (Whitworth et al. 2007).

To see how powerful questions work, let's look at some typical team scenarios in Table 6.1 and contrast a nonpowerful (but common) question with some powerful question alternatives.

TABLE 6.1 Powerful questions for agile teams (adapted from Whitworth et al. 2007)

Scenario	Instead of asking...	Try powerful questions...
The team has been in conversation for a while, and you think they need to hear a specific team member's opinion.	What's your opinion?	What do you make of it? What is possible here? What is the part that is not yet clear? What else?
The team is diving into solution details, and you think they should stay in the "visioning" state longer.	What are other options?	What is here that you want to explore? What other angles can you think of? What is just one more possibility?
The team has decided on a solution but isn't moving into action.	What do we need to do to get started?	Is this a time for action? If your life depended on taking action, what would you do? If you had free choice in the matter, what would you do?
A team member is rehashing a story of something that happened in the past.	Why does this keep coming up?	What is the essence of that? What do you make of that?
A team member is unsure about a course of action.	What do you need to be sure about this?	What will this get you? What is your prediction? What are your best experiences from similar cases? What did you do in order to succeed then?

Scenario	Instead of asking...	Try powerful questions...
The team keeps coming around to the same conversation.	Why are we talking about this again?	What seems to be the main obstacle? What concerns you the most about...?
The team is evaluating options.	Is this a viable option?	What is the opportunity here? What is the challenge? What is your assessment?
The team is stuck.	How do we get past this?	How else could a person handle this? If you could do anything you wanted, what would you do?

When you speak a powerful question, it will often be followed by dead silence, especially if the team has never heard this type of question before. The silence is normal. They are reflecting. During the silence, look around at the team members, not demanding them to talk but silently inviting them to talk. When they are ready, they will.

Powerful questions reinforce your role as their coach because they carry no judgment. They are truly open. When you ask a powerful question, you offer a living example of your belief that they are the ones with the answers.

WHY DO YOU ASK WEIRD QUESTIONS?

After asking this powerful question, "What does your history tell you?" and hearing the animated conversation that resulted, I might offer this as a bit of learning as well: "I asked this question not to satisfy my own curiosity but to open a new line of inquiry for you. Perhaps now you can see another possibility, something that wasn't here before. Maybe a slight shift has happened and something will come of this a few days from now. Maybe we've just wasted five minutes, but your minds are now refreshed."

A team member may respond by saying something such as, "Oh, yeah. It was good for us to come up one level and reconsider where we are in the bigger picture. I get why you ask these questions."

Over a short period of time, team members catch on to the powerful questions a coach asks and, often, will take up this type of questioning themselves. It's another way they imbibe your coaching to become self-managing.

Powerful Challenges

Challenging clients has long been a tool used by professional coaches (Whitworth et al. 2007). With a challenge, the coach moves the team past where they would normally stop. They won't necessarily accept the powerful challenge (because you're going to make it audacious), but they will often go further than they would have without the challenge.

It is amazing the things that hold teams back. They accept limitations placed on them by their organization, by prior experiences (once bit, twice shy), and quite often by themselves. Sometimes, they need an "unreasonable" challenge to move them off their well-worn path.

Let's say that you've been observing the team in a design conversation, and you notice that they're not dreaming very much. They're coming up with some ideas, but they're not very interesting, let alone astounding. You feel a challenge coming on.

First, tune in to the content of their conversation. (Yes! Pay keen attention to the content now.) To challenge them, you need to use the material they give you, so listen for it. Whatever they say, go one better. Amplify their thoughts, or take their idea in a totally new (and wild) direction. Be big, be bold for them.

If they have just decided that their new process can take up to 200 new callers a day, you inject this: "What would it take to amp that up to 2,000 new callers a day?" The point is not to get them to accept the 2,000 number but to have them break through the assumptions and limitations holding them at 200 callers a day. Get them dreaming a little bit, and, in so doing, watch them come up with something even better, maybe even astounding.

When to Sit with Them, When to Sit Back

The coach's physical location in the team room matters when facilitating during team conversations. When the team is new, sit with them. Be physically close to the conversation but still mostly silent. When you decide to speak your observation or offer a powerful question or challenge, you will be right there with them. This helps them get used to the types of things you offer, and they notice that you contribute on a different level than anyone else. They clearly see that you pay attention at the whole-team level so that you can help them have higher-quality conversations.

Once a team manages the basic elements of quality conversations themselves and you find yourself offering powerful observations, questions, and challenges less often, sit back. Physically and energetically, sit back from the main area of the team room. Still be with them and pay attention. Interject from your position at the fringe of the team room when you see the need. Contribute your carefully considered observations, questions, and challenges from your vantage point in the periphery, removing yourself from the center. They don't need you there anymore.

When you're not actively involved in the content of a conversation, it's easy to go unconscious. This happens whether you are sitting with the team or away from them.

You might find that your mind wanders off somewhere. Perhaps you find yourself making menu plans for dinner, rehashing a fight with your kid, or worrying about how the team will be viewed at the end of the sprint. This is normal. The research coalesced in Wikipedia on this subject offers this:

> Estimates for the length of human attention span are highly variable and range from three to five minutes per year of age in young children to a maximum of around twenty minutes in adults. Continuous attention span, or the amount of time a human can focus on an object without any lapse at all, is very brief and may be as short as eight seconds. After this amount of time, it is likely that an individual's eyes will shift focus or that a stray thought will briefly enter consciousness. Fortunately, these short lapses are only minimally distracting and do not tend to interfere with task performance.

Most conversations I've observed last more than twenty minutes, putting the agile coach at risk for a wandering mind. Regardless of the conversation length, the less-than–eight-second ability to continuously concentrate can be a trap, too. If you're like me, a short concentration lapse is enough to send your mind into a whole new world that has nothing to do with the job at hand. For me, short lapses definitely affect task performance when I'm observing other people's conversations.

Whether you're like me or whether you can continuously concentrate for long periods, sooner or later your mind will wander. It's up to you to bring it back. Focus, wander, attention. This is your practice. Focus on the conversation. Whoops! My mind has wandered. Bring the attention back. Over and over again (Devin).

To increase your ability to pay attention, you may find it useful to keep your hands or mind busy on a background activity. Doodling or making paper clip sculptures are two of my favorites. Others read the latest agile blogs or surf fractal art images online. These are fine ways to help you keep your attention on the team. Of course, you need to be aware when the background activity has become foreground and has taken center stage in your attention. When this happens, drop the background activity and remember focus, wander, attention. Come back to the team. They are why you are here.

Most of the time, you will probably sit away from the main action. You have helped the team conduct quality conversations, and more than that, you have passed on the skills they need to manage the quality of the conversations themselves. There will certainly be times to come back to the main action, though.

When it gets tense or you notice anxiety, you may decide to come forward and sit with the team again. Sometimes just lending your physical presence and full attention diffuses the tension. Maybe this happens because each person knows that they have been heard, at least by you. Other times, a powerful observation, question, or challenge helps them break out of their holding pattern.

Or, perhaps it's time for the team to pick up a new skill. Maybe you notice that they need to build more collaboration muscle or acquire the ability to navigate conflict. The best time to offer new skills like this happens in the moment, when it can be put to immediate use. So, be on your toes to take advantage of situations as they present themselves.

SEE ALSO	Everything an agile coach does with a team is done with the purpose in mind of transferring skills to the team. Two essential skills for teams are working together in collaboration and conflict. Building the team's collaboration muscle is the subject of Chapter 10, "Coach as Collaboration Conductor." Chapter 9, "Coach as Conflict Navigator," offers models and tools that help teams weather conflict well.

Professional Facilitator and Agile Coach

There are many skills an agile coach can apply with great effect from the world of professional facilitation. I encourage you to do your own research and find the tools that will help you the most. I have specifically steered away from many formal facilitation techniques in this book because so much good material already exists on that subject.

As you pick up more facilitation skills, remember to apply them within the purpose of coaching agile teams. Facilitating for agile teams is not about using techniques to drive them through one formal conversation after another as one would do on a project that gets done through a series of meetings. The context of an agile team means that team members stay in constant conversation with one another, both formal (as in a meeting) and informal (all the time). Facilitating for agile teams stays focused on teaching them the ropes of the formal meetings and then using keen coaching senses to observe them in action and help them make their interactions better, all the while relying on them to know where to go next.

A Refresher

Let's lock in the ideas from this chapter:

- Every agile meeting has a specific purpose that answers the question, "Why do we do this meeting, anyway?" Coach teams to achieve the purpose, using it as a check to ensure they are getting as much out of the various agile meetings as possible.

- Intervene with the team more in the beginning, when you are teaching them agile, and step back as soon as you can to support their continuous self-organization.

- Make a conscious decision before offering anything to a team and only offer the things that carry benefits that far outweigh the interruption.

- Get good at being a keen observer.

- Get out of the content and get into the facilitation so you can help the team improve the quality of their interactions.

- Become skilled at delivering powerful observations, powerful questions, and powerful challenges. This takes practice, so get to it.

Additional Resources

Tabaka, J. 2006. *Collaboration Explained: Facilitation Skills for Software Project Leaders*. Boston: Addison-Wesley. This book is a staple on my bookshelf and is used every time I coach new coaches. Don't let the word *software* in the subtitle of this book make you think it is only relevant for software development teams.

Davies, R., and L. Sedley. 2009. *Agile Coaching*. Raleigh: Pragmatic Bookshelf. This book provides page after page of practical tips for coaching during the standard agile meetings and goes deep into coaching technical practices.

Derby, E., and D. Larsen. 2006. *Agile Retrospectives: Making Good Teams Great*. Raleigh: Pragmatic Bookshelf. This book contains the five-step retrospective "formula" that I follow to this day. It is also chock-full of activities that help a team see their working methods in a different light and come up with ideas that will make a significant impact to the way they work together.

References

Cohn, M. 2005. *Agile Estimating and Planning*. Boston: Addison-Wesley.

———. 2004. *User Stories Applied: For Agile Software Development*. Boston: Addison-Wesley.

Davies, R., and L. Sedley. 2009. *Agile Coaching*. Raleigh: Pragmatic Bookshelf.

Devin, L. A random collection of favorite acting exercises. Unpublished manuscript.

Pichler, R. 2010. *Agile Product Management: Creating Products that Customers Love*. Boston: Addison-Wesley.

Tabaka, J. 2006. *Collaboration Explained: Facilitation Skills for Software Project Leaders*. Boston: Addison-Wesley.

Whitworth, L. K. Kimsey-House, H. Kimsey-House, and P. Sandahl. 2007. *Co-Active Coaching: New Skills for Coaching People Toward Success in Work and Life, Second Edition*. Mountain View, CA: Davies-Black.

Chapter 7

Coach as Teacher

An agile coach takes on the job of teacher many times throughout the life of a team. There is much for the team to learn. Right from the start, agile coaches teach agile at its simplest and most powerful. Then, they constantly coach teams to come back to the simple and powerful, where agile thrives.

This chapter details prime teaching times and topics: teaching agile during team start-up, during restarts, and during unexpected moments; teaching the roles in agile; and continuously holding people to the best expression of those roles.

The first time to teach comes up fast—at the outset of the team. Done well, the team start-up can be jet fuel to a team, helping them to go further and faster than they ever imagined.

Then, when things go awry, the coach teaches again, giving the team a little remedial tutoring or going deeper into an area where they have gone beyond the basics or unnecessarily complicated agile and lost their way.

By the time you finish this chapter, you will be able to answer these questions:

- What do I teach the team during the start-up? What do they need to know before they get going on the work?
- How much time should I expect to spend preparing for the start-up session?
- How do I integrate new team members into the team?
- How can I ensure the agile "leadership" roles—product owner, agile coach, and agile manager—are well understood and healthy?
- What tools can I use to help teams when they are operating under unclear roles?

Teach During the Team Start-Up

When a company wants to "go agile," they turn to you, the coach, and ask, "How do we get teams started?" This creates a flurry of questions in your mind. What do I need to know before starting up a team? How much do teams need to know about agile before they "go"? What do they need to know about each other? About the product to be built? About what they will become as a team? You sense something crucial and fleeting about this moment, and you are right. Although you reinforce agile constantly as the team works together, the team start-up allows you to teach agile at its most basic and potent. This time will not come again.

Powerful team start-ups transpire in a day or two; they need not take several days or a week. Those that go long often delve further than needed into team building or get deep into the work, both of which are better done in the sprint as a team pursues shared goals. Team building, especially, resonates more with people done in the context of the work rather than an "event" for its own sake. So, keep the start-up short and specific.

By the end of the start-up, the first sprint will have started. You will have smoothly moved the team members from a collection of individuals into a new team in its first sprint, with no pause between the two. To do so, address these main areas during the start-up (Vizdos 2005):

Learn about the process to be used.

Learn about the team.

Learn about the work ahead.

Go!

When you design the start-up, allot more time for learning about the process and the work ahead and less time for learning about the team. All three are equally important at some point in the team's life together, but at the start, focusing the team on a task orientation rather than a relationship orientation sets them up for better success (Gratton et al. 2007). Later, when conflicts start to arise, you can lean on a relationship orientation, but for now give more air time (and attention) to the work at hand.

SEE ALSO How to manage conflict with your team is the subject of Chapter 9, "Coach as Conflict Navigator."

Let's dive in to the first of the three start-up areas, learning about the process.

Learning About the Process

Learning about the process to be used certainly includes the agile framework of choice. For this, you are their teacher. But it may also include disciplines or tools from Six Sigma, lean, user-centered design, or Extreme Programming, or it may be a training ground for company standards or procedures. If these or others are to be used, then ask experts to teach the team about them (if you're not one). Then, you enter the picture again to help the team decide how tools and ideas from other disciplines can fit within the agile framework. To do this, they need to learn the agile framework first.

If team members have been on agile teams before, your teaching takes the form of light training disguised as "getting on the same page." With a team new to agile, you have the gift of a truly new start. Teach agile completely, fully, and compellingly to them.

People who have worked on agile teams before think they "know agile" and don't need training on agile practices, principles, values, and roles. As depicted in Figure 7.1, they have often unknowingly adopted the rituals and limitations of their prior teams and may have strayed far from the core of agile. They don't recognize it yet, but "my agile" is not "your agile" and looks nothing like "his agile." Worse still, all versions may be far from agile done well.

Teaching agile to experienced agilists starts with the coach saying, "I know you are experienced in agile. Let me take ten minutes to show you my version of agile so that we can make sure we are synchronized in our understanding of it. It's from this version of agile that I will coach you, so it's important that you know where I am coming from."

Then, deliver a short whiteboard talk that trains them on the agile framework to be used. The agile frameworks most often used are lightweight and simple—easy to convey in ten minutes if you get good at your whiteboard talk. So, practice your whiteboard talk, and be able to deliver it simply and credibly anytime, anywhere.

SEE ALSO   Especially for a team of experienced agilists, set your expectation that they will be high-performing right at the start using the tools offered in Chapter 2, "Expect High Performance."

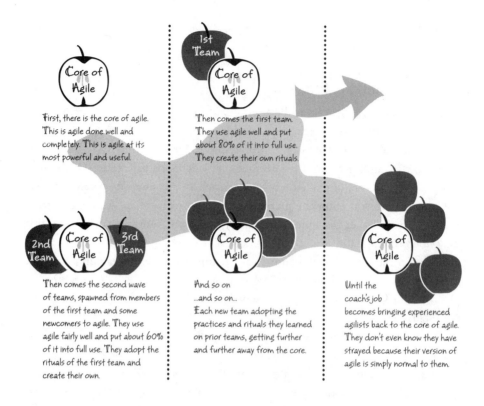

First, there is the core of agile. This is agile done well and completely. This is agile at its most powerful and useful.

Then comes the first team. They use agile well and put about 80% of it into full use. They create their own rituals.

Then comes the second wave of teams, spawned from members of the first team and some newcomers to agile. They use agile fairly well and put about 60% of it into full use. They adopt the rituals of the first team and create their own.

And so on ...and so on... Each new team adopting the practices and rituals they learned on prior teams, getting further and further away from the core.

Until the coach's job becomes bringing experienced agilists back to the core of agile. They don't even know they have strayed because their version of agile is simply normal to them.

FIGURE 7.1   The progression of agile teams creates the need to train team members to come back to the core of agile.

These short ten minutes bubble up different experiences of agile. People recognize where agile had been tailored before they joined the team and now understand that they have never used some parts of the framework. People see how prior teams have loaded agile practices down with rituals that no longer serve. With these revelations bubbling to the top, the coach starts a discussion about the core of agile and how it has been used (or misused).

TASK CARD TECHNOLOGY

On each new team, we inherit the burdens of generations of prior teams without knowing it. Even a simple thing such as printing task cards can become an unnecessary burden. One team stopped dead in their tracks during sprint planning because the mail-merge routine they used to print task cards failed.

They were convinced they could not continue planning; then the coach got out a few markers and showed them that writing task cards by hand would work well, too. As they wrote task cards longhand, they discovered something amazing: They talked to each other more. They got into details about how the tasks would work and who was best equipped to do what. They explored alternative approaches to getting the work done. They discovered a new depth to planning. And, they were amazed to find that it took about half the time it used to take.

Printing task cards may not be an especially bad idea, but it's not part of the core of agile. Most certainly, printing task cards solved a particularly difficult problem for some team in the past (whatever that was), but it was no longer relevant, and was even harmful, for this team.

During this discussion, take up the position of teacher strongly. Bring this team of experienced agilists back to the core of agile. Along the way, do not denigrate them for the rituals and changes their prior teams (and they) made to agile. Since we ask people to inspect and adapt, the "drift" away from the core is expected and can be a perfectly healthy maturing of their use of agile. As their coach, help people become aware of the adaptations they bring to this new team and differentiate where they may have applied "copy and follow" over "inspect and adapt." In so doing, the whole team decides whether to use the adaptations. In this discussion, hold the position of one who knows the core of agile solidly and helps the team see this new start as a beginner would, full of possibility to get agile right.

With new agilists, you have the treat of a completely fresh start! Teach more than a ten-minute whiteboard talk to help embed the values and principles of agile from the beginning. Use activities from your own training as an agile coach. Choose the ones that make agile visceral and relevant to them.

Whatever you do, light training or more in-depth, stick to the core of agile. Monitor yourself closely, and consciously choose which, if any, rituals from past teams you will bring to them. Something almost universally accepted but perhaps not seen as the core of agile, such as user stories, may be just fine to bring forth. The layout of the team's storyboard and what color cards their stories and tasks should be written on, not so much, even if this ritual seems innocent enough. This team is different. They may not encounter the same obstacles prior teams encountered, so you need not bring forth those particular remedies.

Keep it simple, knowing that agile has in it everything they need to face whatever comes their way.

Learning About the Team

Learning about the team starts with learning about each individual on the team and, from there, creating a shared team identity. For this part of the team start-up, your teaching takes on the flavor of a tour guide, helping them discover new things about themselves and others.

> *The art of teaching is the art of assisting discovery.*
>
> —*Mark Van Doren*

Individuals shape into a team when they learn first about one another as human beings and then grow from that understanding into a sense of who they can become together. In the start-up, plan activities that allow team members to relate to one another on a human level wherein they discover each other's skills, talents, and anything else they bring that will help achieve the goals of the work ahead. This sets the stage for self-organization and cross-functional behavior.

With the lessons about one another as a fresh source of insight, guide the group to create an identity as a team. Let them dream a shared vision of themselves together as one team and imagine how they will act to achieve that vision. Through this you establish, right from the start, that making the team is a product in itself, to be held just as important as the other products they will make together.

Learning About Each Other as Individuals

Dozens of excellent activities help people break through their shyness so they can share their hopes, dreams, skills, perspectives, and goals with one another when in a new group. You'll find them using "team building" as an Internet search word. A note of caution: As you find such activities, refrain from bringing activities to the team that have as their goal making everyone feel good about one another and sing "Kumbaya" together. We use activities under the "team building" heading to help people learn about one another so they can depend on each other as they pursue shared goals. No fluffy stuff here.

A few activities that have become my standard fare in building this type of understanding are Journey Lines, Market of Skills, Constellation, and Values. Journey Lines yields a deep understanding of each person's past—their accomplishments and disappointments, their skills and talents, and a bit about their lives under the surface. Market of Skills, an alternative to Journey Lines, primarily highlights people's skills and talents. Constellation provides a window into how team members like to work and don't like to work, what motivates them and what kills their drive, what they aspire to become, and what they'd rather avoid. The Values activity invites each person to discover and express those essential things about them that make them who they are.

Journey Lines A journey line (Tichy 2002) graphs a person's professional journey. Starting as far back as they want, each person draws the ups and downs of their journey on a flip chart. As you can see in Figure 7.2, the journey line often looks like a roller coaster with notes at each high and low point to remind the person of that particular event. Some include details of their home life as well as their professional life. Some stick to the professional facts. It doesn't matter. No two are ever the same, and they all work fine.

After everyone has completed drawing their journey lines (about ten minutes), each person presents theirs to the team. As one person speaks, the rest of the group jots down anything that sticks out for them: skills the person has that will be useful for the project on which they are about to embark, talents that are interesting and may be useful later, or experiences and values that make that person who they are. Each person reads aloud the notes they took, and they stick the notes up on the journey line. Here are some examples of notes from Journey Lines activities:

- "Accounting background—may come in handy as we get into interfaces with the bean counters."

- "Assisted mentally ill patients in a hospital—I know you can do anything if you can do that."

- "You really honored yourself through every career decision. You never compromised who you are."

Through sharing one's journey and being truly received by the other team members in the form of the notes, each person is affirmed for who they are and what they bring. And the entire team builds a foundation for working cross-functionally because they now know each other's backgrounds.

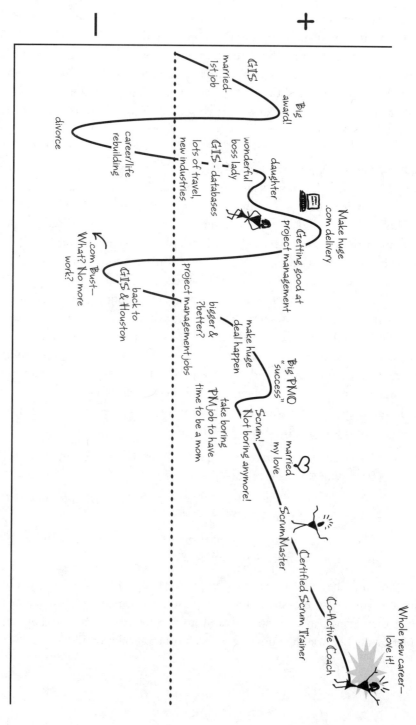

FIGURE 7.2   Sample journey line

FIGURE 7.2   Sample journey line

The results of Journey Lines are sometimes astounding. One such case happened for me during a "new" team start-up. The team members had worked together for years over cubicle walls and had come together for their first-ever agile experience. As one person presented her journey line, she got to a hard bit—the year she had cancer. As she talked about the impact of cancer on her life, I noticed another team member getting emotional. After a few minutes, this team member started to cry. Through tears she said, "I sat in the cubicle next to you that whole year, and we never knew about each other. I had cancer then, too."

> *There is nothing more empowering than being seen, celebrated, and known for who you are.*
>
> —*Karen Kimsey House*

Deep connections get started through Journey Lines. Perhaps not as apparent as in the cancer situation, they nonetheless have started to grow beneath the surface. Even if deep connections don't appear to happen at all, the Journey Lines exercise plants the seeds by making the skills, expertise, and overall background of each team member visible and an acceptable topic of conversation. With this knowledge, teams set the stage for being self-organized and cross-functional. Without it, how would they know what each of them brings?

Market of Skills   Although I have never had anyone walk out of the room when I introduced the Journey Lines activity, there are those who find it uncomfortable at first. If, as their coach, you find it uncomfortable, then don't do it. Instead, substitute the Market of Skills activity, used extensively by Certified Scrum Coach and certified systemic coach Bent Myllerup in his team start-ups. As with Journey Lines, "participation in the Market of Skills activity strengthens the team's awareness of their combined skills as well as the areas in which team members can support and educate each other. The activity is both an appreciative aspect of team identity and a way to know one's teammates better" (2009).

Here's how it works:

Imagine that each team member owns a booth at a market. Within 20 minutes, each person makes a poster that answers the following questions:

- Which competencies, skills, and abilities related to the team are available at your booth?

- What is available under the counter of your booth? (In other words, which competencies, skills, and abilities do you possess that may not be relevant to the goal of the team?)

- Which competencies, skills, and abilities would you like to achieve or learn from some of the other team members?

Next, each person presents their poster. During the presentation, everyone else notes the following (one note on each sticky label):

- The competencies and so on that you are especially excited that this person offers (this could be on green sticky labels).

- Other relevant competencies, skills, and abilities that you know this person possesses but didn't mention (this could be on red sticky labels).

- How you can help the person to gain the competencies, skills, or abilities the person wants (this could be on yellow sticky labels).

After the presentation, the other team members individually give their feedback and post the sticky labels near the person's poster (Myllerup 2009).

Myllerup says to be specific with team members about what type of feedback is constructive, especially for the "how I can help you" feedback. This activity should not be used as a launching pad for offering advice or criticism that the person presenting their Market of Skills poster has not requested.

Either Journey Lines or Market of Skills gets you to the same place—teammates understanding one another's skills so they can figure out how to share work. With this as the basis, move on to guide the team in an activity that helps them learn about work styles and preferences.

DEALING WITH TOUCHY-FEELY RESISTANCE

People often ask whether I get a lot of resistance when I work with a team through a learning activity like Journey Lines, Market of Skills, or Constellation. I don't. Perhaps it's the way I invite team members to participate, perhaps it's the fact that I just assume they'll go along, or perhaps it's that I believe in the method and the results so I'm not tentative as I approach it. They go along, and I have never (yet) had anyone walk out or even kick up a big fuss. You might do well to assume success and see how it goes.

What if it's a no-go and the team says, "Absolutely no touchy-feely stuff"? One thing other coaches find useful is letting the team in on the purpose and one possible outcome of the activity. If the activity goes off well, there may be many outcomes, some never yet seen by the coach, so be open as you mention an outcome.

Using this method, when you introduce Journey Lines, for example, you could say, "Journey Lines is one way that we can get to know one another's skills, talents, and backgrounds so that you can figure out how to rely on one another once we're into the sprints. More than that can happen, so remain open to the experience, but that's one common outcome and the basic goal as we work through Journey Lines."

This approach also works for people with limited mobility or other circumstances that require them to alter the activity to fully participate. If they know one thing the activity should generate, they can figure out alternate ways to get the same result.

Constellation Constellation (Adkins and Blake 2009) starts in an open space, with enough room for people to walk around. Choose any object and put it on the floor. The object represents the center of the constellation. Invite the team members to stand around the center object and tell them that you are going to read some statements to them. Let them know that for each statement, they should gravitate toward or away from the center object as if it were a scale. The closer to the center object, the more true that statement is for them, and the farther away, the less true it is for them. Start with a few statements, like these, to warm them up:

- I enjoy time alone.
- My happiest times are when I'm in nature.
- I like to make things with my hands.
- I thrive being around people.

After you read the statement, each team member moves closer to or farther away from the center object to mark how much the statement rings true or untrue in their life. They move at the same time, with no one paying much attention to where anyone else moves. Once in their chosen location, invite them to look around and see where their teammates stand. Encourage them to take a good look at the "constellation of people" created for the statement. Make sure they understand the purpose of the activity—to learn about one another.

After the warm-up statements, move into more targeted statements designed to raise work preferences and needs:

- I like speaking in front of people.
- I avoid conflict with people who have more seniority than me.
- I like surprises.
- I do not like uncomfortable silence and work to fill it in.
- I enjoy public recognition.
- I get quiet in uncomfortable situations.
- I am a perfectionist.
- I enjoy debates.
- I like to facilitate meetings.

Again, invite them to notice their whole-team reaction to these statements in the shape of each constellation.

After reading your preconstructed statements, ask the team to create their own. Invite them to write statements on scraps of paper for you to read to the group. Sometimes people come up with pointed statements that indicate potential areas of concern. Statements can also indicate someone expressing a need they have to see who else has that need, too. Other times, the statements are little "tests" one team member has for the rest, just to see how people react to certain conditions, even those that they want the team to explicitly avoid.

Here are some examples of team member–generated statements:

- I thrive in micromanaged environments.
- I feel more of an accomplishment working individually than as a team.
- I feel comfortable providing direct feedback.
- I need time to think about something before I work on it.
- I am frustrated when there is a lack of order.
- I think agile is going to work for us.
- I don't mind bending the rules to get things done.
- I am comfortable using agile even if it lessens my personal influence or control.

Viewing the constellations resulting from these statements shows the team what their teammates will and will not do, what they do and do not believe, and what they will and will not tolerate. This provides a more solid basis from which the team will self-organize because it generates a better understanding of the people on a team. Perhaps, a month or two later, someone says, "Oh, I see why you're being so quiet. It's not that you don't care or have no opinion; you just shrink when people raise their voices. I remember you were almost out the door when we did the constellation and the coach read the statement, "I am comfortable in a shouting match." Understanding established. A stellar outcome, indeed.

> *What I hear, I forget.*
> *What I see, I remember.*
> *What I do, I understand.*
>
> *—Kung Fu Tzu (Confucius)*

Success with Constellation happens when you ask this question and then let them talk with one another, "Where were you surprised about the shape of a constellation?"

Values   The Values activity (Kouzes and Posner 2007) allows people to explore their inner world in another way—through values words. Each person receives a deck of the same values cards. Written on the cards are words such as the following:

Decisiveness	Happiness	Patience	Teamwork
Humor	Independence	Challenge	Diversity
Prosperity	Spirituality	Productivity	Growth

One card is left blank in case someone has a values word they want to write in. There should be many values cards, perhaps 50 or so, enough to cause people to make trade-offs between one value they hold dearly for another they hold more dearly.

Here's how this works: Each person sorts through their deck of values cards, placing them in two piles, important to me and not important to me. Then, they take the cards in the "important to me" pile and sort just those into two piles as before. They repeat this, each time sorting the ever-smaller "important to me" pile until there are only five values cards remaining: the most important ones.

Then, each person writes their five values on a big flip chart or whiteboard with their name at the top so all the values from all the team members are seen at once. Then they step back and consider the lists. As they do this, ask a few thought-provoking questions and wait for the answers: What do these lists tell us? What here surprises you? Which would you like to understand more deeply? Where are we divergent? Where are we harmonious?

In the ensuing conversation, guide the group so that each person increases their understanding of their teammates and themselves. To do so, encourage curiosity rather than judgment. No one gets to be wrong (Coaches Training Institute 2008).

To help everyone learn about the people on their team, conduct one or two activities such as Journey Lines or Market of Skills, Constellation, Values, or another one you discover or create yourself. Each of them establishes a deep understanding of one another as human beings, which is so needed as people work toward shared commitments in the sprints to come. They also set the stage for what happens next—learning about the team.

Learning About the Team

With the awareness of one another created from the previous activities, launch into learning about the team. "The team" has yet to emerge. It will be whatever this collection of bright, complex, curious, willful, powerful people wills it to be. It is the first product they create together.

The guiding lights for this product—the team—are a shared vision and team norms.

Create a Shared Vision   Teams need goals at multiple levels: What's in it for me? What's in it for us as a team? What's in it for my company? What's in it for the world? A shared vision encompassing these varied and rich dimensions will survive the shifting winds of conflict and change, which are sure to blow as the team works together in the months to come.

Creating this vision starts from the individual out. On scraps of paper, ask each team member to write their name and the completion of this sentence: "When this project is over, I want to say I have…." These might be skills some hope to add to their tool kits; for others it might be a quality such as having more patience or acceptance. Whatever they are, have the team members write each one on a separate piece of scrap paper. Then, post the scrap papers in a big circle on a flip chart. Have each person read theirs aloud. Then, ask the team, "Do you agree to support this?" Most of the time, the answer is a no-brainer "yes" because the person's goal does not compete with getting the work done or with another teammate's desires.

Sometimes, though, individual goals clash. It's better to surface these now and recognize their existence, but don't try to resolve them. The clash can't be resolved now because it hasn't really happened yet. It will come later, as the team works together. Perhaps the team cannot support two people finishing their Six Sigma black-belt projects in the same sprint. That's a clash. Deal with it then, when you have information and options for this particular instance of a clash.

Your focus stays here: This activity explicitly gives people permission to talk about their personal hopes in the context of this new team. It opens the door for a continual conversation about goals and how best to support them for one another.

Once the "What's in it for me?" part has been done, turn your attention to the team as a whole. Recall some of the insights that arose during the previous activities where the team members learned about one another. Guide them to create a succinct and meaningful statement of what they desire to become together. Place this statement at the top of the flip chart, written big and bold. Some examples:

- We are a creative group of people, bringing out the best in each other to create products that matter.

- We deliver excellent and useful products and listen to our customers and ourselves so that we can be great, not just good.

- We don't mess around. We face reality and use it to our advantage, relying on the strengths and desires of every team member to overcome adversity and be better for having done so.

With a statement of who the team will become in place, move on to the third level of goals: What's in it for my company? Often, the vision statement for the team's project or product or the hoped-for impact on customers or users serves as the basis for this goal. Start with it, and guide the team to make it meaningful for them. This often means excising wishy-washy words and "corporate speak" to let the real goals shine through. Invite a team member to write the reworked statement in the center of the flip chart, bounded by the scrap papers of the individual goals. These are some examples of company-level goals:

- We are re-creating our website so that we can attract more patients and keep them by making it easy for them to get the services we offer.

- We make it pleasurable for our customers to get their problems resolved so that we can retain them and gain a top score for customer service from industry analysts.

- We are staging a takeover of the online tax software market with our new and totally revolutionary tax preparation software.

The final level of goals is "What's in it for the world?" If the team's endeavor does not benefit the world in a remarkable way, invite them to look on a smaller world scale: "Our product helps low-income people make it to the next paycheck" or "Our project saves the jobs of 1,000 people in our area." Skip this completely if thinking about what's in it for the world is too depressing. Sometimes the work teams are asked to undertake simply does not benefit the world.

> *I never teach my pupils; I only attempt to provide the conditions in which they can learn.*
>
> —*Albert Einstein*

If you are lucky enough to work with a team whose product will have a big world impact, guide them to be big, too: "Our product turns the tide on health care so that the individual becomes the most powerful part of the whole system" or "Our project saves the lives of 100,000 children at risk."

Once crafted, write the "What's in it for the world?" statement inside the circle of individual goals. Let it live there with the company goals statement. Figure 7.3 shows a completed shared-team vision chart.

Write these goals statements in straightforward language and in the present tense—as if they are already true. This creates vision. Wrapping up this activity pulls all the goals together into a unified whole, which also creates vision.

When you wrap up this activity, let the team know it's no mistake that the company and world goals live inside the individual goals; by attending to individual growth, we create the environment that lets us achieve the business goals. Then, draw their attention to the team vision statement written in huge letters at the top of the chart.

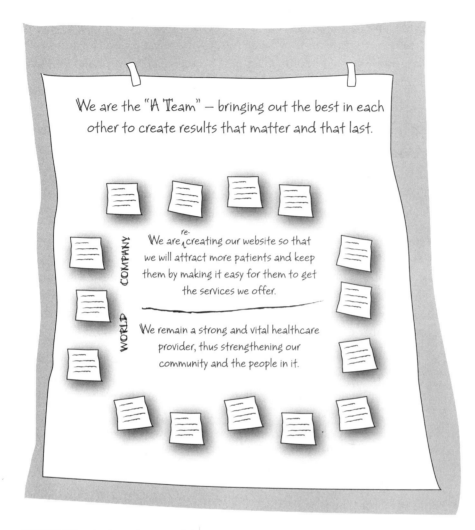

We are the "A Team" — bringing out the best in each other to create results that matter and that last.

COMPANY

re-
We are creating our website so that we will attract more patients and keep them by making it easy for them to get the services we offer.

WORLD

We remain a strong and vital healthcare provider, thus strengthening our community and the people in it.

FIGURE 7.3   A shared-team vision

The team vision and individual goals are their beacon, their big "A" Agenda. This Agenda outlives projects started and finished, business goals sought and accomplished, and products launched and retired. That's why the company and world goals, big though they may be, are the little "a" agenda. They represent the team's pursuit at this particular point in time.

Both big "A" and little "a" agendas have their uses (Whitworth et al. 2007), and it's the big "A" that rights the boat when the waters get rough.

When this happens, read this team vision statement aloud, and perhaps remind people of the commitments they made to support one another. The conversation that results often guides the team back to their best selves and their best expression as a team.

SEE ALSO	You can find more examples of shared-team vision statements in Chapter 9, "Coach as Conflict Navigator," where they are presented as a tool teams use to deal with conflict.

All these goals taken together comprise this new team's shared vision. This vision gives them a destination to start moving toward.

Create Team Norms   With the shared vision as a warm-up, the team can easily dive into creating team norms. The best team norms are more than stand-up time, core hours, and whether or not people can eat in the team room. Those may be on the list, too, but the team norms that help most during the hard times are ones that express the following (Adkins and Blake 2009):

- **Shared values:** If you did the Values exercise previously, this one is easy. Primed with what they have learned about one another, they come up with things they will value as a team. If this is the first time they have considered values as a team, ask for characteristics of the best teams they have witnessed. Use this as a way to get the juices flowing. These are some examples of shared values:

  - Being bold isn't bad.
  - Share the work = share the credit.
  - Notice when someone needs help and offer it.
  - Preserve open communication, even when not comfortable.
  - Success of the team is more important than success of the individual.
  - Keep it simple.
  - Don't struggle for more than 30 minutes before asking for help.
  - Be truly open so we can get the most creative solutions.

- **Rules for living together:** The "no stinky food" rule goes here. These are typically easy for teams to come up with as they contemplate sharing a space together or remember what it was like to share space with their last team.

- **Logistics:** These norms are important, too, but they are the easiest to come up with. Core hours (if not all day), sprint length, and stand-up time are typical logistical norms.

- **Being together in conflict:** You might as well do the uncomfortable work of preparing for conflict now. It saves heartache later. Ask questions that prompt the team to think about how they want to be with one another in conflict.

  - In what ways will we call out conflict in the moment?

  - How will we get back to "the dream" of our shared vision when we are deep in conflict?

  - Under what circumstances would we be willing to call it quits as a team?

Let this conversation have breathing space—these are hard questions.

Allow team members to write the list of the team norms as they consider each of these categories. Encourage them to find a place in the team room where the list will be big and visible so they can easily use it as a reminder.

Learning About the Work Ahead

The final part of the team start-up has arrived! Learning about the work ahead entails these three activities: envision, review the product backlog, and get going. The product owner takes center stage as the team learns about the vision for the product and the work that lies ahead. Once again, you act as their guide, ensuring the team gets the learning they need. The start-up ends with agreed-to goals for the first sprint, which moves the team swiftly into action.

Envision

Invite the highest-ranking person you can find to paint for the team a vision of the product to be created by them. This person's opinion matters to the team. It's someone they want to impress and who has a vested interest in the product because the company has conferred formal authorization to this person to achieve company goals. More than likely, this person sponsors, or pays for, the project. The one holding the purse strings has great influence. Use it.

Prep this person to speak about the importance of the project at two levels: company and personal. It's useful to know how this high-ranking manager expects the product to impact the company. It's better still to know why the product and the business impact are important to the person. This gives the team something more real to grip than the cold, lifeless bullet list of expected improvements.

The high-ranking manager delivers the vision and leaves. The product owner takes that vision and, if needed, fleshes out the details of the high-level objectives, turning them into tangible goals for the team.

At this point, revisit the "What's in it for the company?" and "What's in it for the world?" goal statements. If needed, update them now that the team has more firsthand information. Or, avoid the update, and wait to fill in these goal statements until this point in the start-up session.

Sometimes, hearing the vision gives the team enough of a glimpse into the work ahead to get going. Other times, they need more to make it real. In this case, use a visioning exercise to put flesh on the bones. One such exercise is the Newspaper Projection.

Newspaper Projection   Tell the team, "Imagine it is a year from now, and the product is a resounding success. It surpasses all expectations and is touted as a total breakthrough. The *Wall Street Journal* (or substitute your favorite newspaper) has written an article about the product and the way it was created, citing it as a model for others to come. Write that article. In it you might interview customers and team members, detail the positive impacts of the product, or explain the special way in which the product was built."

Then, let them write. Give them about 20 minutes to write their article. Encourage them to make it light; this does not have to be Pulitzer Prize–winning material. It just has to be meaningful to them, so encourage them to make it so.

Then, each person reads their story. As they do, another team member captures any words or phrases that stick out for them on a flip chart. This continues until all have shared their stories and all have captured notes. All during the sharing, there will be laughter and a sense of excitement, maybe a bit of silliness. Let it all happen without interfering. When all stories have been shared, draw the team's attention to the list of words and phrases on the flip charts, and ask whether they feel any of these causes them to update the "What's in it for the company?" or "What's in it for the world?" goals statements. If so, update them.

Review the Product Backlog

At this point in the start-up, individuals have started to come together as a team, and they know what they are meant to accomplish together. They can now get into the nitty-gritty of the work ahead.

The product owner walks through the product backlog, answering questions about items on the backlog and asking the team to identify missing items. At this point, the product backlog does not have to be robust or even written well. The product owner needs to have stocked it with enough items to get going with the first sprint, though. As the coach, ensure the product owner has done so and that the product owner can also accurately represent the business goals of each item. As the product owner reviews the backlog, coach the group to engage in high-quality conversation that builds a shared understanding of what they are about to do together.

> **SEE ALSO** Facilitating teams so that the quality of their conversations improves is covered in Chapter 6, "Coach as Facilitator."

Get Going

As the product owner completes the product backlog review, ask the question, "Product owner, what short phrase, like a newspaper headline, encompasses the goal for this first sprint?" A sprint goal helps at two levels: to serve as a "true North" compass point so the team knows they are on the right track as the sprint progresses and to "minimize variation by limiting the type of requirements worked on in a given sprint, for instance, by choosing items from the same theme, [which] facilitates close teamwork and can help increase velocity." A sprint goal can also serve as handy shorthand for communicating what the team is up to (Pichler 2010).

With the sprint goal created, you have officially begun the team's first sprint planning session. Call out that this has happened and that in the future they will flow through these same two steps to plan every sprint: Agree to specific product backlog items for the sprint, and create user stories with tasks. At this point, turn to them and say, "Go! You are already in sprint 1."

Prepare for the Start-Up

Now that you know the basic set of activities and goals for a team start-up, let's layer on the pre-work. There are three levels of preparation for a team start-up from good enough to targeted, each requiring more preparation than the last.

- **Good enough:** Using the guidelines in this chapter, create your own "formula" for a team start-up. Choose the activities that make the most sense to you, and create a standard agenda, which can be a set of questions they answer as they go through the start-up or a list of topics. While in the start-up, follow your agenda, and adjust to the team's needs on the fly, just as you will do the rest of the time you coach them. Good enough is truly acceptable because the magic happens in the conversations and insights the activities spawn, so you need not fret about creating the perfect start-up agenda.

- **Insightful:** An insightful start-up seeks to satisfy the goals of the main players such as the product owner, senior team members, and managers. Ask them, "Imagine that we're leaving the team start-up session and you turn to me and say (Tabaka 2006), 'That was perfect! The start-up couldn't have been better.' What was it that happened that made the start-up perfect?" Using these answers, string together activities that achieve the learning goals of the start-up, plus any specific outcomes people desire. This takes a moderate amount of preparation, usually a few hours' time to talk with the main players and design an insightful agenda.

- **Targeted:** To design a targeted start-up, spend time talking with as many team members as you can. Also, spend time observing the team members in action, other agile teams, and the surrounding organization. Notice people's ability to interact with one another positively and collaboratively. Notice whether impediments arise and whether they are dealt with or ignored. Notice common problems that seem to affect multiple people or multiple teams. Notice whether agile values and the agile manifesto are alive and useful for teams and managers. Then, plan a team start-up that addresses any "ills" you observed. Add activities that teach the part of agile that, if done well, would cure the ill or prevent the team from falling ill in the first place.

ROUGH STARTS WORK, TOO

I thought for sure this team would fail. We started out with their managers saying, "Use agile, use lean, use user-centered design. Use whatever you want and whatever you think will work best." What really happened was that the winds of politics were blowing and managers couldn't agree on one approach, so they told their self-organizing team that they could pick and choose from many. So, the managers' nondecision decision rolled downhill.

As the team's agile coach, a big part of me wanted to mandate Scrum and tell them they could weave in user-centered design and lean as secondary processes. Another part of me heard a nagging voice in my head that said, "Trust the team."

I listened to the nagging voice and decided to design a targeted team start-up rather than force the use of Scrum. Given the political situation, I interviewed every person on the team as well as the managers who were pointing in different directions. I created activities that allowed them to choose their approach. I taught them the intentions of each Scrum practice so they could decide for themselves whether they would adopt it. Experts in lean and user-centered design taught those methods and processes. The team then chose from this smorgasbord the particular parts they would adopt.

The team decided they would do the daily stand-up and have a storyboard but not put effort estimates on the tasks. They decided they would focus on the artifacts produced by user-centered design first and do so on a deadline-by-deadline basis rather than be bounded by the rhythm of timeboxed sprints. They decided the retrospective was a waste of time. They reasoned they were all professionals and didn't need any "kindergarten" treatment. Lean was completely forgotten, and no one noticed.

It was, as I could have predicted, a mess. The product owner couldn't tell the team's progress because the tasks were not granular enough to see momentum on a daily basis. So, he asked for regular written status reports from each team member instead. I retaught the use of the storyboard, tasks, and task estimates. The team politely listened and went on as before.

Team members worked separately until just before a big deadline approached. Then they worked together at a frantic pace, to the frustration and resentment of all. I pointed out that it didn't have to be this way. The team politely listened and went on as before.

The product owner constantly slipped in "little things" because some user stories carried on for quite a long time without the boundary of the sprint to stop them. The team produced results because the "superstar" performers pulled long hours to do so. By this time, they were feeling the effects of their decisions, and I remained quiet.

No one was happy—not the team members and certainly not the product owner because even though he had received the products he desired from the team, he was frustrated with their lack of predictability. I didn't save them from

Continued

themselves, so they remained unhappy. They got unhappier still until, one day, one of them said, "I think it's time for a retrospective."

In the retrospective they talked about how they felt—how they felt about their products (good), how they felt about the quality of their products (not so good), how they felt about making the deadlines (pretty good), how they felt about what it took out of each of them to make the deadlines (not so good), how they felt about each other (really bad), and whether they wanted to continue working this way (absolutely not!). So, they changed. We reviewed the intentions of the Scrum practices again, and they adopted more of them. They talked about the values that underlie those practices and why those values were important to them. Through this conversation, two months after they had started together, they completed part 1 of the team start-up: learning about the process to be used. The rest of the start-up activities became meaningful to them as they realized they needed to know more about one another to really share the work and as they wanted to know more about why they were doing the project beyond the bullet list of expected results.

If a team gets off to a rough start, that's OK as long as you don't save them from themselves. Educate throughout, coach, and abide by their choices. Let them feel the natural consequences of their decisions and then, when they are ready, guide them back to the core of agile.

Let's say you notice that other teams have "fallen ill" from poorly executed roles. Prevent this ill from spreading to the new team by teaching agile role definitions right from the start. Where you might have given an overview of the roles as part of your standard agenda, this time, you choose to go deeper. You might ask the product owner to talk about the changes he intends to make to be good at his role. You might talk about the changes you will make to achieve the next level of coaching proficiency. You might ask the team members how they will know when the roles are being fully executed and then invite them to use those answers as a measuring stick to assess how well the people in those roles are doing over time. Addressing an ill during the team start-up makes it blameless if done as a topic you simply teach more deeply.

Designing a targeted start-up takes more time, usually several hours over several days. But the extra time may be well worth it, because the increased impact is often greater than the additional up-front effort.

Team Restart

Restart teams when team membership or team goals change significantly. You need not do everything you did in the initial start-up, just the parts that have changed or need bolstering. If team membership changes, ensure that you teach agile again. The ten-minute whiteboard talk does the trick. Regardless of the reason for the restart, take advantage of this time to address lingering team ills with a little retraining and positive reinforcement.

Teach New Team Members

Try though we may to avoid it, team members come and go. People move on to other opportunities, or the team realizes they need to add someone with a special skill set.

Keep team membership as stable as possible, and coach the team to only introduce or take away team members between sprints. Remember the rule: The people who made the commitment deliver the commitment.

When a team member leaves, ensure the team acknowledges the person and their contribution. This happens naturally in most cases, so you probably don't need to do much coaching here.

When a team member joins, offer a short tour of the team room. Point out the team norms list hanging on the wall. Stand in front of the storyboard, and explain how the team uses it to stay in sync with one another during the sprint. Talk about the team's shared vision and anything else hanging on the walls that hints at the rules, nature, and identity of the team. Let the person in on the team's personality: the inside jokes, the toys in the room, or the gags they have pulled. Give this tour when the other team members are present so they can jump in with a short story or two so that the welcome is made by many.

Then, teach the new team member agile. The ten-minute whiteboard talk works nicely for this. In this talk, you express agile at its most powerful by keeping to the core. If the team falls short on a particular practice, point this out as the growing edge of the team. If some practices go completely missing from the team's operation, teach the practice to the new team member anyway, and point out where they fall short. Teach the new team member agile done well first, and teach the particular team's use of agile second. This way, you help avoid the team member unconsciously believing that this team's agile = agile.

This ends your teaching job (for now). Let other team members take it from here. They are probably anxious to tell the new person many things about the product and themselves.

As each agile practice occurs, come back to the new team member and check in. You may say, "You just experienced the sprint planning session. Now we're in the sprint and delivering on the commitments the team—including you—made." Help this person connect each agile practice they experience with the whiteboard talk you gave at the beginning.

SEE ALSO	Setting the expectation for and following through with one-on-one coaching is covered in Chapter 5, "Coach as Coach-Mentor."

Also, within a few days of joining, sit down with the new team member and just talk. Get to know this person—where they've been, what they want, and where they are on their agile journey. Set the expectation that coaching conversations happen every once in a while, sometimes for no reason at all and sometimes so you can be their guide to help them use agile well.

Use Teachable Moments

Teachable moments occur frequently and unexpectedly as the team works and converses together. They naturally arise and create a backdrop for just the right learning at just the right time. Use teachable moments well and lightly. Don't use them to launch into a retraining or to introduce a whole new area. Remember, the team's job in the sprint is to sprint! When you take advantage of a teachable moment, teach just enough to convey the lesson without impacting the team's momentum.

Teach Agile Roles All the Time

So many problems arise from poorly executed roles that these deserve special teaching attention.

The team's role is intuitive, and by and large teams completely internalize agile and the part they play—getting work done and not allowing anything to stop them.

The biggest role problems come from people on the edge of the team—the agile coach, the product owner, and a host of agile managers. To clear the way for the team to perform, these roles must be defined unambiguously so they can work well together. Herein lie rich teaching and coaching opportunities.

First teach people their roles. Any time is a good time to do this. Teach them during the start-up session if the organization at large lacks a clear understanding. If the roles function, in general, don't teach them as an overt lesson; just help people perform them better as teachable moments occur.

Once the roles are taught and everyone understands what everyone should be doing, ask the team to expect that people will fill their roles completely. Anything less gets called out as an impediment and dealt with as such.

Teach the Product Owner Role

The product owner role has enormous impact on a team because direction setting and constant strategic decision making come directly from the person in this role. A poor product owner creates a languishing team, one half alive, just going through the motions. A good product owner helps keep the team moving in the right direction. A great product owner accelerates results and stays open to allow astonishing results to emerge.

A good product owner can help make a team. A poor product owner will certainly break a team. Neither of these is good enough; aim your coaching squarely to help people grow into great product owners.

To help great product owners surface, first teach them to be these things for their teams:

- **Business value driver:** All decisions and trade-offs, including when to stop the project, are made through considering which alternative gives the most business value *now*.

- **Daily decision maker:** Be fully present with the team to engage in conversation and make decisions as they arise so that the team can move forward unimpeded.

- **Vision keeper:** Keep the big picture of the product in the team's sight, and direct them toward it each sprint.

- **Heat shield:** Protect the team from all outside noise and pressure, allowing them to focus.

- **The one ultimately responsible:** Be completely invested in the product. The team's work is not just another job assignment—it matters to your career—so you graciously accept the burden of being the final person answerable for the business results of the product.

Let these phrases create a vision of great product ownership in the product owners you coach. Invite them to explore what these mean to them and where they feel comfort and discomfort. Discomfort signals a growing edge for them and a fertile place for you to coach.

To help them ground the vision in specifics, offer these examples in Table 7.1 to illustrate desirable and undesirable behaviors.

TABLE 7.1 Product owner behaviors

Do	Don't
Say "what" needs to get done.	Say "how" the work will get done or "how much" effort the work will take.
Challenge the team.	Bully the team.
Demonstrate a commitment to building a high-performance team.	Focus on short-term deliveries only.
Practice business-value-driven thinking.	Stick to the original scope and approach "no matter what."
Protect the team from outside noise.	Worry the team about changes until they become real.
Incorporate change between sprints.	Allow change to creep into sprints.

With this definition of product ownership in mind, start a discussion with the product owner using questions such as these:

"What parts of the role feel like a good stretch for you?"

"What parts of the role do you feel you have mastered?"

"What parts will you have to make yourself do?"

"What about the team and the organization must you believe in order to keep yourself from doing the 'Don't' things?"

"What should I, the agile coach, watch for to help you keep these essential beliefs in operation?"

Through this conversation, help them firm up their understanding of the role and create a future vision of themselves as a great product owner. Discover together where their growing edge lies, and set an expectation that you will coach them there to help them on their way. Make the stakes clear: A healthy team needs a great product owner.

Selecting a Product Owner

As the agile coach, you may be asked to help select a product owner for a team. The managers starting up the work will say, "We have a couple of people in this business area who could be a good product owner for this team. How do we choose one?"

To help them, remember this memory-jogger: CRACK. An effective product owner is Committed, Responsible, Authorized, Collaborative, and Knowledgeable (Boehm and Turner 2003):

Committed to the work and engaged in it fully, like any other team member

Responsible for the outcome so that "skin in the game" is a reality

Authorized by the person paying the bills to make decisions about the product under development and to know which decisions can be made solo and which require consultation with others

Collaborative as a normal mode of interacting with people

Knowledgeable about the business purposes of the endeavor and the business domain itself

First, measure prospective product owners using the CRACK qualities.

Then, if needed, slip into teaching mode again. Conduct a conversation with each prospective product owner in which you teach the product owner role to them. Let them know what you and the team expect of them. Discuss how the role feels to them. Will it be a stretch to work side by side with team members so frequently? Or, does it feel like a welcome breath of fresh air to be so closely involved? As they talk about the role, pay attention to their words and tone. Do you hear a lot of opportunity in the way they talk about being a product owner, or do you hear a lot of "Yes, but…"?

With CRACK and the conversations about the product owner role, you have two useful tools to help select a product owner for the team. Select the person who has the makings to become great.

Teach the Agile Manager Role

There are a bevy of agile managers orbiting agile teams: team members' functional managers, stakeholders, and managers of other teams, just to name a few.

This role is not a formal part of Scrum or any other agile framework, although it exists in most organizations. Michael Spayd, agile coach and organizational change expert, had already formalized much of the thinking about agile managers when he and I started working on this role together. We noticed that these managers—located in the middle of their organizations—were also being squeezed in the middle. They were squeezed by their teams as those teams blossomed into self-organized powerhouses that resist all attempts to be managed. They were squeezed by the top brass who want the fruits of agile but still long for the illusion of certainty that schedules, status reports, and steering committee meetings represent. A new reality dawns for agile managers: When their teams deliver, the squeeze lets up, and they get to breathe again.

To help teams deliver, managers boost agility. To boost agility, they need a view of their new role as:

Organizational change artist: Guides the organization through agile adoption (and re-adoption)

Boundary keeper: Reinforces healthy role boundaries both within the team and between the team and the greater organization

Value maximizer: Manages the portfolio of projects like a product owner manages a portfolio of user stories, always asking what the highest business value project is *now*

Lean manager: Uses lean thinking to improve organizational flow so that the value teams deliver can be realized without delay

Organizational impediment remover: Finds the gritty courage it takes to remove entrenched impediments

Team champion: Offers observations from the team boundary and releases the team to reach their fullest potential by truly believing they can

The agile manager is like water—patiently, water can carve away the hardest surface, and it will always find a way to flow. Making things flow so the team delivers again and again is an honorable (and challenging) job. In so doing, agile managers offer their highest service to the team.

AN AGILE MANAGER RESCUES HER TEAMS FROM ADMINISTRIVIA

One of the best agile managers I have seen in action met the challenge of status reporting in a simple and powerful way.

Together with coaches from the teams she "managed," she created an executive status whiteboard in the hallway, near where the directors and vice presidents sat. She and the product owners (with the coaches along for the ride) met in front of the board on a regular basis to check in with one another. They color-coded some key health indicators for each team: red = bad, yellow = getting bad, and green = good to go. Some of the key health indicators were

- Current sprint on target?
- Next release on target?
- Product owner's direction clear?
- Sponsor satisfied so far?
- Sponsor confident in future delivery?
- Team actively taking their next step toward high performance?

With these indicators in red, yellow, and green and the impediments clearly listed, the board became an impossible-to-miss status report.

Senior leaders absorbed the status of projects in less than the time it took to walk past the whiteboard. It was right there in their faces.

In addition to the self-service view of status, this astute agile manager used the board to give a heads-up display of "what have we done for you lately?" by listing recent chunks of value delivered and new chunks planned, real business metrics improved by these deliveries, and what's up next for each team.

She could have asked each team to create a custom status report, which would have interrupted their work and been pure overhead for them. Instead, she preserved team focus and worked with the natural rhythms of agile. The regular check-in became a useful tool for each of the teams. It was their time to discuss common impediments, share solutions, rave about accomplishments, and keep everyone aware of what each team was doing now and what they had coming up. It was also time for them to pause and ask themselves, "Do we need help on this?" This way, the manager-level impediments were raised early, when there was still time to clear them before they stopped the team.

Whenever an executive had a question about a particular project, this agile manager simply pointed to the status board in the hall. Pretty soon, extra requests for status faded away, and she was free to focus on providing greater value: ensuring healthy teams and clearing impediments. In short, boosting agility.

This vision describes a lot of things to do, all without managing agile teams directly. To provide such a low-touch way to guide teams, Mike Cohn offers this model: Containers, Differences, and Exchanges (CDE). In a nutshell, agile managers exert control over the following:

- The containers within which teams work, specifically their physical location, organizational position, and team assignment

- The differences between the backgrounds of team members, going for a mix of people that will yield a high level of team interaction

- Transformational exchanges in which team members are changed or influenced by their differences and interactions (Cohn 2009)

Using CDE, managers can appropriately influence teams from the outside without hampering the teams' self-organization.

With the vision of the agile manager role in mind and the CDE model at their disposal, offer agile managers another slant on their agile role. Teach the manager that self-organized teams need them to interact differently with them than they have before. Specifically, the agile manager will do the following:

- Add items to the product backlog through the product owner only.
- Direct questions or observations to the agile coach or product owner.
- Remain silent during the daily stand-up.
- Attend sprint reviews and give direct feedback.
- Remove impediments when asked. Otherwise, the agile manager will leave the team alone to get the work done.
- Satisfy requests through simple means that work with the cadence of agile teams rather than adding a distracting layer of bureaucracy on top of them.

Just as you did with the product owner, open a discussion with the agile manager about the nature of this role. What about the role feels exciting to them? Daunting? Anxiety producing?

Make it clear that performing this role well yields greater team delivery. Greater team delivery yields success for them. Everyone wins.

Teach the Agile Coach Role

Finally, we come to the agile coach role. You've been carefully considering the agile coach role, and you've probably already concluded that the responsibilities and richness of this role cannot be contained in a few short phrases. This is true. Yet the phrases serve their purpose to jog our memories and make something powerful and evolving easy to grasp. Know these phrases, understand their meaning in your own life, and use them well when teaching others what it means to be an agile coach. Tell the people you teach, "An agile coach is a…"

Bulldozer: Helps the team bulldoze impediments to get them out of the way (Cohn 2005)

Shepherd: Guides the team back to agile practices and principles when they stray (adapted from Schwaber 2004)

Servant leader: Serves the team rather than the team serving you (Cohn and Schwaber 2003)

Guardian of quality and performance: Examines both what the team produces and how they produce it to offer observations that help them tune the human system they are (Douglas 2007)

SEE ALSO	For a deeper dive into being a servant leader, see Chapter 3, "Master Yourself."

The agile coach helps the team navigate unpredictable waters and adapt as things happen to them, all the while paying close attention to the outer world of the team and the inner world of one's thoughts and impulses, carefully acting only on those impulses that promote the team's self-organization. To help you discern which impulses to act on, Table 7.2 provides a short list of desirable and undesirable agile coach behaviors.

Teach this role definition to the team and the people who surround the team. Then, ask the team to hold you accountable for moving toward the highest expression of this role—and getting better at being an agile coach all the time.

TABLE 7.2   Agile coach behaviors

Does	Does not
Guides and facilitates	Direct or drive
Keeps everyone focused on delivering business value	Stick to deadlines and approaches that no longer work
Has a keen interest in the team's overall performance	Become attached to specific outcomes from the team
Coaches the team for high performance	Get involved in task-level direction
Promotes the skills and growth of every team member	Become the only voice of the team

The Roles Are Interlocking

These roles, each one complete and strong in itself, do not stand alone. As shown in Figure 7.4, it takes all three, operating well together, to give teams a chance at creating astonishing results and unleashing agile as a competitive advantage weapon for their company.

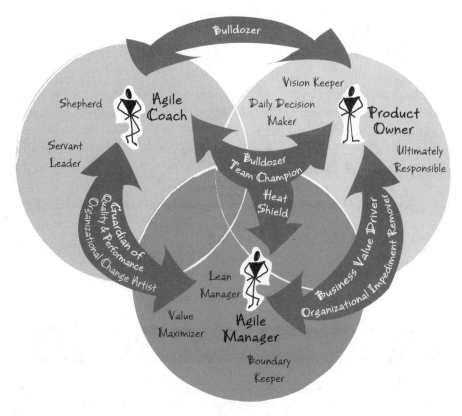

FIGURE 7.4 Interlocking roles in agile

Let's pay special attention to the places where the roles help one another. Often, the activity of bulldozing impediments takes two—a coach and a product owner—stronger together. Just because the coach and product owner bulldoze together does not mean the responsibility gets diluted between them, however. The role boundaries are not fuzzy or porous, so the accountability still rests with the agile coach.

All the "overlaps" are this way. One role gets support, strength, vitality, and help from the others. Yet, that one role remains accountable. It keeps things clear in the midst of complex situations when one might be tempted to run away from one's own accountability. No running away is allowed.

Let's look at overlaps between the agile coach and agile manager. The agile coach is fully focused on being the guardian of quality and performance from inside the team boundary. The agile manager brings a different perspective, one step away from the team boundary. Both have observations to offer the team to help them get better each time. And, although the agile manager's position gives credence to their role as the organizational change artist, support from the agile coach is essential. They work together to move the organization through all the changes it will experience as it uses agile and faces its company's demons.

The product owner interlocks with the agile manager through their single-minded focus on achieving business value. They are business value drivers, allowing business value to be the only standard by which progress gets measured at both the team and portfolio levels. The two also join forces as organizational impediment removers, because organizational impediments are the big ones that restrict value delivery and the gnarly ones that often need to be double-teamed.

Although the product owner gets top billing for being the heat shield for the team, it takes the agile coach, the product owner, and the agile manager—all standing hip to hip—to create a shield big enough and thick enough to keep the noise and politics at bay.

Finally, all three roles have an element of team champion in them. They must all truly believe that the team can accomplish anything to which it applies its effort, intelligence, and passion. As team champion, all three roles look for ways to uphold the team and help them believe it, too.

The three roles interlock with one another and, in so doing, support the team's efforts to produce real product in a short period of time. Interlocking sometimes means locking horns, too. The roles can pull at one another and become full of dynamic tension. For example, as the product owner demands more and moves toward bullying the team, the agile coach protects the team so they can learn to do it themselves. Discussions may not always be polite as the roles pull against one another. View this as normal and desired. The roles are meant to be this way. Dynamic tension provides the edge needed for creativity and truth. It's all for the sake of value delivery.

Role Clarity

Agile roles are not titles, so they can be taken up by anyone who has the ability and desire to do them well. They have nothing to do with the organizational structure surrounding the team. Yet, both informal roles and formal titles exist and can clash. The agile coach stays watchful for these clashes and helps people maintain healthy boundaries between their team roles and their organizational titles.

It is unhealthy, for example, when the product owner also serves as the team members' direct manager. Clash. It's a bit unhealthier still if the product owner also serves as the agile coach's direct manager. Double clash. This team suffers from unclear dual-role boundaries. Here are other unhealthy role boundaries:

Product owner as both project manager (schedule slave driver) and agile coach

Agile coach as subject-matter expert and team member

Agile manager as agile coach

In small companies where human relationships are already healthy, teams may be able to work (mostly) with people playing multiple role-title combinations as long as the combo does not mash up agile coach and product owner. In all other situations, it erodes trust because team members do not know "what part" of the person interacts with them at any given time. They may fret, "Is this person speaking as the product owner, as my boss (the one who writes my performance appraisal), or as my coach?"

To help expose unclear roles, agile coach and coauthor of *Agile Coaching* Rachel Davies helps team members work together to review the responsibilities of each role. She starts by asking each person to list on separate pieces of scrap paper what they do and what other roles do. Team members compare notes, and in the conversation that follows, they often discover duplication between the roles and responsibilities that no one owns (2009).

Here's another way to go at it. To avoid role and title jumbles, use this rule of thumb when something needs to be done, but who should do it is not clear: Carefully consider whether you are the right person to do it. Ask yourself, "Am I the source? Am I the one who should suffer if it goes wrong? Does this fall within my area of responsibility? Is this part of *my* commitment? If the answer to any of these is "yes," then you are likely the person to rightfully take ownership. If the answers are "no," then hand it off to the person in the appropriate role.

Use this yourself to avoid loading the agile coach role with noncoach responsibilities. Teach this far and wide so others may do the same.

A Refresher

Let's lock in the ideas from this chapter:

- Powerful team start-ups are jet fuel to an agile team. Get good at conducting them.
- Teach agile during the team start-up, and bring all team members back to the core of agile.

- Focus the team on the work ahead, and help them better relate as human beings so they can determine how to best self-organize.

- Teach agile when new people join the team and when teachable moments arise, but do so lightly.

- Teach everyone about agile roles, and ask them to expect that the people around them will completely fulfill their role. Anything less is an impediment.

- Expect the agile coach, product owner, and agile manager roles to interlock with both harmony and discord.

- Constantly seek role clarity for yourself, and train others to do the same.

Additional Resources

Adkins, L. 2008. Interlocking Roles in Agile. YouTube. Use this video to practice getting good at teaching agile roles. Also, show it as a training aid when you teach teams.

Cohn, M. 2009. *Succeeding with Agile: Software Development Using Scrum*. Boston: Addison-Wesley. This book contains tons of useful advice, models to use, and stories that will help in your use of agile. It includes a chapter on leading self-organized teams, which is essential reading for agile coaches, product owners, and agile managers.

Pichler, R. 2010. *Agile Product Management: Creating Products that Customers Love*. Boston: Addison-Wesley. See this book for details on the product owner's role.

References

Adkins, L., and K. Blake. 2009. Coaching Agile Teams to Constructively Navigate Conflict. Orlando: 2009 PMI Global Conference Proceedings. Constellation activity adapted from Center for Right Relationship, Organization, and Relationship Systems Coaching training curriculum.

Boehm. B., and R. Turner. 2003. *Balancing Agility and Discipline: A Guide for the Perplexed*. Boston: Addison-Wesley.

Cohn, M. 2009. *Succeeding with Agile: Software Development Using Scrum*. Boston: Addison-Wesley.

————. 2005. Certified Scrum Master Workshop.

————, and K. Schwaber. 2003. The Need for Agile Project Management. *Agile Times Newsletter*. Both gentlemen used the term *ScrumMaster* rather than coach. The application of their ScrumMaster definition to agile coaching is Lyssa Adkins' change.

Coaches Training Institute. 2008. Co-active coaching training course curriculum. San Rafael, CA: Coaches Training Institute.

Davies, R. 2009. Personal correspondence with Rachel Davies.

Gratton, L., A. Voigt, and T. Erickson. 2007. Bridging Faultlines on Diverse Teams. *MIT Sloan Management Review*. Vol. 48, No. 4: Massachusetts Institute of Technology.

Kouzes, J., and B. Posner. 2007. Leadership Challenge Workshop.

Myllerup, B. 2009. Building Scrum and Agile Teams for Efficient and High-Performance Development. Executive brief. www.executivebrief.com/article/building-scrum-agile-teams-efficient-performance-development/P2/.

Pichler, R. 2010. *Agile Product Management: Creating Products that Customers Love*. Boston: Addison-Wesley.

Schwaber, K. 2004. *Agile Project Management with Scrum*. Bellevue, WA: Microsoft Press.

Tabaka, J. 2006. *Collaboration Explained: Facilitation Skills for Software Project Leaders*. Boston: Addison-Wesley.

Tichy, N. 2002. *The Cycle of Leadership: How Great Leaders Teach Their Companies to Win*. New York: HarperCollinsBusiness.

Whitworth, L., K. Kimsey-House, H. Kimsey-House, and P. Sandahl. 2007. *Co-Active Coaching: New Skills for Coaching People Toward Success in Work and Life, Second Edition*. Mountain View, CA: Davies-Black.

Chapter 8

Coach as Problem Solver

Iused to solve problems for teams. All the time. I was greatly rewarded for doing so. In fact, I was rewarded not only for solving the problems of the day but for looking ahead and solving problems I thought were coming even though they hadn't happened yet. We called it *issues and risk management*. People said I was a great project manager because I could solve all kinds of problems, and in a plan-driven world, having a project manager who was also a good problem solver proved essential. When one holds on to a plan so tightly, one must keep reality at bay, or at least "solve for it."

Some common situations of the past illustrate this. My program manager tells me she has just accepted a huge change request with no corresponding change to the client's delivery expectation. "Solve for it," she says. My client tells me that my team misunderstood the specification, and we should have known better, even though the new understanding means a lot more work that we don't have the skills to perform. When I go to my boss for help, she simply says, "Solve for it." Two team members don't see eye to eye about the order in which we have planned to build the system. They come to me to complain and then expect me to "solve for it." After a while, I found myself making decisions for the team and solving more and more problems that they should have been

---

By the time you finish this chapter, you will be able to answer these questions:

- Whose job is it to solve problems? Where does the agile coach's responsibility lie compared to the team's responsibility?
- What tools can an agile coach use to detect problems?
- How can an agile coach see problems clearly and decide what to do about them?

able to solve themselves. Somehow, I became central. People could not function unless I "solved for it."

When I started working agile, I brought my problem-solving skills with me. I continued to "solve for it" on behalf of the team members. Sometimes I solved a problem before the team even realized there had been a problem. I was inflicting my help on them.

During this time, I was fortunate to have a persistent agile mentor, Mike Vizdos. Mike has been around agile a long time and has worked on scores of agile teams, but you wouldn't know it from the way he chooses to interact with his apprentices. Feeling no compulsion to prove himself to anyone, Mike goes about his work quietly, sometimes completely silently. When he chooses to speak, it's straight to the point, no-frills, and can often knock you right off your feet. If Mike caught me in the act of solving a problem for a team, he would simply give me a look from across the room that seemed to say, "Do you really want to do that?" Sometimes that was enough, and other times, in the throes of solving so deeply, I didn't see "the look." A short while later I noticed that I felt crowded somehow. Waking from my problem-solving mania, I realized that someone was standing very close to me, just off to the side in my peripheral vision. It was Mike. When I acknowledged him, he gently smiled and quietly said, "You're doing it again." Waking from my reverie, I realized that I had fallen into the problem-solving mode once more—doing something for someone else, which really means doing something *to* someone else. Sometimes Mike would have to stand almost body to body with me before I got the hint. These behaviors are hard to break.

After one such time, Mike and I stepped out of the team room for a mentor-apprentice chat. He said something that struck me to the core and freed me from my incessant need to solve the team's problems. In his no-frills manner, he came straight to the point, "It's the team's commitment, not yours." It was a mantra echoed many times by Mike's meaningful glances and played over and over in my head until it finally sunk in. As I released my need to "solve for it," I immediately recognized that the team filled the void, something I would have never believed they would do based on my experience as a project manager. But this was a new world, an agile world, where teams not only could but felt obligated to "solve for it" themselves and do it far better than me. I could fully relax, knowing they had it well in hand.

Even so, ingrained behaviors die hard.

A few years later as an accomplished agile coach, I was caught solving problems on the team's behalf again—just at a higher level this time. I say I was caught because I truly did not recognize that I was "doing it again" until the team brought it to my attention. I had been working with some of their managers tackling questions such as "Should we start up another team or add scope and people to the current team?" "Should we switch out product owners to see whether the one having problems on Team A would have the same problems on Team B?"

These are questions for agile managers to wrestle with, no doubt, and they brought me in to help them because I had a good view of what was happening across teams. So, I jumped in and started solving. The teams eventually got wind of the changes being discussed and said, rather emphatically, "Involve us in decisions that impact us!" Shamefaced, I learned the lesson again, this time from a group of courageous people who could be courageous because of the working environment I had helped them create. Although some decisions may ultimately be management calls, they were right; no one should make decisions without consulting the people who have to live with the result.

My lesson: Take the problem to the team.

Does "Take the problem to the team" mean that an agile coach does nothing to see danger coming or notice problems right under her feet? Certainly not. It just means that she doesn't go looking for danger, identify a potential problem, assess options, choose a solution, and implement it all by herself. She need not be alone to do all that work anymore. And that's a good thing, too. When the team takes their rightful place as problem solvers, she can clearly see how often she must have wrongfully solved the problems of the past for them.

This chapter helps coaches see problems clearly and enlist the help of the team. After all, they are the people to whom the problem ultimately matters.

An Agile Problem Solving Rubric

When working as an agile coach, take this problem-solving rubric along for the ride:

A problem is brought to your attention, or you detect a problem.

Pause (really, take a pause), and reflect on the problem to see it clearly.

Take the problem to the team.

Allow the team to act (or not).

Remember, it's their commitment, not yours. Whether they act or not rests with them, not with you. Whether they follow through with the actions they planned or not has everything to do with them and nothing to do with you. It's their commitment. If you take it up and carry it for them, you have just excused them from doing what it takes to meet the promises they made.

Yet, people insist on bringing you problems, and as you look around, you see even more problems. What should you do about that?

Problems Arise and Are Sought

When problems are brought to you, it's easy to want to jump to solutions, especially with the problem-bringer standing right in front of you. The temptation to solve pulls at you. Resist the temptation, and instead escape the eyes boring into you so that you can get time to reflect. Very few problems require immediate action, and those that do, such as fire, harassment, and bodily harm, are ones you already know how to deal with. Violations of basic human decency also call for your in-the-moment action. In all other cases, let there be space.

Also, let your problem detector rest. Even if you see a potential problem on the horizon, know that all things change so quickly that you need not bring that problem to the team now. If you take up a potential problem on their behalf, you are making it a problem in the present.

Instead, the next time you see a potential problem, hold yourself back from addressing it, and see whether it becomes a real problem. When I started holding myself back, I realized how few of the future problems I worried about actually came true. So much happens so fast that many problems "out there" just go away before the team gets there. When I grasped this new awareness, I realized how many times I must have been the one to *create* a problem for the team by unnecessarily bringing it to them. That represents a lot of wasted effort and heartache!

Hold yourself back, and if the problem becomes real later, deal with it then. If you truly cannot do this, then bring the potential problem up with the team, and ask whether they're worried about it. If they aren't worried, drop it. They know better than you.

But what if you're convinced they don't know better than you? If you're at the beginning, with new team members or people new to agile, then invoke the Teaching style of coaching and teach them what you think they are missing. If they're violating a rule of agile and you feel strongly that they should do it "by the book," then put your foot down. Otherwise, it's your opinion of which way they should go vs. theirs, and theirs should win. They are the ones who have to live with the consequences.

SEE ALSO When to invoke the Teaching style vs. other coaching styles is covered in Chapter 4, "Let Your Style Change."

Problems, Problems Everywhere

Having problems does not indicate a problem in itself, so welcome problems because they bring with them the chance for the team to overcome, grow, and become stronger together. People will bring you problems, and you will trip over problems lying there in plain view. As if this weren't enough, you also seek out symptoms that point to problems. As the agile coach, attend to multiple perspectives to detect these symptoms:

- **The process level:** How are we doing with agile?

- **The quality and performance angle:** How can the team produce better?

- **The team dynamics dimension:** How can the team become a better team?

From these perspectives, you muster the courage to carefully consider this question, "Where are we weak?" This question reverberates for all teams, new ones and old ones, poorly performing ones and high-performing ones. Every team has something to work on next.

> *The problem is not that there are problems. The problem is expecting otherwise and thinking that having problems is a problem.*
>
> —*Theodore Rubin*

Problems at the Process Level

To detect problems at the process level, use health checks. A health check, often in the form of a questionnaire, lists required elements and qualities that jog our minds to help us remember the basic ingredients of agile. From this, we consider anew whether the team truly adheres to their agile process. A few good health checks are included in the "Additional Resources" section of this chapter.

Any health check offers a fresh perspective. Most of them I have found are specific to either Scrum or Extreme Programming, making them software development–centric. Even so, they serve as a good starting point, and if you're not developing software but can substitute the word *product* for *software* in your head, you may be able to use them as is. If not or if you are using some other brand of agile, then use one of these as a base and create your own version by backing out the parts that don't apply and adding your own.

Basic insights from a health check come when the agile coach uses it to reflect on the team's process, asking, "How are we doing with agile?" Richer insights come when the health check gets carried out in two steps with the whole team: questionnaire and conversation. Enlisting the help of a peer coach, someone from the outside, makes the richness even greater. Not only does the outside perspective bring new ideas, but the peer coach can create a completely open environment—one in which team members feel free to discuss anything, even to complain about their coach (you!).

Problems from the Quality and Performance Angle

To expose lurking problems, inspect the products the team created together. With a dispassionate eye, consider the things they created and ask, "Did the team produce real value?" and "Is the quality something they should be proud of?" As guardian of quality and performance, the agile coach has all the authority (and responsibility) needed to look at the team's products with a critical eye.

This does not mean that the agile coach becomes an expert in the team's product or subject matter. Testers and others who validate the team's products already exist on the team. That's covered. It does mean that the coach faces quality and performance problems squarely, from a commonsense perspective. From this reasonable stance, the coach considers questions such as, "If this product were a hamburger, would I serve it to my kid?" and "If I were the customer, would I be happy to pay for this?"

From these honest answers to oneself, the coach can then move on to the next reflection, "How can the team produce better?"

Problems in the Team Dynamics Dimension

Changes that knock one team flat barely cause a ripple for another team. What's the difference? Examining dissimilar reactions and thinking about a team's emotional maturity can help an agile coach detect problems with team dynamics, especially when coupled with careful thought about this question: "How can the team become a better team?"

> *It is better to know some of the questions than all of the answers.*
>
> —James Thurber

Ellen Braun, an accomplished agile manager, noticed that different behaviors emerge over time as telltale signs of a team's emotional maturity, a key component in their ability to adjust as things happen to them and to get to the tipping point when "an individual's self interest shifts to alignment with the behaviors that support team achievement" (Braun 2010).

Team Dynamics Survey   Ellen created a list of survey questions she first used as personal reflection while she observed teams in action. Using these questions the same way, as a pathway to reflection, an agile coach can gain insight into potential team problems or areas for emotional growth. Using them with the team will be more insightful, perhaps as material for a retrospective where the team has the time and space to chew on the ideas that come up. While the team sprints, though, mull them over on your own, and notice what they tell you about team dynamics (Braun 2010).

- How much does humor come into day-to-day interaction within the team?

- What are the initial behaviors that the team shows in times of difficulty and stress?

- How often are contradictory views raised by team members (including junior team members)?

- When contradictory views are raised by team members, how often are they fully discussed?

- Based on the norms of the team, how often do team members compromise in the course of usual team interactions (when not forced by circumstances)?

- To what extent *can* any team member provide feedback to any other team member (think about negative and positive feedback)?

- To what extent *does* any team member actually provide feedback to any other team member?

- How likely would it be that a team member would discuss issues with your performance or behavior with another team member without giving feedback to you directly (triangulating)?

- To what extent do you as an individual get support from your team on your personal career goals (such as learning a new skill from a team member)?

- How likely would you be to ask team members for help if it required your admission that you were struggling with a work issue?

- How likely would you be to share personal information with the team that made you feel vulnerable?

- To what extent is the team likely to bring into team discussions an issue that may create conflict or disagreement within the team?

- How likely or willing are *you* to bring into a team discussion an issue that is likely to have many different conflicting points of view?

- If you bring an item into a team discussion that is likely to have many different conflicting points of view, how often does the team reach a consensus that takes into consideration all points of view and feels workable to you?

- Can you identify an instance in the past two work days when you felt a sense of warmth or inclusion within the context of your team?

- Can you identify an instance in the past two days when you felt a sense of disdain or exclusion within the context of your team?

- How much does the team make you feel accountable for your work?

Mulling over these questions solo or posing them to the team will likely generate a lot of raw material to consider. When you step back from the many answers, perhaps one or two themes jump out at you, signaling the "big things" to address.

BART Analysis   If you don't like the survey questions or want a "second opinion," try boundary, authority, role, and task (BART) analysis.

TRY THIS

Use either the survey questions or the BART analysis questions to reflect on team dynamics. How do you imagine the team members would answer these questions about themselves and their team? What themes or issues emerge as you reflect on this? Then, at the next opportunity, run these same questions by the team. See what they say. Their answers may surprise you and give you an even deeper view into the nature of their "teamness" (and your ability to be "right" about what's going on with them).

BART analysis comes to us agile coaches from the group relations (GR) domain and asks us to consider the impact of these four dimensions on team dynamics: boundary, authority, role, and task (Green and Molenkamp 2005).

When teams go wrong, the source of trouble can often be linked directly to one or more of these dimensions of team life.

To look for problems, apply this BART analysis customized for agile teams by agile coach Den Mezick (adapted from Mezick 2009):

Roles

- Are all formally defined roles in your agile framework occupied by specific individuals? For example, is there one and only one product owner and agile coach (or your equivalent terms for these roles)? Do team members know the definition of their role, "team member"?

- Are all formal roles functioning within role boundaries (but not beyond) and done well and completely?

- Is any one person taking up more than one formal role defined in your agile framework? If so, what is the impact to the use of authority and boundaries on the team?

- If the team has added additional formal roles, are these roles completely described? Are the people occupying them performing them within the formal role boundaries and doing so well and completely?

Tasks

- Does the team get great clarity about their team purpose from a shared mental model they can each express?

- Can someone distinguish all the different tasks needed to accomplish the team's purpose (such as a product owner with a prioritized backlog)?

- Which histories and past experiences do people "import" from prior, similar situations? How does this affect their ability to see the true nature of the current tasks at hand?

Authority

- Is authority for each role clearly specified, understood by all, and adhered to?

- Do team members "take up" formal authority appropriately? For example, does the team appropriately "take up" their authority over the daily stand-up meeting?

Boundaries

- Do people work within the boundaries of the authority granted by their agile role? If not, what are the effects of these authority-boundary issues?

- How do team members grant one another the authority to claim tasks within the sprint? How does this change over time during the sprint? How does this change across multiple sprints?

- What are the various "turf" boundaries on the team? Are these turf areas "markers of identity" for one or more team members (Green and Molenkamp 1995)?

As you reflect on the answers to these questions, remember that we coach agile teams to first uphold agile and then "inspect and adapt" to continuously improve. For the first one, upholding agile, look for places where the people filling basic agile roles are not performing in those roles completely or are overstepping their boundaries or authority.

Sometimes, through inspecting and adapting, teams alter or add agile roles. Scrutinize these carefully. Teams commonly make changes to agile roles without recognizing it. Without thinking, people can even occupy a role and act from that role. These "unconscious" roles signal danger for an agile team. When you detect them, remember that agile grants great leeway in how teams get their work done, so very few strictures exist. However, to have a workable agile team, the members must be aware of the agreed-to roles and the boundaries and authorities that go along with each of them (Green and Molenkamp 1995).

Once you have raw answers to the survey questions and/or BART analysis questions, you will probably find that more questions get raised in your mind. At the same time, you may be circling in on some preliminary conclusions. Maybe problems lurking under the surface have come into the light of day, or maybe a situation that has been bothering you suddenly has an "answer." Before acting, you need to step back to get a clear view of the things that surfaced so you can decide what to do about them.

See Problems Clearly

Once a problem has been brought to you or you have detected it, chill out. You need reflection time to see it clearly to get past the symptoms and down to one or more potential causes. Some strategies for reflection are sleep on it, question yourself, pair with another coach, and go to the source.

Sleep on It

I have found that most problems that come up on agile teams can be solved by strengthening or reaffirming an agile practice. Although lightweight, agile frameworks are also amazingly complete. So, sleep on it. Let your mind relax, and see whether you wake in the morning with the answer. Perhaps an agile practice comes to mind. Perhaps something deeper, something that reaffirms the nature of agile itself, arises.

Once an agile manager asked me, the agile coach, to have the team produce a special status report for her. I didn't understand her request because we were doing sprint reviews and that should have given her all the status information she needed. When I spoke with her about it she said, "Well, the sprint review is really for the team, so I don't get much out of it." Stunned, I probed a little deeper to learn why she, one of the intended beneficiaries of the sprint review, was not getting what she needed from it.

As we talked about her sprint review experiences, I came to see her point of view. In past sprint reviews, as team members showed each piece of the product completed, they went into great detail about how they built that piece and all the blind alleys they went down before they finally created it successfully. By the time they were done with their story, the "why we built this thing anyway" had gotten lost. With it, the agile manager's interest in the sprint review had also gotten lost.

As I reflected on past sprint reviews, I realized that her experience might not be unique. I could clearly recall that at about ten minutes in, a number of stakeholders were twiddling with their mobile email devices. Maybe they felt the same way, that they were there to show support for the team but weren't supposed to get anything out of the sprint review for themselves.

So, I slept on it. I went to sleep that night thinking, "What in agile already gives us what we need in this situation?"

On the drive to work the next morning, it hit me. We already have what we need, and we're already doing it—the sprint review. Could it be as simple as reaffirming the purposes of the sprint review? I wondered.

Question Yourself

As one might say to a doctor who smokes cigarettes, "Physician, heal thyself." This goes for you, too, agile coach. Those powerful questions that you wield and use on the team can be used on you, too. When sitting with a problem, ruminate on questions such as these:

- If I could do anything in the world, what would it be?
- What's at stake here?
- If the situation were already perfectly solved, what would it be like?

SEE ALSO	You can find powerful questions, including what they are and how to use them, in Chapter 6, "Coach as Facilitator."

You may not follow the answer you immediately come up with. In fact, if you're letting the powerful question have its way with you, you're probably thinking of big, bold answers—crazy things you might not really do. That's OK. Let the wild ideas come. Somewhere in there will be the angle that makes the situation come into clear focus.

Although brainstorming may surface possible actions to take, maybe even brilliant ideas, you will not act just yet. Taking action requires the team's involvement.

Pair with Another Coach

If you really want powerful questions to do their work on you, pair with another agile coach who can pose the questions to you. And then, allow that coach to help you "get big" as the two of you brainstorm audacious answers. Give the coach permission to offer unbridled ideas to help you come up with unexpected viewpoints on the problem at hand.

Pairing with another coach turns out to be good, solid practice in general. As you build your reciprocal coaching relationship with a peer, you create a place where you can bring your most vexing problems. In this place, resting in this relationship, you receive advice from an outsider's perspective and perhaps a challenge or two.

Go to the Source

Once in a while, a coach who apprenticed with me will e-mail with a problem. I'll make an appointment to talk with that coach in two day's time. Even if the problem sounds urgent, as they all can, I'll postpone the conversation for that long.

I'll tell the coach, "In the meantime, why don't you review the agile mani-festo and the 12 principles that stand behind it? See which of these are not true for the team. Oh, and do you remember the High Performance Tree? Have a look at that, too, and see whether there is a value or high–performance charac-teristic that feels weak for this team."

AGILE MANIFESTO AND 12 PRINCIPLES

Although the wording in the agile manifesto and 12 principles is software-centric, if you substitute *product* for *software* to address your nonsoftware context, they still work beautifully. The software-centric tendency honors the roots and point of view of the originators.

Agile Manifesto

We have come to value...

- Individuals and interactions over processes and tools
- Working software over comprehensive documentation
- Customer collaboration over contract negotiation
- Responding to change over following a plan

12 Principles

We follow these principles:

1. Our highest priority is to satisfy the customer through early and continu-ous delivery of valuable software.

2. Welcome changing requirements, even late in development. Agile pro-cesses harness change for the customer's competitive advantage.

3. Deliver working software frequently, from a couple of weeks to a couple of months, with a preference to the shorter timescale.

4. Businesspeople and developers must work together daily throughout the project.

5. Build projects around motivated individuals. Give them the environment and support they need, and trust them to get the job done.

6. The most efficient and effective method of conveying information to and within a development team is face-to-face conversation.

7. Working software is the primary measure of progress.

8. Agile processes promote sustainable development. The sponsors, devel-opers, and users should be able to maintain a constant pace indefinitely.

9. Continuous attention to technical excellence and good design enhances agility.

Continued

10. Simplicity—the art of maximizing the amount of work not done—is essential.
11. The best architectures, requirements, and designs emerge from self-organizing teams.
12. At regular intervals, the team reflects on how to become more effective and then tunes and adjusts its behavior accordingly (Beck et al. 2001).

SEE ALSO You can learn how to establish and use the High Performance Tree in Chapter 2, "Expect High Performance."

By the time the conversation rolls around a couple of days later, I usually hear the good news I hoped for. The coach exclaims, "You know, the answer was right there! It's number four in the list of principles. We're not involving the businesspeople in our daily work. It was so simple and so hard for me to see."

The agile manifesto, 12 principles, and High Performance Tree represent more than lofty statements of intent and agile excellence. They are diagnostics, useful on a daily basis. When confronted with a problem that feels hard to get your arms around, go to these sources to see what wisdom they have to share.

Resolve Problems

Once you have an idea of what's going on or even if you have thought about it (a lot) and have come up empty-handed, take the problem to the team.

When you address the problem with them, ensure that you balance problem solving with their ability to sprint. Raise only those problems midsprint that must be attended to immediately. Let the others wait until the retrospective. And let some wait even longer. Sometimes a problem is just not ripe or can't be seen clearly enough yet.

SEE ALSO Especially when agile is new, people around you may not be comfortable with this problem-solving approach. They may see it as too laid-back as their need to "solve for it" grabs them and holds on tight. Various managers surrounding the team may push you to solve the team's problems or may try to solve the problems themselves. Turn to the list of performance measurements in Chapter 12, "When Will I Get There?" This list can help you come up with solid reasons for your actions. When managers try to solve problems for the team, they need you to teach them their new agile manager job. A vision of this new job and advice on how to dissuade them from solving problems is covered in Chapter 5, "Coach as Coach-Mentor."

Taking the problem to the team can be done in a number of ways that we will explore one by one:

- Address it directly.
- Reaffirm agile.
- Reveal the system to itself.
- Use the retrospective.
- Add a revealer.

Address It Directly

Simple and straightforward, addressing the problem directly means that you state the symptoms you see, float your hypothesis, and ask the team what they want to do about it.

This may be the method you have used the most in the past. Although familiar, if you want to get to the deep source of the problem and effect lasting change, this method comes up short. It engages the team as problem solvers only within the narrow band of what you already see. Yet, some situations call for it, especially when the problem truly seems clear-cut or when the team acquires something new, such as knowledge, a new practice, or even a new team member.

For example, you notice the team's velocity has slowed over the past few days. From the looks of the storyboard, a tremendous percentage of the total work seems to be in progress. You might say, "Hey, everyone. I see a couple things: The burndown chart looks a bit flat, and the storyboard looks like a lot of work is happening at once. Hmmmm…I could guess that we have too much going on simultaneously. What do you think?"

When you float your hypothesis, make it light and open. If you present it in too much detail or with too much ferocity, then they won't be invited to challenge it and tell you what's really happening. Plus, you being wide open illustrates that you are willing to be wrong. When you do this, you model a powerful way of being in an agile team—a way of being that allows people to float ideas without being attached to them, which is an essential ingredient for innovation.

Reaffirm Agile

Remember the team that left its sprint review attendees wanting more status information? After sleeping on it, I wondered whether the solution was as simple as reaffirming the purposes of the sprint review. To find out, I tried it.

SEE ALSO	You can find the purposes of the sprint review and other standard agile meetings in Chapter 6, "Coach as Facilitator." Talking in value-first order is also described there.

As the team prepared for the next sprint review, I took the opportunity to reteach the purposes of the sprint review, getting back to the "why" of it. I paid particular attention to the show-and-tell purpose of the sprint review. I shared with them the manager's experience and suggested that they learn to talk in value-first order and then go into technical details, but only if needed. They liked this idea because it didn't mean adding anything new to the way they were working, such as a customized status report. All they had to do was come home (again) to the idea that the sprint review exists to show what was created so they can get direct feedback from stakeholders in a low-tech, high-impact way. Talking in value-first order supports this purpose because it allows everyone to focus on the reason we're all together in the first place—producing business value. Deepening the team's understanding of the sprint review did the trick. *Voila!* Problem solved (by them).

Reveal the System to Itself

One of the cornerstones of team coaching says that the job of the coach

> …is not to repair or "fix" the system but rather to reveal its nature to its members. Armed with new awareness the systems' members can become "response-able" to better perform the tasks of the system. This mirroring process empowers the self-regulating function of the system (Center for Right Relationship 2008).

Thinking of an agile team as a system, perhaps as an ecosystem more than a machine, you can apply this principle when presenting a problem to the team.

Assume that a system seeks to restore its own health or, at least, will continue to produce at least one possibility for further change (Center for Right Relationship 2008). Given this, the only job of the agile coach is to reveal the system to itself through observation that invites exploration. As the coach, you simply state what you observe and then allow silence.

People will eventually talk, and when they do, the coach remains focused on helping the team reveal more about their (eco)system to one another. Wherever it goes, the coach follows, asking questions and then remaining silent so that team members can uncover more and more and get a richer view of what's going on. Then, having attained this view, they will naturally move to correct what needs to be corrected.

The coach does not need to drive this to a conclusion or wrap it up with a neat bow. Sometimes things are not ready to be corrected or, upon further examination, it becomes clear that they really don't need to be corrected. The coach leaves this alone, trusting that the team will move to restore themselves at the appropriate time.

Use the Retrospective

Once you detect problems, design a retrospective that will likely raise them. Choose activities that invite the team into different ways of thinking about how they've worked together. Often, the unfamiliar activities give them new slants on the situation and bring into light the problem you have been noticing. This means that you need to spend time designing the retrospective. The "what did we do well, what do we want to change, what do we want to add" formula will likely not be inspirational enough to break team members out of their well-worn thinking patterns. So, do a good job for them by breaking out of your well-worn patterns to offer them new ways to inspect how they work together.

| **SEE ALSO** | See Chapter 6, "Coach as Facilitator," for advice on designing retrospectives that pack a punch. |

Having designed a good retrospective, then relax. If the problem is big enough, it will find a way to come out. You need not have nailed the perfect retrospective activity; you just need to have something that helps people tap into different ways of thinking and relating to one another.

If the problem doesn't come up in the retrospective, you may choose to bring it up by addressing it directly, or you may choose to wait, assuming it is just not ripe. If the team displays signs of being in relationship with one another during the retrospective and having a meaty conversation that yields insights, follow them along their line of thinking and let the problem you detected drop. They're getting somewhere.

If the team dances on the surface of issues without really getting into them, your primary job becomes helping team members relate to one another so they can get to a meaty conversation that allows problems to come out. In this case, keep following the scent of the problem you detected until they get into a real conversation about that one or until the conversation leads them to another, more pressing problem.

Add a Revealer

Sometimes you see a problem and, upon reflection, you think you have discerned the breadth and depth of it but are not sure. In this case, it can be helpful to add something to the team's process that will allow the problem to reveal itself to the team (and you). That "something" is anything that coaxes a problem forth, simply and with low effort from the team. For example, if I notice that the team seems to be losing a lot of work time to "outside things" such as laptops failing or impromptu all-hands meetings, I might suggest that we start a pain snake (Schlabach 2008). Any time their work gets interrupted by something that has nothing to do with the work itself, they write the interruption on a scrap of paper and post it on the pain snake wall. Pretty soon, a trail of scrap papers winds all over the wall, resembling a snake. Almost effortlessly, the pain snake has revealed the problem (or problems). In my experience, people don't pay too much attention to the pain snake as it grows during the sprint, and this is appropriate since their job entails only sprinting. So, let the snake be. In the retrospective, though, you can use the details of the pain snake to great effect to help the team understand the problems and see whether they are widespread or contained, big or small, easy or hard.

What if you suggest a revealer and the team doesn't use it? Just let it die a quiet death. It may take two or three tries at different revealers before the team grabs on to one and uses it. Maybe later they'll realize that they want to resurrect one you introduced a while ago. A wise woman once told me, "We need 100 doors, because we don't know which one people will come through." Indeed.

A Refresher

Let's lock in the ideas from this chapter:

- It's their commitment, not yours.
- You receive problems from others and detect problems by yourself, and then you stop to reflect on them.
- Having the courage to ask "Where are we weak?" is an agile coach's constant practice and sacred duty.

- Once you see a problem clearly or you have considered it well but have come up with nothing, take it to the team. See what perspectives they add to help everyone understand it. Then ask what they want to do about it (if anything).

Additional Resources

Process Health Checks:

Cohn, M. 2009. *Succeeding with Agile: Software Development Using Scrum.* Boston: Addison-Wesley. A whole chapter of this book, entitled "Seeing How Far You've Come," offers a few assessment models used as health checks, as well as sound advice about creating your own.

Kniberg, H. Are You Really Doing Scrum? www.crisp.se/scrum/checklist. This checklist starts with the bottom line: Your process is fine if you are delivering working, tested software (or product) every four weeks or less, if you are delivering what the business needs most, and if your process is continuously improving. If these three are not 100% true, read on to the rest of the checklist.

Vodde, B., and J. Sutherland. Nokia Test. http://jeffsutherland.com/scrum/2008/08/nokia-test-where-did-it-come-from.html. This health check has been altered over time by various agile practitioners. It examines your process at two levels: Are you doing iterative development? Are you doing Scrum?

Or, make up your own process health check!

jlampl. 2008. What is Group Relations Conference? www.youtube.com/watch?v=N-LuFdBpCGM. View what people say about how GR conferences work, and consider attending one. GR conferences are completely experiential and designed for the attendees to get some real insights about how group relations work and how you, as a person, step into roles, boundaries, authority, and tasks under various circumstances.

References

Beck at al. 2001. Manifesto for Agile Software Development. www.agilemanifesto.org.

———. 2001. Principles Behind the Agile Manifesto. www.agilemanifesto.org/principles.html.

Braun, E. 2010. Helping Agile Teams Tip Toward Greater Emotional Maturity. www.agilejournal.com/component/content/2648?task=view.

Center for Right Relationship. 2008. *Relationship Systems Coaching Model.* Organization & Relationship Systems Coaching core curriculum.

Green, Z., and R. Molenkamp. 2005. The BART System of Group and Organizational Analysis: Boundary, Authority, Role, and Task. www.it.uu.se/edu/course/homepage/projektDV/ht09/BART_Green_Molenkamp.pdf.

Mezick, D. 2009. BART Checkup for Teams. www.newtechusa.com/agileboston/notes/BART-checkup.htm.

Schlabach, K. 2008. Snake on the Wall! http://agile-commentary.blogspot.com/2008/12/snake-on-wall.html.

Chapter 9

Coach as Conflict Navigator

We were warned this would happen. Ken Schwaber and Mike Beedle told us to expect it. They said that the very nature of people being together—all with different backgrounds and perspectives—would bring it out (2001). Anyone who has spent time with an agile team can attest to this. What is it? Conflict.

Patrick Lencioni of *The Five Dysfunctions of a Team* fame names fear of conflict as one of the five dysfunctions, citing it as a main reason that teams, even good ones, struggle (2002).

Jean Tabaka, professional facilitator and agile coach, reveals that one of the hallmarks of highly collaborative (read: high-performance) teams is that they use conflict constructively. They live in a world of constructive disagreement (2006).

These experts tell us to face conflict and turn it into a force for good, yet many conflict resolution models see conflict as something to be "solved," as if conflict were a mechanistic system one can take apart, fix, and put back together.

By the time you finish this chapter, you will be able to answer these questions:

- As the team's agile coach, where does my responsibility to resolve conflict begin and end?

- What can I use to see the level of conflict on the team more objectively so I can help the team see it, too?

- Which ways of responding to conflict match best what's happening on the team?

- What methods and tools can I use to address conflict?

- What should I do when one person complains about another to me? What if someone complains about me?

- What can I do about conflict that seems to come up over and over, even when we've resolved it?

My experiences of conflict on agile teams don't even slightly resemble machine models, and the people in conflict are certainly not mechanisms. They resemble tropical storms more than machines—blowing hard, pelting everyone around them with their unpredictability, and often dissipating just as fast as they came on.

Working together day after day is an intense human experience, with all the glories and warts that emerge from constant interaction between these astonishing, disappointing, challenging, infuriating, magnificent, normal human beings we call team members. On an agile team, especially, we see this, and in our pursuit of excellence we know that conflicts arise and that we can expect both harmony and disharmony. Navigating conflict is our new mind-set, in which we help teams move from conflict to constructive disagreement as a catapult to high performance.

The Agile Coach's Role in Conflict

Coaching teams to navigate conflict may feel unfamiliar or uncomfortable to you. It did for me, even though books, articles, and studies on the subject abound. As a plan-driven project manager, I didn't have to "go there" in the face of conflict very often because team members joined the team and left the team as we moved from phase to phase. If my feeble attempts to resolve a conflict failed, no big loss. Sooner or later, the team members in conflict would move on to other projects. With agile, however, team members stay together throughout the project. They do not move on, nor does the conflict.

Given this, the agile coach faces conflict squarely, skillfully determines the severity of it, mindfully decides whether to intervene and how, generously teaches teams to navigate it, and courageously refuses to settle for a team that shrinks from greatness by avoiding it.

As their coach, you help teams navigate conflict. You show them a method. You can't give them a full-color, waterproof chart that marks the shoals and hazards. You can give them something more precious, more powerful. You can give them a guide, a framework, so that they create their own charts, whenever they need to do so.

Five Levels of Conflict

An agile team humming along in the rhythm of steady momentum will display conflict all the time—minor quips at one another, rolling eyeballs, heavy sighs, emotional voices, stony silences, tension in the air. You'll witness dry wit, teasing, "just joking" comments, or just-short-of-snide remarks, all in the range of normal for an agile team.

These behaviors signal normalcy for any group of people who spend considerable time together and who create a shared history. It happens in neighborhoods, community coffeehouses, churches, and agile teams—especially agile teams—where team members sit arm's distance apart for hours on end every day while they create products together, all the while responding to the built-in pressure of the timeboxed sprint.

Conflict, ever present, can be normal or destructive, and the two can be hard to tell apart. An author of many books on conflict, Speed Leas offers us agile coaches a framework we can use to determine the seriousness of the conflict (1985). This model, well suited to agile teams, looks at conflict in a deeply human and humane way. As depicted in Figure 9.1, it forms an escalation path of conflict from "Level 1: Problem to Solve" to "Level 5: World War."

FIGURE 9.1   Five levels of conflict

Level 1: Problem to Solve

We all know what conflict at level 1 feels like. Everyday frustrations and aggravations make up this level, and we experience conflicts as they rise and fall and come and go. At this level, people have different opinions, misunderstanding may have happened, conflicting goals or values may exist, and team members likely feel anxious about the conflict in the air.

When in level 1, the team remains focused on determining what's awry and how to fix it. Information flows freely, and collaboration is alive. Team members use words that are clear, specific, and factual. The language abides in the here and now, not in talking about the past. Team members check in with one another if they think a miscommunication has just happened. You will probably notice that team members seem optimistic, moving through the conflict. It's not comfortable, but it's not emotionally charged, either. Think of level 1 as the level of constructive disagreement that characterizes high-performing teams.

Level 2: Disagreement

At level 2, self-protection becomes as important as solving the problem. Team members distance themselves from one another to ensure they come out OK in the end or to establish a position for compromise they assume will come. They may talk offline with other team members to test strategies or seek advice and support. At this level, good-natured joking moves toward the half-joking barb. Nastiness gets a sugarcoating but still comes across as bitter. Yet, people aren't hostile, just wary. Their language reflects this as their words move from the specific to the general. Fortifying their walls, they don't share all they know about the issues. Facts play second fiddle to interpretations and create confusion about what's really happening.

Level 3: Contest

At level 3, the aim is to win. A compounding effect occurs as prior conflicts and problems remain unresolved. Often, multiple issues cluster into larger issues or create a "cause." Factions emerge in this fertile ground from which misunderstandings and power politics arise. In an agile team, this may happen subtly, because a hallmark of working agile is the feeling that we are all in this together. But it does happen.

People begin to align themselves with one side or the other. Emotions become tools used to "win" supporters for one's position. Problems and people become synonymous, opening people up to attack. As team members pay attention to building their cases, their language becomes distorted. They make overgeneralizations: "He *always* forgets to check in his code" or "You *never* listen to what I have to say." They talk about the other side in presumptions: "I *know* what they think, but they are ignoring the real issue." Views of themselves as benevolent and others as tarnished become magnified: "*I* am always the one to compromise for the good of the team" or "*I* have everyone's best interest at heart" or "*They* are intentionally ignoring what the customer is really saying." Discussion becomes either/or and blaming flourishes. In this combative environment, talk of peace may meet resistance. People may not be ready to move beyond blaming.

> *Whenever two good people argue over principles, they are both right.*
>
> —Marie Von Ebner-Eschenbach

Level 4: Crusade

At level 4, resolving the situation isn't good enough. Team members believe the people on the "other side" of the issues will not change. They may believe the only option is to remove the others from the team or get removed from the team themselves. Factions become entrenched and can even solidify into a pseudo-organizational structure within the team. Identifying with a faction can overshadow identifying with the team as a whole so the team's identity gets trounced. People and positions are seen as one, opening up people to attack for their affiliations rather than their ideas. These attacks come in the form of language rife with ideology and principles, which becomes the focus of conversation, rather than specific issues and facts. The overall attitude is righteous and punitive.

Level 5: World War

"Destroy!" rings out the battle cry at level 5. It's not enough that one wins; others must lose. "We must make sure this horrible situation does not happen again!" Only one option at level 5 exists: to separate the combatants (aka team members) so that they don't hurt one another. No constructive outcome can be had.

What Level of Conflict Is Present?

To determine the level of conflict in a team, an agile coach must spend solid time with the team members. This means direct observation over a period of days or weeks to see the conflict in its natural environment. Observing for a few minutes here or there will not be sufficient. Make sure you have spent enough time with the team to observe what's going on before you draw conclusions about the level of conflict.

Determining the level of conflict present on a team is not rocket science. It's actually not science at all; it's observation, conversation, and intuition. And everyone views it differently. Although you may discern an overall level of conflict on a team in a given moment, be aware that team members experiencing the conflict may be doing so from different levels. That's what makes this so fascinating.

Speed Leas's framework will help you become more objective so that you can get past your own judgments and preconceptions to see what is truly present in a team. In the end, though, simply do your best to navigate uncharted waters knowing you may not be 100% correct. Be rigorous enough to feel that you have given the team your full and useful attention, and move forward from there.

While observing, pay attention to these three things that help assess the level of conflict: Hear complaints, feel the energy, and focus on language.

Hear Complaints

Team members may complain to you directly. You may hear complaints openly in the team room. Or you may see team members "secretly" complaining to one another in whispered hallway conversations. While you are observing, remember that you need not act to resolve these complaints. There is something deep inside many of us that wants to "make it all right." When people complain to us, we think we need to "solve" it, so we move into action immediately. Resist this. Listen compassionately, take in what the complainer is saying, and make it clear you care so much that you are spending the time needed to see the full scope of the conflict.

Feel the Energy

Notice how the team room feels when you first walk in. Is there a hum of earnest and coordinated effort? Are people in motion together, in conversation, at the whiteboard, or at their computers? Is there a sense of purpose and forward momentum? Or, are people coming in and out? Are conversations fragmented or being held more than once? Is there a feeling of stop and start and then stop again? Or is there something lurking just below the surface?

You've probably seen conflict lurking below the surface on teams: barely disguised disregard, sidelong glances, rolling eyes, or words that halt conversation for an eternal heartbeat while people think, "Was that meant to be a put-down? Did she really just say that?" When the energy in the team room feels heavy with the emotional residue of these types of actions, you can bet the team is at level 2 or maybe even higher.

Notice whether the conflict lies subsurface or right out there for all to see. Throughout the day, feel the energy of the team. Pay attention when the energy seems to become more positive or more negative and ask yourself, "What happened just before that shift in energy? Was it one particular thing, or has this been building up?" Pay attention to whether the team uses mostly positive, forward-moving energy or mostly negative, stagnating (or swirling) energy. Feeling the energy gives you another clue to help assess the level of conflict.

Focus on Language

What people say and how they say it is the main key for assessing the level of conflict on an agile team. The team will be in conversation frequently, so there will be many chances to focus on language. Table 9.1 lists examples of typical language heard at each level. Use these to help you hone in on the words people use when they talk to one another while experiencing various levels of conflict.

TABLE 9.1   The language people use can tell you what level of conflict is happening.

Conflict level	Language example
At level 1, team members engage in conflict openly and constructively. Conversation "self-management" happens among team members who use questions and open-hearted statements to ensure that everyone gets heard, that what was heard is understood, and that what is understood is true, whether it's a true fact or a need.	"All right, I hear you, but I think you're forgetting the fact that…" "Did we just have a misunderstanding? What are you thinking I'm saying?" "Stop! We've been here before. I am tired of this conversation. What new information makes us think we need to open this again?" "Oh! I see what you're saying now. OK…I still don't agree with you. Here's why…" "Barb, I just remembered that you value order. Is that the main thing here? Doing the rollout this way violates your sense of order."

Continued

TABLE 9.1 The language people use can tell you what level of conflict is happening (Continued).

Conflict level	Language example
At level 2, the conversation changes to make room for self-protection. At this level, what's not being said gives clues as much as what is being said. To create a shield, people don't reveal all they know, so be on the lookout for conversations that just don't add up.	"You knew that the support team didn't come through for us when they said they would. Why didn't you tell us?" "Yes, I broke the build, but I think we need to look at the bigger picture. There are worse things going on in our team than one broken build." "You're doing the same thing you did last time that didn't work."
At level 3, distorted language such as overgeneralizations, presumptions, magnified positions, and either/or emerges. Real issues get lost.	"If only she weren't on the team." "She always takes over every conversation." "They always take shortcuts, and we're left to clean up after them." "I don't know why she's being so nice these days. Is she setting me up?" "I don't even know what we're fighting about anymore. We just don't get along."
Level 4 becomes more ideological.	"They'll never change, so it's not even worth talking to them." "They're wrong, plain and simple." "We need more people on our side." "We're right!"
Level 5 features full-on combat.	"We have to win. There is no option." "It's us or them." "The world must be warned so this will never happen again."

Having discerned the level of conflict happening on the team, what should you do? The next sections reveal several techniques that answer this question so you can help teams navigate conflict when they find themselves in the midst of it.

What Should You Do About It?

The goal of navigating conflict is to de-escalate. Knock it down a notch or two. As the agile coach, the first and most important question to answer is "Do *I* have to respond?"

First, Do Nothing

Agile teams—even new ones and even broken ones—can often navigate conflict by themselves, even conflict up into the level 3 range. So, sit back for a while and witness their moves. See whether they make progress. Even if it's not perfect or the "complete" job you could do for them, if team members navigate the conflict well enough, leave them alone. To help you live with the uncomfortable feeling of watching a team's bumbling attempts to deal with conflict, remember these words from Chris Corrigan in *The Tao of Holding Space*: "Everything you do for the group is one less thing they know they can do for themselves" (Corrigan 2006).

The team's bumbling is better than your perfect plan. Remember the goal of supporting the team's self-organization (and reorganization). Your discomfort is a small price to pay.

But what if you've decided to intervene? If you feel you have observed long enough (which should feel like a really long time) and decided to intervene, there are a few response modes you can employ: analyze and respond, use structures, and reveal. These come in order from least to most powerful for the goal of fostering self-organization.

Analyze and Respond

This may be the most comfortable response mode an agile coach can use because it feels familiar and at least somewhat analytical. To use analyze and respond, the agile coach considers these questions (Keip 1997):

What is the level of conflict?

What are the issues?

How would I respond as side A?

How would I respond as side B?

What resolution options are open?

What should I do (if anything)?

When using the analyze-and-respond mode, remember that no one has the whole story. Each person's perspective is valid and needed. If there are ten team members, you can bet there are at least ten perspectives, each of which is true in the eye of the beholder.

> **SEE ALSO** What is your knee-jerk reaction when conflict arises? Agile coaches must be able to name that reaction and consciously choose it or reject it in service to the team. See Chapter 3, "Master Yourself," for ways to keep yourself solidly rooted when unexpected things happen with teams. Things like conflict.

Table 9.2 provides a map of successful response modes at each level. Look to this to help answer the question "What resolution options are open?" when addressing conflict in the whole-team setting (Keip 2006).

TABLE 9.2 Conflict navigation response modes at each level

Conflict level	Successful response options
Level 1: Problem to Solve	Collaboration. Seeking a win-win situation. Consensus. Learning where every team member's head is with regard to the issue and, in time, arriving at a decision everyone can back.
Level 2: Disagreement	Support. Empowering the other to resolve the problem. Safety. Anything that restores a sense of safety, such as collaboration games or regrounding in the team's shared values.

Conflict level	Successful response options
Level 3: Contest	Accommodate. Yielding to the other's view when the relationship is more important than the issue. This is a successful short-term strategy only and becomes a liability if used often over the long term.
	Negotiate. When the "thing" the conflict is about is divisible, such as the use of a shared resource, negotiation can work. Negotiation will not work when the issue revolves around people's values. Values are not divisible, and one person giving in to another in violation of their own values feels like a sellout.
	Get factual. Gather data about the situation to establish the facts.
Level 4: Crusade	Establish safe structures again. Use "shuttle" diplomacy, carrying thoughts from one group to the other until they are able to de-escalate and use the tools available at lower levels of conflict.
Level 5: World War	Do whatever is necessary to prevent people from hurting one another.

When the team de-escalates, they get more options for dealing with the conflict as the tools from the next level down become available to them.

The analyze-and-respond mode for navigating conflict may feel comfortable to you—an easy shoe to slip on. If that's the case and if it seems the best choice for your current level of skill and confidence, use it. However, you should know that it is the weakest response mode for building high-performance teams because it puts the coach in the driver's seat. It also relies completely on analytical thinking, which is just one small way to think about conflict. So, as you feel ready, try the next two response modes.

Use Structures

One step up on the power curve of response modes entails using the "bones" of agile to navigate conflict. The bones are those principles, values, or roles that help the team understand how to get the best from using agile.

Research suggests that it may be misguided to address interpersonal conflict on a team head-on. The way a team performs will likely influence people's perceptions of their interpersonal interactions, not the other way around (Hackman 2002). We often think that by addressing interpersonal conflict we can enhance team performance. But perhaps that's not true, especially on new teams, where the agile coach can best help by adopting a task orientation. A task orientation, rather than interpersonal orientation, works best with a new team because "the team is still trying to learn the specifics" of their purpose together and to "clarify people's [informal] roles" (Gratton 2007). Given what this research tells us, a coach should first attempt to address conflict by addressing performance.

Agile coaches can turn to the bones in order to address performance as the door to navigating conflict. In professional coaching terminology, the bones of agile are analogous to structures—"devices that remind people of their vision, goals or purpose, or the action they need to take immediately. Collages, calendars, messages on voice mail, and alarm clocks can serve as structures" (Whitworth et al. 2007).

With agile, the makings of structures abound: the practices and principles inherent in agile methods, the agile manifesto, values, the purposes of recurring events such as sprint reviews or stand-ups, role definitions, and the focus on removing waste. All of these serve as fertile ground for creating structures that help the team become conscious of dealing with conflict in the context of getting better at a particular bit of agile. Choose one of these bits to bring to the team—or reaffirm it—when the team experiences conflict. Pick the one you think will get to the core of the conflict. Pick something inspiring. You can find much inspiration in the simplicity and depth of agile methods. You need not look far to find a piece of agile the team can use to create a structure that will serve.

SEE ALSO   Refer to Chapter 6, "Coach as Facilitator," to learn the purposes of each of the standard agile meetings.

Here's an example: Dealing with conflict that seems never-ending about how "good" good needs to be, perhaps you choose to recall the principles behind the agile manifesto to the team members (Beck et al. 2001). After reacquainting themselves with the principles and engaging in some lively discussion, the team creates a big, bold poster that hangs in a place of honor in the team room. It reminds them that they agree to tread the fine line between good, good enough, excellent, and perfect. Figure 9.2 shows the resulting structure: their poster.

We will balance these

Continuous attention
to <u>detail</u> enhances
agility

Simplicity:
The art of maximizing
the work <u>not done</u>
is essential.

How are we doing today?

FIGURE 9.2   One team's structure for dealing with unsolvable conflict

Each day, after stand-up, the team looks at the poster and asks one another, "How are we balanced between these two today?"

As in this example, use structures to indirectly navigate conflict. Through them, you don't address the conflict head-on as a problem that must be solved. Instead, you bring the conflict up and then address it in the context of teaching or reaffirming agile—a practice, a value, a mind-set, a vision—with the team. This allows your guidance to be forward-moving and positive rather than punitive.

Note that this does not mean ignoring the conflict or sidestepping it. You still tackle it. You just do so by holding up a bit of agile done well and asking team members to think about whether they embody the best intentions of that bit. Using this response mode, the structure the team creates becomes a call to action for each person. In so doing, you effect change through inspiration rather than consternation.

Reveal

The most powerful intervention in the face of conflict calls you to reveal what you know. Give the team the benefit of the knowledge you now have. Reveal this entire model to them. Give them the language of levels of conflict and how to assess the current level. Teach the team members to recognize their own knee-jerk responses and consciously choose which response option best serves the team given the level of conflict they are experiencing.

In so doing, you give the team a powerful self-management tool, a framework to use again and again to navigate conflict as it arises.

This doesn't mean that you get a "pass" for coaching. You still need to be part of the discussions, especially at first when team members first learn the framework. Your role changes, though. Instead of being immersed in the content of the conflict and the framework simultaneously, you can let them worry about the content, which frees you up to become the boundary keeper for the framework. In this role, you ensure that the framework is used as intended, not warped to fit someone's position and not used as a way to "label" and weaken others or make their position wrong.

TRY THIS

The next time conflict breaks out in the team, try revealing instead of "resolving." If the team has just successfully de-escalated the conflict on their own, bring it to their attention, and then ask some questions: What level of conflict do you think you just experienced? How could you tell? What happened to cause the de-escalation?

If they are in conflict and not de-escalating, intrude in the conversation, and ask the same questions, only change the last question to be something like "What will need to happen for the level of conflict to de-escalate now?"

Often, the best time for teaching the team a new framework comes exactly when they need it most—in the middle of the problem itself. So, use those moments of conflict to reveal the model and start asking questions that cause the team to become aware so they can self-correct.

Getting yourself out of the loop remains the goal, but you can do this only once the team becomes proficient in using and truly upholding the framework. Even then, observation every now and again can still be good.

When you see the framework used well, team members ask one another a whole new class of questions as they navigate conflict. They may ask, "At what level are we?" or "What is going on that makes this so?" or "I notice a lot of generalizations in the way we're talking about that; do we need to de-escalate to get constructive again?" or "Do we need a break from one another?"

You also may see the conflict framework used as a tool for recognizing and adjusting one's own conflict level before it leaks out into the team. One team member may say to another, "I realized I was getting into crusade territory and needed to back down. You know how much I care about this, but I know that getting up on my high horse isn't going to help anyone. So, I'm thinking about other ways to bring this up."

Teams that actively navigate conflict and de-escalate regularly can learn to thrive in level 1 conflict. Here, they live in a world of constructive disagreement. They dance on the edge of discomfort—just enough so that they can come up with the best ideas and build upon one another's thoughts to find astonishing new possibilities. In so doing, they use conflict as a catapult to high performance.

Carrying Complaints

An agile coach helps the team see that conflict is normal—and useful—if it remains constructive. Conflict seething just below the surface is clearly not constructive, however, and often leaks out around the edges as complaints.

Team members know that one part of the agile coach's job revolves around removing impediments to work, making the coach a popular target for complainers. Some agile coaches may have even practiced dealing with complainers if they took the Certified ScrumMaster (CSM) course and their instructor used a set of "typical" complaint scenarios that go something like this:

> A team member comes to you and says that the architect on the team has such bad body odor that she cannot stand to work near her. With summer coming, she is worried the architect will run everyone out of the team room. As the team's coach, what do you do?

> A developer comes to you fuming because Joe, a developer, broke the build—yet again. He is convinced that Joe is sloppy and doesn't care about anyone but himself. He says that the rest of the team is ready to "vote him off the island." As the team's coach, what do you do?

> A team member comes to you complaining about the lead tester taking personal calls in the team room. As she talks, it becomes clear that she is really steamed about the loud, personal conversations she has to sit through several times a day. She thinks he is rude and has questionable morals. She wants you to make it stop. As the team's coach, what do you do?

I've actually played out one of these scenarios in real life to a real team member. It was the one about body odor. I'm not kidding. As the agile coach, I thought it was my job to "resolve" the problem, so I went to the odor-offender and told her. It was uncomfortable and awful, and I felt like the lowest of the low as I watched her face crumble before me. But, it was over quickly, was relatively painless (for me), and ended there. She became more self-aware, her odor improved, and everyone was happy. The indirect confrontation method worked, or at least seemed to on the surface. And I thought I did what was best for the team. But did I?

I can't think of many other scenarios in which the indirect method would work and one might rightly argue it didn't work in that one either. By carrying the complaint from complainer to offender, I ensured that there would be no full understanding of the situation from both "sides." In fact, as the intermediary, I helped create sides by reinforcing a division in the team. This was probably a minor infraction given the body odor issue but would be significant in many other situations.

Most complaints arise from situations more complicated than this one and feature both parties contributing to the wrongdoing. Not clear-cut, these situations feature feelings that have come to the boiling point, where ideas of right and wrong create divisions and situations in which people feel vulnerable, hurt, and unappreciated. These are the more common situations. They call for something better than the coach carrying the complaint from complainer to offender.

The next time someone brings you a complaint, try this three-step intervention path (Keip 2006). Ask the complainer the following:

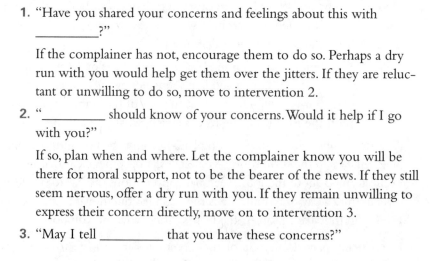

1. "Have you shared your concerns and feelings about this with
   _____?"

   If the complainer has not, encourage them to do so. Perhaps a dry run with you would help get them over the jitters. If they are reluctant or unwilling to do so, move to intervention 2.

2. "_____ should know of your concerns. Would it help if I go with you?"

   If so, plan when and where. Let the complainer know you will be there for moral support, not to be the bearer of the news. If they still seem nervous, offer a dry run with you. If they remain unwilling to express their concern directly, move on to intervention 3.

3. "May I tell _____ that you have these concerns?"

Whenever possible, get the complainer to address the grievance directly, either alone or with you in tow. Avoid triangulation, when one party talks about another party to someone else, at all costs.

Going to intervention 3 puts you in the spotlight as "the carrier" of the grievance and prolongs the situation. If intervention 3 is the only option, though, remember this: Never carry anonymous complaints. Let the complainer know that you will reveal who has the complaint.

If you relay an anonymous complaint, you open yourself up to manipulation, and you model that talking behind team members' backs is OK. It's not. It wasn't OK in middle school; it's not OK now. Healthy agile teams live in a world of courage and respect. Make it clear that you expect this and uphold it yourself.

TRY THIS

Try the three-step intervention path. Ask a friend to play out these scenarios with you. The friend will be the complainer, and you will be the coach.

A team member casually mentions that he came in over the weekend to correct another team member's work. In his opinion, it was a job poorly done. He tells you that he was willing to do it this one time, but in the future he expects you to set the other team member straight.

A team member tells you that she will be taking an unexpected day off because another team member did that to her last week, which caused extra work and a lot of frustration. This week, she's going to "get back" at the other team member by taking a day off. She feels she deserves it and wants the other person to know how it feels to be let down.

A team member comes to you and asks that you talk with two others on the team who speak too softly to be heard during the stand-up. He says he is embarrassed to bring it up himself because he has a slight hearing problem, and he's not sure if his inability to hear them is his issue or theirs.

Then, have your friend play out a scenario that you think might be brewing in your own work situation. See how well you do with "live ammo."

If the complainer rejects all three options, then do something very difficult: Cease to consider it a problem. Really, cease to consider it a problem. To help you do this, remember that as the agile coach, you are in this for the long haul needed to create a high-performance team. The short-term win of temporary team harmony or the fleeting feeling of a problem solved isn't good enough for you (or them). With this perspective, you can see that not every complaint calls for resolution.

Sometimes, people just need to vent. As the coach, you are the wise and calm one who hears them and allows them to get it out and let it go. This opens the door to healing. Fully listening while they vent may be all that is needed.

Other times, people try to add you to their gossip chain—not a place you want to be because no gossip is harmless. As the coach, know that someone who wants to gossip doesn't want to resolve the complaint. Hear them fully, give them your observation that they don't seem ready to resolve the complaint, and let them know that you will take no action.

Or, people may be complaining to you so they can enlist you in their war. Don't sign up. You can tell when someone tries to enlist you because you won't get a firm and positive response to this question, "Are you ready to resolve this without blaming?" In fact, if you sense resistance as you ask the three questions, then pause and switch to this question, "Are you ready to resolve this without blaming?" Most of the time, people will say "yes" and then keep talking. Listen extra carefully. As they keep talking after they say "yes," pay close attention so you can hear the "but." Here's an example: "Yes, I have always wanted to resolve this without blaming, but Jeff is so stubborn that he just won't listen to reason." If there's a "but" in it, there's a good chance the person cannot yet resolve the issue without blaming. So, let them have their say and then just leave it. By listening and offering your honorable help, you have done all that can be done (for now).

Chronic complainers deserve special treatment. If the same person comes to you time and again with complaints but does not take you up on any of the aboveboard resolution options you offer, then address their chronic behavior. Ask the complainer to consider the destructive influence that harboring resentments has on the team and on him as an individual. Let this person know that only so many "free passes" can be given to a chronic complainer and that the complaints department may have to shut its door to them if they are not willing to take steps to rectify at least some of the situations they complain about.

When You Become the Subject of the Complaint

Addressing complaints aboveboard can be uncomfortable. No one likes confrontation, especially when they can't get someone else to do it for them. When you handle complaints in the open, you will stir things up—so much so, in fact, that you may find *you* become the subject of complaints. When someone passes along anonymous complaints about you, ask these questions to bring the conversation to a constructive place:

"May I ask how you feel about this? Is it a concern for you, too?"

"I would welcome a chance to talk with <the complainer>. Would you be willing to help us get together to talk?"

Remember that, as the agile coach, you model the behavior that helps the team get to high performance. In this regard, imitation is definitely the highest form of flattery. Face complaints about you head-on and hold fast in your absolute refusal to carry anonymous complaints. Then, see what happens. The best outcome possible is that you hear one team member say to another, "Have you shared your concerns with her directly?"

Unsolvable Conflict

Do you ever get the feeling that some conflict just can't be solved? The team members in conflict address the issue, and it seems to go away, but then it comes back. Maybe it's all dressed up in a new situation or with a different level of intensity, but the conflict is a familiar visitor who has turned up on the team's doorstep again. If the team uses humor as a stress reliever, you may even hear the conflict turned into a sarcastic half-joke, "OK, team, just to put you on notice. Julie hates me again." Sounds almost like a marriage, doesn't it?

Agile Teams Are Intimate

Dr. John Gottman's 30-year research into what makes marriages work and fail offers this: 69% of issues in marriages are perpetual (1999). They do not go away. There is no way to solve them. In the extreme, you can divorce and remarry with the likely result that you will have traded one set of perpetual issues for another.

How does information about conflict in marriage, a very personal and intimate relationship, relate to agile teams? To answer this, listen for the conversations that happen during a typical day on a healthy agile team. You'll hear talk about things like mammogram results, coping with elder parents, frustrations with visiting in-laws, upcoming vacation plans, advice on raising kids, and much more. On exceptionally healthy teams, you hear team members talk to one another at an even deeper level of intimacy. They discuss their fears about the upcoming performance evaluation cycle, whether they feel valued on the team, and how their work on the team does or does not mesh with their personal growth goals. Relationships on agile teams are intimate. The reality of unsolvable conflict is as valid in this context as in a marriage.

The world of professional coaching applies Dr. Gottman's research to groups of all sorts (Center for Right Relationship 2008). Business partners, teams, organizations—they all benefit from the coaching perspective that some conflict is simply unsolvable. It sounds hopeless, but don't lose hope. Although it's true that unsolvable conflict exists, coaches are taught all is not lost—there is a "way out."

Rather than focusing on unraveling and resolving conflict, the "way out" is to navigate through it by increasing the positivity in the group. Simply put, increasing positivity means increasing the number of positive interactions among the team members. We, in the agile community, can follow this path and apply the same thoughts and tools to our teams when they experience unsolvable conflict.

Take the first step by teaching the team that unsolvable conflict exists and is expected and normal. Tell them that the way to live successfully with unsolvable conflict is to increase the number of positive interactions between them to help navigate the conflict when it arises.

> Injustice can be eliminated, but human conflicts and natural limitations cannot be removed. The conflicts of social life and the limitations of nature cannot be controlled or transcended. They can, however, be endured and survived. It is possible for there to be a dance with life, a creative response to its intrinsic limits and challenges.
>
> —Sharon Welch

Scientific studies prove this. Several parallel research efforts, going back as far as 15 years, independently deduced the positivity/negativity ratio in individuals, teams, and marriages. For marriages, the "magic" ratio is about five positive interactions to one negative interaction (Gottman 1994) For teams, it's three to one for high performance and five to one for the most high-performing. (Losada and Heaphy 2004) That's what we need to stay on the side of life that lets us ride on the surface of a turbulent ocean of conflict. At least three to one, and five to one is even better. Are you receiving your recommended allowance of positivity? Are the team members you coach?

To boost the positivity/negativity ratio on teams, help them avoid misunderstanding buildup and use a shared vision.

Avoid Misunderstanding Buildup

Have you ever noticed that team members sometimes talk past one another? Perhaps they talk more than they listen, leaving true understanding behind. Or, maybe a team member's voice has yet to be heard. Someone has something to say but fears the risk of speaking up. Without knowing this, the team moves on and leaves that team member in the dust.

As their coach, you note these things because you pay attention to the quality in the conversation, but the team—embroiled in the work—probably doesn't notice. They need you to help tune their ears so they can learn to listen for quality in the conversation. When they do this, they will avoid misunder-standing buildup, and they will increase the positivity in the relationships. All of this makes unsolvable conflict livable.

Consent and Consensus Checks

Use the following two simple tools to help avoid misunderstandings and, as a by-product, increase the positivity in the group: consent check and consensus check. Use a consent check when it sounds like all the voices that want to be heard have been heard and the group is generally moving toward a shared conclusion. On the flip side, use a consensus check when all voices are not being heard and it is unclear whether the team is moving toward a shared conclusion.

Let's say you are in a retrospective and the team is discussing whether to change their stand-up time to 1 p.m. Through the conversation, you notice that most people have spoken and no one has been talked over or ignored. The general energy of the group feels upbeat, and it seems they are in sync with one another. In this case, you might ask for a consent check: "Is there anyone who objects to moving the stand-up to 1 p.m.?" Purposely phrased in the negative, this question gives explicit permission for a team member to voice an objection.

The conversation about moving the stand-up time to 1 p.m. could take a different tone. Let's say that some of the team members are in favor of moving the stand-up time and have spoken about the virtues of doing so. Others have raised minor concerns, and they have been discussed. At one point, someone tried to get a word in edgewise and was not successful. You have a gut feeling that the team is not moving together in the conversation. You think that there might be something unspoken here—some need or concern left unsaid. In this case, you may call for a consensus check. Professional facilitator and coach Jean Tabaka offers us a good description of the Fist of Five method of check-ing consensus (Tabaka 2006). To do it, say something like, "Let's see where we are with this idea of moving the stand-up to 1 p.m. Let's do a consensus check. Ready? 1, 2, 3." On "3," each team member holds up a hand showing one to five fingers, to correspond with their level of agreement to the statement. Here's what they mean:

Five fingers: I love this idea. I wish I had thought of it myself.

Four fingers: I'm happy with this idea and am glad we came up with it.

Three fingers: I can live with and support this idea. (This is the definition of consensus.)

Two fingers: I have reservations about this and would have trouble supporting it.

One finger: I have grave misgivings. I can neither support it nor live with it.

Then, everyone looks around to see whether anyone has one or two fingers in the air. If so, they are invited to speak their point of view. Because everyone "votes" from their conscience at the same time, team members are not swayed by others' votes. In this way, Fist of Five often surfaces unheard voices and helps neutralize conversation dominators.

Consent check and consensus check are two ways to ensure that team members are invited to speak, the team is called to listen, and overall understanding of one another—and with it, team positivity—increases.

Use Their Shared Vision

When coaching business partners, activities that help surface "the dream behind the conflict" are often employed to improve the working relationship (Center for Right Relationship 2008). In "the dream behind the conflict," the partners are coached through an activity that calls to mind the reasons why the partnership was a good idea in the first place. In so doing, they remember the excitement of the "dream" and regain the big-picture view of the partnership's purpose. With this big picture purpose in mind, they often see that the unsolvable conflict is secondary, maybe even unimportant.

On agile teams, we usually don't have the luxury of a voluntary relationship forged in mutual interest to fall back on in times of conflict. Teams are most often created by managers and announced to the team members, with no "dream" of what the team can be together, short of delivering some product. Even so, that doesn't mean the team must remain devoid of a shared dream.

SEE ALSO	Teams need goals at multiple levels. Chapter 7, "Coach as Teacher," presents multiple levels of team goals and why each is important, including the "dream" of what the team seeks to be together. Team start-up is a great time to set these goals so they can be used later when the going gets rough.

A shared dream, or vision, gives teams a beacon they can use to light the way back to their best selves and their best expression as a team when unsolvable conflict has caused them to wander off the path. This vision differs greatly from the laundry list of business goals the team must satisfy to be deemed successful. It is about something bigger than that: It's about them. In coaching terms, this vision is called the big "A" Agenda (Whitworth et al. 2007) and is often expressed as a compelling statement that sums up what the team has set out to be together. Here are some examples:

> "We will successfully improve the customer experience through collaboration, passion for what's right, and out-of-the-box creativity, all the while playing to each other's strengths and downplaying our weaknesses."

> "This year, we are focused and are holding our customers and external partners to the focus we all agree to. Our belief is that focus will improve our results and the way we work together."

> "We will deliver a website that draws in new customers, and we will do so by becoming the best cross-department team the company has ever seen. We want people to ask, 'How did they do that?'"

When unsolvable conflict arises, point to the vision statement hanging on the wall of the team room to call the team back to their shared dream. If that doesn't work, try asking these questions: Does this vision of us as a team still apply? What is the meaning of your current conflict in the context of this vision? Having recalled the vision, does the conflict even matter? Sometimes the conflict falls away as team members give one another sheepish looks, and shared laughter once again rings out. Sometimes a conversation ensues, perhaps releasing the conflict in deference to the vision or in changing the vision if it has become stale or meaningless. In either case, having a shared vision lets the team see that unsolvable conflict is normal and can be navigated as long as they use the vision as their beacon.

A Last Word on Conflict

These techniques don't add up to a magical solution. Knowing conflict frameworks, choosing responses, handling complaints, and increasing team positivity don't address conflict in themselves. The "magic" happens when you see the skills and mind-sets you've imparted take hold in the team's actions.

You know you've had the intended impact when a vision statement on the wall prompts a conversation that allows the team to see that their ongoing conflict is a small part of what they are together. Or when a team member catches herself moving toward destructive conflict and apologizes to the team as she chooses a better course. Or when team members address complaints with one another out loud and in the moment. That's the real magic.

A Refresher

Let's lock in the ideas from this chapter:

- Resolving their conflict is not your job. Helping them see it and choose what to do about it is.
- Pay close attention to the team when in conflict, and consciously decide whether to intervene.
- Use the five levels of conflict to more objectively see what's going on. When ready, reveal the five levels so the team can use them, too.
- Given that much of the conflict that arises on agile teams is unresolvable, offer the team ways to live with it.

Additional Resources

Gottman, J., and N. Silver. 2004. *The Seven Principles for Making Marriage Work.* New York: Three Rivers Press. It turns out that the research, advice, and tools for making marriage work also work for many other types of relationships, including teams. As a side benefit, you may also improve your marriage.

Leas, S. 1998. *Discover Your Conflict Management Style.* Herndon, VA: Alban Institute. This short workbook presents various conflict responses and uses a quiz to help you discover your default conflict response.

References

Beck at al. 2001. Manifesto for Agile Software Development. www.agilemanifesto.org.

———. 2001. Principles Behind the Agile Manifesto. www.agilemanifesto.org/principles.html.

Center for Right Relationship. 2008. Organization & Relationship Systems Coaching core curriculum. Benicia, CA: Center for Right Relationship.

Corrigan, C. 2006. The Tao of Holding Space. www.archive.org/details/TheTaoOfHoldingSpace.

Hackman, J. R. 2002. *Leading Teams: Setting the Stage for Great Performances.* Boston: Harvard Business School.

Keip, M. 2006. Handout from conflict class conducted at First Unitarian Universalist Church of Richmond, Virginia, in 2007 (adapted from Leas 1998).

————. 2006. Adapted from "carrying complaints" intervention path handout from conflict class conducted at First Unitarian Universalist Church of Richmond, Virginia, in 2007.

————. 1997. Handout showing the "analyze and respond" steps of conflict resolution from conflict class conducted at First Unitarian Universalist Church of Richmond, Virginia, in 2007.

Leas, S. 1985. *Moving Your Church Through Conflict.* Herndon, VA: Alban Institute.

————. 1998. *Discover Your Conflict Management Style.* Herndon, VA: Alban Institute.

Lencioni, P. 2002. *The Five Dysfunctions of a Team: A Leadership Fable.* San Francisco: Jossey-Bass.

Losada, M., and E. Heaphy. 2004. The Role of Positivity and Connectivity in the Performance of Business Teams: A Nonlinear Dynamics Model. *American Behavioral Scientist* 47 (6): 740–765.

Schwaber, K., and M. Beedle. 2001. *Agile Software Development with Scrum.* Upper Saddle River, NJ: Prentice Hall.

Tabaka, J. 2006. *Collaboration Explained: Facilitation Skills for Software Project Leaders.* Boston: Addison-Wesley.

Gottman, J. 1994. *What Predicts Divorce: The Relationship Between Marital Processes and Marital Outcomes.* London: Lawrence Erlbaum.

Gottman, J. 1999. *The Marriage Clinic: A Scientifically Based Marital Therapy.* New York: WW Norton.

Whitworth, L., K. Kimsey-House, H. Kimsey-House, and P. Sandahl. 2007. *Co-Active Coaching: New Skills for Coaching People Toward Success in Work and Life, Second Edition.* Mountain View, CA: Davies-Black.

Chapter 10

Coach as Collaboration Conductor

In high school, I was in a garage band. I had forgotten this until someone reminded me of it at my high-school reunion. He said, "Were we really as bad as I think we were?" And I said, "Uh-huh. We were pretty bad." We were dedicated, though. We practiced at a friend's house day in and day out, but we never hit our stride. Given the squeaks, wrong chords, and out-of-tune notes coming from our respective instruments, we didn't have even a slim chance of sounding like a real rock band, even though we convinced ourselves that we rocked.

Years later, I see clearly why we never hit the big time. We were all new to playing together, and each of us was still focused on learning how to make our instruments sound like they were supposed to sound, each person's attention completely absorbed by controlling their own instrument. No attention could be spared to put all those sounds together to make a real band. Even though we practiced hard, we remained a handful of teenagers playing individual instruments side by side. It was still a great time.

Although I haven't been in a band for many years, I love music, and I especially enjoy the symphony. The music delights my senses, true, but I go to the

> **By the time you finish this chapter, you will be able to answer these questions:**
>
> - What is the difference between cooperation and collaboration? Why does it matter?
> - How do I help each team member learn to cooperate and collaborate? How do I build the team's collaboration muscle?
> - Why do the team's ideas feel uninspiring, and what can I do about that?
> - What practical exercises help the team collaborate?

symphony to watch the conductor. I sit there mesmerized as the conductor waves his baton in the air, cueing the oboes, quieting the violins, and making a stern face that tells the French horns to come in strong. Accomplished musicians in their own right, each person in the symphony knows how to make their own instrument sing, and together they create music that stirs the soul. Yet they all submit to the conductor's baton, giving the conductor final say. Conductors are amazing.

But conductors are nothing compared to the Shanghai Quartet. I've heard them only once, but that experience has stuck with me for years. When my husband and I arrived at the hall to hear the Shanghai Quartet, I noticed that the stage was bare save for four chairs set up in a shallow semicircle. Before long, the musicians and their instruments took the stage. They sat down and, a few seconds later, started to play. I was so astounded that I must have jumped in my seat or made some kind of startled sound, because my husband looked at me. When I looked back at him, I noticed the astonished look on his face, too. His look told me that I had not imagined what just happened. These four guys sat down, and with no one looking at anyone, no one counting down, no one doing even as much as taking in a big breath, they just started to play.

When they played, each hit their instrument at exactly the same moment, filling the hall with lush sound, big enough to startle. As they played, they managed the music themselves, shifting and correcting as the piece went on. No conductor needed. Although the music was glorious, I couldn't wait for each piece to end so that I could watch them start the next one.

Each time, the same thing happened. That is, nothing happened, and then, all of a sudden music burst forth from all four instruments at once in perfect timing with one another but with no one leading or even giving so much as a tiny nod to kick it off.

I had never experienced anything like this before. Like so many things do, it had me reflecting on the nature of teams. A team that could work together as seamlessly as the Shanghai Quartet would be unstoppable. I ruminated, "What would it take for a team to develop abilities like this?"

This chapter takes you through the steps needed to bring collaboration to your teams. Maybe they sound like the high-school garage band now, each person asserting themselves in conversations that feel jerky and out of rhythm. Maybe, individually, they are already accomplished collaborators and find themselves in a symphony conducted by you or an alpha team member. In both cases, more and better ways of working lie beyond.

Collaboration or Cooperation?

Before bringing collaboration skills to your team, make this choice with them: Will cooperation serve us, or do we need collaboration to achieve our goals? Because some problems teams face are best solved through collaboration and others through cooperation, teams need to find the right balance that will work for them. Collaboration yields that old adage: The whole is *greater than* the sum of the individual parts. Cooperation yields the sum of the parts. Let's explore these in greater detail so that you'll have a framework that helps you determine which of these approaches fits the team's situation.

If the work the team has been charged with does not require innovation and they are content to use agile practices mechanically, you may choose to stop at cooperation. There's no shame in this. Cooperation features the smooth flow of work-in-progress from one team member to another and between the team and the wider organization. When cooperating, the team moves itself toward their shared commitment through daily fine-grain coordination of everyone's efforts. People talk with one another defenselessly and build understanding of the whole and of their respective parts as they achieve real results regularly.

Getting good at cooperation and choosing to leave collaboration to the side may be the right direction if the team you coach does not need to be innovative, specifically if the problem at hand doesn't call for imaginative or break-through thinking. Cooperation, easier to get working and far less emotionally and time intensive, comes to us "for free." It's built into the way agile works.

Cooperation heralds a huge step forward, especially compared to the way most organizations have worked in the pre-agile era. With cooperation, at least people aren't interacting with one another through long e-mail trails designed more to place blame than to solve the issue at hand. At least they jointly create their own plan and excitedly pursue it, rather than plodding through the execution of a task assigned to them by someone else. At least they face issues and resolve them in the moment, rather than scheduling meetings a week from now to talk about something that needs to be addressed today. Animated inter-action, two-way conversation, real understanding, and progress are all hallmarks of cooperation.

Cooperation feels so good and works so well that you can be duped into thinking that cooperation *is* collaboration. It's so much better than what I had previously experienced that I was fooled by it until I learned the difference. Collaboration needs cooperation as its base, but it adds the essential ingredient for yielding innovative, breakthrough, astonishing results: emergence.

A prolific agile blogger and author of a forthcoming book on agile management, Jurgen Appelo, offers this definition of emergence (2009):

> When a property of a system cannot be traced back to any of the individual parts in the system, it is called an emergent property. Your personality is an emergent property of your brain. It cannot be traced back to individual neurons.
>
> —Jurgen Appelo

So, too, with collaboration. The ideas that emerge don't come with a straight-path way to trace back to their origins. When collaborating, team members build on top of one another's ideas, each person giving away their cherished vision of what it "should be" so that something better, something that no one of them could have imagined alone, emerges from the ash of their burned and forgotten personal visions. This creates an environment of courageous sharing and vulnerability, an environment where the whole truly can be greater than the sum of its parts. The agile coach sets the tone that allows this environment to grow.

From Cooperation to Collaboration

To start moving toward collaboration, first build cooperation.

Perhaps you notice that the team sounds like a high-school garage band right now. Their conversations seem stilted and lifeless or seem like a cacophony of competing sounds featuring everyone talking and no one listening. Remember that at this stage, it takes every bit of one's attention to learn how to play one's own "instrument," so don't expect that team members will be able to think much about the overall sound just yet. In the high-school garage band situation, your job as agile coach focuses on helping each person learn the skills needed to cooperate.

Once team members have started grooving with basic cooperation skills and have gotten control of their own instrument, they have the chance to sound like a symphony. So, take up the conductor's baton. As the team converses, cue in the quiet people, nullify the advantage of the loud people, and encourage everyone to come in strong. At this stage, you act as the glue that holds their conversation together, encouraging them to build upon what was just said to go beyond the same old ideas. As their conductor, you notice some great sounds coming out of the team symphony, and you smile as you realize the team can now collaborate.

You know, though, that having a conductor limits how far they can go, so you set your sights on helping the team become a conductor-less string quartet.

No one has to cue them to start; they are practiced and know how. No one has to bring out the softer sound or quiet the overbearing sound; they manage those themselves. No one has to remind them to build upon one another's ideas and allow the conversation to flow like a gorgeous piece of music; doing so has simply become normal for them.

Going from a high-school garage band to a symphony to a string quartet can seem like quite a tall order. Take it one step at a time. Start with the individual instruments, and get those working well. In our context, this means building individual collaborators.

Build Individual Collaborators

Being able to collaborate (and cooperate) is not a talent doled out to a precious few at birth. Both arise from learning a set of skills, all of which can be practiced until they become second-nature. In fact, we learned most of what we need to know long ago. Take yourself back to the lessons of your early childhood: Play nice. Share. Say you're sorry when you hurt someone, even if you didn't mean to.

Much of what you do as a coach reawakens this long-ago learning and helps people cast it in a context that benefits them now, in their adult lives. Perhaps you use the adult-speak, "Take responsibility for your emotional wake" rather than "Say you're sorry when you hurt someone." It's the same rule, cast into adult language.

Bring these skills to team members, and encourage them to practice until the skills become powerfully ingrained. As the guardian of quality and performance, you sit in the perfect place from which to teach (or reawaken) these essential skills.

Stay at the individual level to first focus on team members because collaborators are necessary for collaboration, and collaborators must cooperate first. Offer four things to help them become solid cooperators and collaborators: Teach them cooperation skills, expect them to come prepared, encourage their ego, and establish the collaboration zone.

Teach Them Cooperation Skills

To collaborate, each person must start from a place of personal responsibility to learn how to cooperate and contribute to the team. What you need to convey to them "is a specific set of attitudes and behaviors that make 'teamwork' an individual skill, not some elusive outcome of group dynamics available only by the luck of the draw" (Avery 2001).

The book *Teamwork Is an Individual Skill* teaches team members how to adopt the key behaviors and attitudes one needs to be able to cooperate well with others. Among these are the following (Avery 2001):

- Agreeing to "response-ability," which means choosing to respond intentionally to whatever happens in life rather than denying or blaming

- Noticing when your silence has conveyed implicit consent because real "team players" never "go along"

- Using your veto power while also accepting responsibility for moving the group toward an acceptable solution

- Reflecting on your actions to recognize the interplay of your conscious and unconscious intentions

- Telling your truth with compassion instead of delivering "constructive" criticism

These and other lessons are made actionable in Avery's book through behaviors to try (some simple, some hard) along with change-inducing personal reflections. Both help team members develop their repertoire of cooperation skills. Introduce these as you coach team members one on one and as you plan retrospectives that address the team's overall ability to cooperate.

Expect Them to Come Prepared

Having laid the cooperation foundation, we now step into the skills and mindsets of collaboration. Here's the first concept to teach: Collaboration starts inside the heart and mind of each person on the team. Since collaboration starts inside each person, every team member has a professional obligation to arrive at work ready to collaborate. A maxim in the theater tells us this: *On time is already late* (Devin 2009). That is, if we arrive at work on time with our bodies only, having not groomed our minds to collaborate, we are simply late. Unprepared.

Arriving fully "on time" means that team members have done what's necessary to clear from their minds everything but that which is required and relevant for the day's work. This requires each person to discover what helps them clear the clutter and get into the day. In a collaboration seminar I conducted, 30 participants came up with more than 75 ideas for doing just this in less than five minutes. Among them were listen to classical music, make sounds for no particular purpose, look at art, walk the dog, eat breakfast, do nonessential reading, count steps on the way up the stairs, drink coffee and listen to heavy metal, look myself in the eyes in the mirror, and sit on a rock in the woods. None of these is radical or hard to do. All of them are personal and have been done before by the people who listed them (so they know how to do them). All of them bring one's attention inward to quiet one's mind and get ready to be involved with others.

What would the stand-up be like if the team members were on time with more than their bodies? If they arrived on time, mind and body, and ready for the day's work ahead, what would be the difference in their conversations? Do you think they would have more and better ideas? Try it and see.

Expect team members to come prepared for the collaborative day ahead and help them brainstorm ways to get there; then hold them to doing so. When they seem scattered or inattentive, simply ask, "Do you need to take a couple minutes to prepare for the day ahead?"

Encourage Their Ego

To be a good collaborator, one must *not* subordinate one's individuality. Coming up with ideas and dreams that lead to collaboration and innovation requires that team members assert their individuality. The authors of *Artful Making: What Managers Need to Know About How Artists Work* say it this way:

> Artful making [collaboration] requires building up individual ego in group members, while tearing down vanity. The first step is to learn and internalize the distinction, to re-conceive ego and vanity in new terms. Vanity is that inner need to appear before others as we appear to ourselves, or as we'd like to appear to ourselves. Vanity makes you worry about another's opinion of your haircut. Ego, on the other hand, is that sense we have of being a distinct creature in the world, a creature of value. Your ego is who you are, your sense of yourself as an individual, and if it's strong enough, you can live with anyone's opinion of your haircut (Austin and Devin 2003).

Following these definitions, encourage team members to keep their sense of self-value solid while subordinating the need for social approval. As team members work together, support their egos and help them keep them strong while encouraging them to leave their vanity at home. And help them tell the difference between the two.

Establish the Collaboration Zone

In their book *Radical Collaboration*, the authors introduce the Green Zone and the Red Zone, an individual's choice to adopt an attitude that will "either support collaboration or undermine it" (Tamm and Luyet 2004). As you read the attitudes of the Green Zone and the Red Zone in Table 10.1, consider how much the people on your teams display them.

TABLE 10.1 The Green Zone and the Red Zone: a personal choice to support collaboration or undermine it*

A person in the Green Zone...	A person in the Red Zone...
Takes responsibility for the circumstances of his or her life	Blames others for the circumstances of his or her life
Seeks to respond nondefensively	Feels threatened or wronged
Is not easily threatened psychologically	Responds defensively
Attempts to build mutual success	Triggers defensiveness in others
Seeks solutions rather than blame	Is rigid, reactive, and righteous
Uses persuasion rather than force	Uses shame, blame, and accusations
Can be firm, but not rigid, about his or her interests	Is unaware of the climate of antagonism he or she creates
Thinks both short term and long term	Has low awareness of blind spots
Is interested in other points of view	Does not seek or value feedback
Welcomes feedback	Sees others as the problem or enemy
Sees conflict as a natural part of the human condition	Sees conflict as a battle and seeks to win at any cost
Talks calmly and directly about difficult issues	Does not let go or forgive
Accepts responsibility for consequences of his or her actions	Communicates high levels of disapproval and contempt
Continuously seeks deeper levels of understanding	Focuses on short-term advantage and gain
Communicates a caring attitude	Feels victimized by different points of view
Seeks excellence rather than victory	Is black/white, right/wrong in thinking
Listens well	Does not listen effectively

* From *Radical Collaboration* by James W. Tamm and Ronald Luyet. Copyright 2004 by James W. Tamm. Reprinted by permission of HarperCollins Publishers.

Before you start indicting the team members you coach for choosing attitudes that undermine collaboration, read the Green Zone and Red Zone characteristics again. This time, carefully consider which of these applies to you. How much do you exude the Green Zone attitudes? Would others say these ways of being are true about you? Can people tell just by noticing how you work? When do the attitudes of the Red Zone grab you and take hold? How do they affect your ability to collaborate with teams? Stop and go back. Read them again, this time, reflecting on yourself.

Once you've come back from your personal reflection, know this: You need not be perfect and live in the Green Zone always. You are human, too, and your shortcomings are just as instructive to teams as your perfections. However, set the example for consciously striving to live in the Green Zone and recovering when you fall into the traps of the Red Zone. Choosing the Green Zone for yourself powerfully states your intention to create an environment where people consciously choose attitudes that allow collaboration to occur.

SEE ALSO	To teach the team to stay in the Green Zone, you must first do it yourself. This means facing your own shortcomings and working on them. Chapter 3, "Master Yourself," offers ideas for doing just this and for arriving at work mentally prepared to coach teams.

To set a collaboration vibe, first live in the Green Zone personally. Then, simply state your intention to coach the team to stay in the Green Zone. To do this, coach to create an environment that enhances Green Zone attitudes and deflates Red Zone attitudes. Given this, take up the position that the Green Zone is simply normal and expected. It will be upheld through your coaching. Conversely, the Red Zone signals a state to recover from, so let them know that you will coach them to notice when they've entered the Red Zone so that they can choose to get back into the collaborative Green Zone.

Once team members become open to collaborate with one another, ideas start to flow. When they are in the flow and moving along well, expect to hear a surplus of ideas, many more than they will actually use and some that are so far-fetched that they would never be used as is. All of these ideas are necessary fodder for the true innovation that arises.

In my experience, many teams stumble here. Although they come up with more ideas than before, they don't often hit the goal of having a surplus, and the ideas themselves may still strike you (and users of their products) as somewhat uninspiring. When you see this, recognize that you are up against the effects of years of a creativity drought brought about by people's fast-moving, narrow-thinking school and work lives.

Surplus Ideas Required

When we unleash teams and tell them "It's OK to collaborate now—let's hear all those great ideas," it's no wonder the ideas dry up. Needing a surplus of ideas necessitates a creative environment and a willingness to explore possibilities with openness and curiosity. How much openness and curiosity do you notice in the average team member around you?

Marketing maven and mega-creative thinker Seth Godin has this insight to offer:

> It's easy to underestimate how difficult it is for someone to become curious. For seven, ten, or even fifteen years of school, you are required to not be curious. Over and over and over again, the curious are punished. I don't think it's a matter of saying a magic word; boom and then suddenly something happens and you're curious. It's more about a five- or ten- or fifteen-year process where you start finding your voice, and finally you begin to realize that the safest thing you can do feels risky and the riskiest thing you can do is play it safe. Once recognized, the quiet yet persistent voice of curiosity doesn't go away. Ever. And perhaps it's such curiosity that will lead us to distinguish our own greatness from the mediocrity that stares us in the face (Godin 2009).

Further, team members will not come up with the breakthrough ideas, even ones pouring forth from unbridled curiosity, when under constant pressure to produce or when moving from task to task, from sprint to sprint, or from release to release without stopping to breathe. Consider this:

> The challenges in organizations start with the frenetic pace many people feel compelled to maintain. Often…teams simply don't know how to stop, nor do they know how to integrate suspension into normal ways of working together. But breakthroughs come when people take the time to stop and examine their assumptions (Senge et al. 2004).

If a lack of curiosity or creativity exists, bring it to the team members' attention and see what ideas they have for getting their creative juices flowing. Ask them to practice a sense of curiosity, seeing even common things anew. Catch them when they show curiosity and comment on the quality of the thoughts that pour forth when curiosity reigns. To help this along, introduce them to the energizing world of serious play, covered in more depth later in this chapter.

Regarding the frenetic pace many people maintain, agile has you covered. The sprint review and retrospective build in the pause so crucial for breakthroughs to break through.

SEE ALSO	The purposes of the sprint review and retrospective are discussed in Chapter 6, "Coach as Facilitator." Measure the effectiveness of these events by asking yourself whether their purposes were met and whether the team got the pause they needed.

In this pause, especially in the retrospective, ask the team members to suspend their habitual ways of thinking. Design activities that help them look back at the way they worked together from different angles so that they can look at the past sprint anew and discover their unrecognized assumptions. Often, assumptions are thought to be fact until one hears an alternate viewpoint and then realizes their fact is only one of many ways to view the previous sprint. Strive to bring out different angles so that people can excavate their assumptions. With the assumptions laid bare, it becomes possible to see new ways of working, maybe even breakthrough ideas for creating products that make a difference.

Through this work, you help each person see how they can best collaborate with the whole team, and pretty soon, the team becomes ready for you to help them build their collaboration muscle.

Build the Team's Collaboration Muscle

A team's collaboration muscle allows them to engage in the messy and joyful work of collaborating. To create a strong muscle, they need exercise. And to make sure they're exercising safely and that they're pushing themselves just the right amount (not too much and not too little), they need a coach. That's you.

While you are building the team's collaboration muscle, your coaching takes on the character of a symphony conductor. The team needs you to help them get collaboration going, but they don't need you to be their conductor forever. Take care to put down the conductor's baton as soon as they start to manage collaboration conversations on their own.

At the beginning, though, take up the position of conductor strongly as you work at the whole team level. Help them start with team-level cooperation and then move to these collaboration behaviors:

- Speak the unspeakable.
- Build up instead of breaking down.
- Hear all voices.
- Nurture collaboration intimacy.
- Gain faith in emergence.
- Get unstuck.
- Play (seriously) together.

Through it all, as you help them cooperate and adopt collaboration behaviors, continue to be their mirror, reflecting to them their behaviors, both the ones that encourage collaboration and the ones that stifle it.

Start with Team-Level Cooperation

Right from the start, help the team discover what they need to know about each other to achieve cooperation. To do this, they must know what each person brings to the team: their skills, talents, desires, and work preferences. They must know one another as human beings first and workmates second. This creates the base from which they self-organize to get the work done.

> **SEE ALSO** You can find learning activities that get teams to know one another's skills, talents, desires, and work preferences in Chapter 7, "Coach as Teacher."

In getting the work done, team members must cooperate with one another because they share the short list of goals they committed to deliver together. Having shared goals puts them "in each other's business," and we want them to be interdependent in this manner. Being interdependent means that they must converse about the best ways to meet their shared goals and produce something that makes them proud. When they do this, good ideas emerge.

As they begin to cooperate, publically encourage team members to build cross-functional behavior that calls each one to step out of their corporate role or title. If you notice that a technical writer has bandwidth available, for example, yet there is no technical writing to be done today, verbally encourage the technical writer to take on whatever task needs to be done, perhaps a task to define business rules, for example.

Even if it's outside her skills and talents, still ask, "How about taking this business rules task or another one that needs to get done?" Let the conversation about why she can or cannot do this particular task happen in the open, where other team members can take part in the conversation. Maybe, together, they find something else she can do. Now more work will get done, and everyone has seen a positive example of working outside one's role.

Clearly, people are not interchangeable parts, and the cross-functional abilities of each team vary according to the current skills and talents present on the team, as well as their emerging skills and talents. If this conversation nudges the team in the direction of becoming more cross-functional (where possible), it has been successful. We're not trying to make database administrators design graphics for a billboard if they don't have that skill and don't want to attain that skill. We are pushing the edges of people's perceptions of themselves so that they can stretch beyond their role and title restrictions as they desire and as the team needs them to do so. Being needed is a strong motivator.

TRY THIS

To encourage cooperation as a basis for collaboration, teach the team to treat their daily interactions as a game called tit-for-tat. It's played in pairs: Both team members start out cooperating. From then on, each matches what the other person does. If one cooperates, then the other keeps cooperating. If one turns uncooperative, then the other matches that uncooperative behavior, giving the "defector" an immediate reflection of their defection in the relationship. If the "defector" doesn't get the behavior hint, then the other team member tells them they can have it be one of two ways: cooperative or uncooperative. It's their choice (Avery 2001).

Tit-for-tat catches uncooperative behavior the first time it happens. The game aspect provides the convenient excuse many team members need to "call each other out" because games are exploratory, are fun, and keep things light. After a while, they won't need the game as a crutch because cooperation will have become the norm.

Maybe this open conversation has led some team members to realize that building skills beyond their historical discipline can be a distinct advantage. Maybe some conclude that the team's ability to deliver results will be restricted by lack of multidisciplinary skills on the team. Using these revelations as a sign they are ready for more, perhaps you suggest they add cross-training user stories to the product backlog or lobby their managers for different training opportunities. Whatever happens, having simply entertained the conversation about cross-functional work in the open, you have stated your position that working cross-functionally and interdependently makes good business sense and that they signal a healthy team and mark the beginnings of cooperation.

You can tell the team has started cooperating when you notice these things:

- Their conversations feature rich, high-bandwidth interchange where they—most of the time—create understanding of one another rather than the layers of misunderstanding that happen when messages get passed through people and e-mail over a span of days.

- Team members talk about the hard bits and get into the meat of the work, all without walls of defensiveness going up.

- Products in-process move smoothly from one team member to another as they work on making it good together.

Each of these by themselves leaps a team forward in their ability to produce more and better results together. They signify huge improvements, gifted to us by the basic workings of agile. Inviting and comfortable though this team environment may be, don't let them (or you) linger here too long. If they display these cooperation characteristics, then urge them forward toward collaboration. They have the basis for it now.

Allow Them to Speak the Unspeakable

One of the first collaboration skills to build makes it acceptable for team members to speak out about things that make them feel vulnerable or uncomfortable. There's a sense in most organizations I've worked with that one must never look weak or give even the slightest hint that they could perform better than they are performing now. They must appear to all comers that they are 100% flat-out busy providing 110% effort at all times. What a weighty charade to keep up! Yet, the existence of such taboos gives us agile coaches an easy entry point for allowing team members to speak the unspeakable.

In the stand-up, the first time you notice that someone seems to have unexpected capacity but hasn't mentioned it, teach the whole team to say, "I have bandwidth to give today." Let them know that they should loudly and proudly declare their availability for more work because unexpected capacity is a gift for an agile team—one that we do not want to squander. By giving explicit permission for people to turn a "weakness" (I'm not performing at 110%, and I'm afraid someone will catch me) into an announcement (Hey, I have bandwidth to give today), you have helped them speak the unspeakable.

Here's another situation: You notice some team members seem to be struggling alone for hours on end. Perhaps they're really striding forward purposefully, or perhaps they are sitting there looking purposeful but actually spinning their wheels. This happened on one of my teams. When I offered my observation to the team, some team members "came clean" and said that they had been spending a lot of time feeling frustrated because they just couldn't figure out stuff that should be easy and they were embarrassed to show their "weakness" to the team. After some discussion, the team decided to add a new line to their team norms: No one spends more than 30 minutes struggling with something before asking someone else to join them. This created the explicit permission people needed to ask for help. In fact, the team room became abuzz with renewed vigor and positive energy as people popped their heads up several times a day to say, "Hey, I'm spinning my wheels. I need help." The result? More work done better and with a sense of "being in it together" that had been lacking until that point.

If neither of these situations arise on your team, then dig deeper. Look for the things people are afraid to speak about but that occur all the time. Help them speak these unspeakables. In so doing, you help them give up the charade of "having it all together" all the time. This allows them to be vulnerable to one another, a key ability for building on one another's ideas in true collaboration.

Push Them to Build Up Instead of Breaking Down

When the team converses, notice what happens to each idea voiced. Does it get duly considered by the other team members and used as raw material for the next idea? Or, does it get immediately analyzed, poked through and either shot down or put on a pedestal?

If the team has the habit of greeting each new idea with a "breakdown" approach where they first ask, "What's wrong with this idea?" then ask them to tone down that approach a little. Instead, let another approach, called *re-conceiving*, have some sway:

> Collaborators re-conceive a problem or process in light of each other's contributions, using them as material out of which, in combination with their own ideas, they make new, unpredictable ideas (Austin and Devin 2003).

Pay attention to that last part again. Through re-conceiving, the team makes new, *unpredictable* ideas. We need unpredictable if we're going to get astonishing results, the kind agile enables but doesn't guarantee. To increase the chances of seeing the astonishing, encourage re-conceiving wherein we build up ideas, not break them down.

| SEE ALSO | Set producing astonishing results as your basic expectation of a healthy agile team. See how to do this in Chapter 2, "Expect High Performance." |

To do this, you must coach the team to stay vulnerable to one another and keep speaking the unspeakable. Create safety for them to do so, specifically by "demonstrating tolerance for failure, refraining from punitive exercises of power, and participating in team processes rather than imposing rules" (Austin and Devin 2003). Those "don'ts" sound so counter to the definition of agile coaching that they almost don't merit mention, except that coaches are human, too, and may be prone to using them. If this describes you, stop yourself, and instead focus on helping the team bring out surplus ideas—more than they need.

Agile teams with the greatest chance for generating surplus ideas are comprised of people who are different from one another, who come from different backgrounds, and who have different slants on the ways they think about the world. We need every one of these people engaged in re-conceiving. As such, agile coaches must help the team "produce synergy through the discussion and appreciation of different perspectives, because two types of behavior kill synergy: people saying more than they know, and people saying less than they know" (Avery 2001). So true.

To address the killers of synergy, work hard to ensure that every voice on the team gets heard—that all instruments in the symphony get to play their part in the music unfolding around them.

Make Hearing All Voices the Norm

Just as a symphony conductor draws out the flutes and shushes the trumpets, in team conversations an agile coach draws out the quiet ones and shushes the dominating ones. Do this directly, as in, "I notice Marcel has been trying to get a word in for a few minutes now, and no one has noticed" or "We've heard from a few people; why don't we hear from the rest?" Indirect techniques such as Fist of Five work, too (Tabaka 2006). Fist of Five starts off with a nonverbal "vote" featuring people putting their fingers in the air, one through five, to indicate their level of agreement with a statement just spoken. After the vote, the team explores why people voted as they did, and the conversation gets spread across all team members.

Use Fist of Five at both the product and process levels as the team conducts their collaboration conversations. Think of the product as the results of their conversation and the process as what they do in conversation with one another to yield the product.

> *No one can whistle a symphony. It takes a whole orchestra to play it.*
>
> —*H.E. Luccock*

For example, if the team has been talking about getting celebrities to attend the grand opening of the company's new store and only a few people have contributed to the conversation thus far, you might say, "I'm observing something about your conversation. Let's see what you all think. Let's do Fist of Five on this statement: I am excited about this conversation, and I am freely contributing my ideas with ease. Ready? 1, 2, 3." On "3," people put their hands in the air with one to five fingers showing their level of resonance with the statement. If they feel completely excited about the conversation and are freely contributing their ideas with ease, they put up five fingers. If that statement doesn't ring true for them, they put up one finger. If they're somewhere in the middle, they put up an appropriate number of fingers to signify their level of resonance with the statement. Once they vote, have the team members look around. Invite anyone with one or two fingers in the air to speak and share why the statement does not resonate with them. Then let the conversation go where it will.

SEE ALSO   The Fist of Five consensus technique is also described in Chapter 9, "Coach as Conflict Navigator."

If all team members have three or more fingers in the air, then you might say, "All right, thanks for the check. I must have been misreading you all. Carry on." If you feel certain that someone "voted" higher than they really felt, then follow up with them later one-on-one with the straightforward conversation starter, "I thought for sure you were going to put one or two fingers in the air when I asked if you were excited and freely contributing your ideas, but I might have just been making up a story in my own head. What was happening for you?"

If all team members have been throwing their ideas into the conversation and the dominators are driving toward convergence on a specific idea, perhaps to the detriment of building on others' ideas, you might use the same technique but at the product level this time. You might say, "It seems you are drawing to a conclusion here. So, let's see where we stand. Let's do Fist of Five on this

statement: I fully support the idea of holding a lottery to determine which customers get to take pictures with the celebrities at the grand opening. Ready?
1, 2, 3." On "3," people vote, and you ask them to look around and engage the
people who have one or two fingers in the air. If that conversation peters out
without too many new revelations and you still see the split between the quiet
ones and the dominators, you might follow up with a Fist of Five, this time at
the process level. Something like this, "I see that everyone is really behind this
idea. Let's just do one more Fist of Five, this time on this statement: We have
come to the most innovative idea possible." After the vote, let the conversation
start with the ones and twos and go from there.

Whether you choose to address quiet ones and dominators directly, whether
you use a voting method to get the ball rolling, or whether you do something
else doesn't matter as long as what you offer the team supports openness and
transparency. Keep doing something (anything open and transparent) to call
conversation disequilibrium to their attention until they start doing it themselves. Once they do, they will make hearing all voices the norm.

Although they need the conductor early on, they won't need that assistance
forever. As soon as they start to manage the conversation themselves, step out
of the conductor role. Break their reliance on the conductor's baton so you can
give them permission to create even better symphonic wonders than you could
have imagined.

Nurture Collaboration Intimacy

From his experience with agile teams and his research in group relations, agile
coach Dan Mezick offers this:

> Real collaboration between persons requires at least some
> intellectual and/or social intimacy. The intimate state is reached
> when both parties signal willingness to work in a "zone" or
> "field" of trust, vulnerability, openness, mutual accommoda-
> tion, and respect.... Teams who are intimate have the poten-
> tial to be *cognitively intimate*. In this state, most team members
> understand the cognitive styles of most all other team mem-
> bers and can sense and anticipate how other members perceive
> communications, and new information. Cognitively intimate
> team members can sense and anticipate individual and group-
> level misunderstandings in the perception of new material,
> and quickly intervene to clarify, leading to more rapid under-
> standing at the group level (Mezick 2009).

SEE ALSO Chapter 8, "Coach as Problem Solver," gives you a diagnostic tool based on the BART model of group relations: boundary, authority, role, and task. Use this diagnostic when problems exist on the team but are hard to pin down.

You've probably seen this in action on collaborative teams as they conduct a Vulcan mind meld with one another or (correctly) finish one another's sentences. They also immediately sense when someone has gone "off the track" and openly work to bring that person back into the conversation. Encourage teams to create this kind of intimacy, and don't shy away from the word. *Intimate*…a completely appropriate descriptor for an environment in which people work closely together in a creative endeavor that has wooed them away from fierce individuality.

Model Faith in Emergence

To be of greatest service to teams, an agile coach must become free from personal agendas. In so doing, the coach provides a powerful model the team can follow as they collaborate together. Collaboration works when one gives away one's own ideas to the group and allows that idea to be just a piece of a bigger idea yet to emerge. Relaxing one's agenda this way can be challenging for many who desire their idea be chosen, to "win."

SEE ALSO Letting go of your agenda while holding the team's goals and pursuit of high performance intact is the subject of Chapter 3, "Master Yourself."

Holding fast to "win" creates a negative self-fulfilling prophecy. If a team member clutches their ideas close and refuses to let them meld and merge with others, then the bigger, better idea will be blocked from coming forth. Since no collective idea comes forth, the team member doesn't see emergence in action. "See?" she says, "Collaboration wasn't even worth trying because we didn't get anything better out of it anyway." And so on.

The power and beauty of emergence is so moving when it happens that it becomes something to cherish and believe in. Teams who see emergence occur create a kind of faith that something great will emerge, if only they believe it will happen and share fully and openly in the process of coaxing it forth. Once a team has seen the beauty of collaborative, emergent ideas arising, they are powerfully motivated to relax their personal agendas in deference to the force of the collaborative. Breaking the negative self-fulfilling prophecy has to start somewhere, and that somewhere starts with you.

To help the team let go so that emergence stands a chance, light the way. Let go of your agenda when it doesn't serve the team, and take their lead to go to a new place that holds greater promise. Do this transparently, with words and actions that reinforce your position as an agent of emergence rather than a coach pushing an agenda. When they lose faith, restore it by encouraging them to be open, to share, and watch for the emergence unfolding around them.

Help Them Get Unstuck

Teams that get good at all of the cooperation and collaboration skills we've been exploring can still get stuck. Their conversation seems fine, clipping along nicely, and then, all of a sudden, they're slogging through the La Brea tar pits. Painfully making their way through every utterance, their conversation has become grueling.

Help them get unstuck by offering ways for them to get back in touch with one another so the ideas can flow again. Start by noticing it and revealing it, "Hey, everyone, the conversation feels stilted. Let's do something to shake it up a bit and get back to a creative place. What do you suggest?" One team I coached suggested group exercise. Although exercise was a gracious term for their trek down the stairs to the on-site Starbucks, it worked just fine because it changed their perspective and gave them a breath of fresh air. Along the way, people asked about one another's kids, and laughter would ring in the halls as they shared jokes and marveled at how heavy they had let their conversation get. Invariably, someone would come up with a "crazy" idea that served as the perfect starting point for the next round of collaboration conversations. Thus unstuck, the La Brea tar pits were left far behind.

Improvisation games can also help unstick the tar when it takes hold of the team's conversations. Improvisation (improv) games often feature accepting what your fellow "actors" give you as a gift and using it for the next idea. No matter how strange the thing they say or bring to the game, an improv player gladly takes it and builds on it.

TRY THIS

The next time the team gets stuck, bring up the improv encyclopedia website (http://improvencyclopedia.org/games/index.html), and let the team choose a game to play at random. As long as the game features people building on one another's ideas, it will help them break the stilted conversation and get to a place where collaboration can happen again.

Sometimes the team gets stuck because they have lost touch with one another. Their conversation goes too fast in a manic panic, leaving some team members in the dust. Two activities help with this situation: circle counting and silent mind mapping.

When I see collaboration being trounced by a sense of mania, I suggest that team members form a circle and count. This exercise, taken from the theater, helps people get back in touch with one another. Everyone stands in a circle, closes their eyes, and starts to count up from one. Here's the deal: People speak the next number randomly, and they don't use a speaking order or pattern to "game" the game. When more than one person speaks at once, they have to start over at one. The challenge is to see how far they can count, as a group, without talking at once and having to start over. To do this, they must pay attention to one another, and each person must get in touch with the whole group so they can feel when it's their turn to say the next number. Teams find this amazingly difficult at first but over time get better at it. More than that, they crave the break it gives them and call for it when they get too far ahead of themselves in collaboration conversations.

Mind mapping also helps teams get back in touch with one another when they've lost the coherence of their collaboration. It works simply. All team members take a marker, and they all start to draw their ideas in mind-map fashion on a big chart or whiteboard silently. That's the trick—they do it silently. When they accept this seemingly constricting rule, they find that they can get many more ideas out and that they have to pay attention to others' ideas as they get added to the mind map. Everyone should be drawing on the mind map simultaneously, with no leader. After a short while, they will likely find that they are back in touch with one another and ready to keep mind mapping or take the ideas into conversation again.

All of these techniques introduce "play" in the workplace, an essential element for achieving breakthrough thinking.

Teach Them to Seriously Play

I'm serious. Games yield collaborative results that everyone can support. This first became clear to me when I taught teams to play Planning Poker to estimate the relative size of items in the product backlog. At first, we were focused only on the product of Planning Poker, the size estimates, and teams were able to create these with ease and confidence. What we noticed was that the focused conversations that happen in the act of playing Planning Poker created a rich shared understanding of the work to come. This discovery was soon recognized as a significant benefit of playing the game. From then on, the teams ensured they had fully received both benefits. They asked themselves these questions: Can we all support the size estimate? Can we all adequately describe the purpose and general approach for the item just sized?

Planning Poker is just one serious game agile teams play. It's so popular that it may be your team's first introduction to using games to get real work done, but other serious games are coming your way.

Forrester Research has done the due diligence. The result? Forrester takes serious games seriously. In the fall of 2008, Forrester released its research, and the titles of the published findings sum it up: "It's Time to Take Games Seriously" and "Serious Games Uncover Serious Requirements." The analysis concludes that games in the workplace not only yield serious results but also overcome many of the shortcomings inherent in meeting-style conversations (Keitt and Jackson 2008; Keitt and Grant 2008).

> Serious games deserve serious attention. They can circumvent many of the problems with product requirements, including collecting sufficient information across customers, partners, and internal stakeholders to make product decisions. Not only are the games relatively lightweight exercises, but they also use a lighter touch to resolve many debates over product decisions (Keitt and Grant 2008).

Forrester goes on to describe how two industry giants, Colgate-Palmolive and VeriSign, use serious games to generate a surplus of ideas and then pare those ideas down to the ones customers will buy (Keitt and Grant 2008).

One of the games they researched was the online version of the Buy A Feature game, one of a dozen Innovation Games used to tap into what customers really want and will pay for. Buy A Feature and other Innovation Games are tools product owners can use to better perform their role well, specifically the part that calls for them to craft a product vision and direction that hits the mark. Make sure the product owners you coach know about them.

To enhance collaboration on agile teams, agile coaches can also use Innovation Games for a variety of agile team events. Agile coach Mike Griffiths uses three different Innovation Games when he facilitates sprint and release planning sessions. The games, in succession, create a shared vision of what the sprint or release will achieve and then backtracks from that vision to fill in the details and consider the forces "putting wind in our sails" or "weighing us down" (Griffiths 2007).

I use Innovation Games when I teach agile courses. I find the game Speed Boat especially effective in helping tease out all the reasons why people believe agile won't work in their company. This gets depressing fast because this game typically turns up long-standing organizational dysfunctions that seem to have no solutions, so we don't stay here long. Instead, we move to more fertile ground, into another game where each person creates a Product Box that advertises the benefits of a healthy agile person, team, or organization. When people create the product box, they tap into their deep beliefs about what agile can do for them and their world. In the best cases, the resulting vision uncovers something aspirational and resonant in the student's perspective of agile. Even in the most ordinary cases, though, the vision shines through as personal and relevant. Through this vision, students can all of a sudden see useful ways to address the plethora of reasons why agile "won't" work. They see ways that it will, can, and should work, and they perceive new angles to convince others to make it so.

Games, by their very nature, enhance collaboration and help people step fully into their work to offer their best ideas, some of which surprise even them when they just "come out" in the course of playing a game. To help your teams collaborate, get serious about games.

Call It Until They Can

While the team works with these collaboration skills and practices again and again, they need you to "call it" (Avery 2001) when they slip into their old, familiar patterns. When you see something that dampens collaboration, "call it" in a way that invites them to do the same. To do this, "call it" in the open and keep it light. You're not punishing anyone; you're just saying, "Hey, I see something here. Do you?"

Reveal the Heart of Collaboration

Once the team has acquired the skills of collaboration, they are ready to go from being a wonderful symphony, conducted by you, to an amazing conductor-less string quartet. They will need to deepen all the collaborative skills you have taught them until they become so "in tune" with one another that they flow with the collaboration rather than concentrating on the skill of collaborating. Arnold Steinhardt, first violin of the Guarneri Quartet, a string quartet revered for their conductor-less playing, tells us what it means for his quartet to be "in tune" with one another:

> In the heat of performance, we send Morse code out in four directions—ensemble signals, significant glances, even smiles or lifted eyebrows as something goes especially well or perhaps not well at all. Michael rolls his eyes at me because David has not done the planned bowing, John and Michael lock glances as they play an inner-voice passage, second violin and viola in unison, or I look over my music stand at David, intent on following him as he deals with a difficult cello solo, his chin jutting forward with the effort. These visual exchanges are, like spices in a fine dish, necessary and energizing ingredients in our performances (Steinhardt 1998).

What will be your team's "necessary and energizing ingredients" in their pursuit of innovation together? Only they can discover them. To help them do so, first stop helping them. Tell them it's time to go conductor-less, and let them know that you are putting down the conductor's baton. You won't be bringing out the quiet voices, you won't be calling for an improv game, and you won't be challenging them to build on each other's ideas. They will do all these things, and more, themselves. You can still be there in case an emergency conductor moment arises, but for the most part, let them know that you look forward to the sounds and abilities of an accomplished string quartet.

Once the team becomes proficient collaborators, reveal the heart of collaboration to them. We've already explored the first of these collaboration maxims in this chapter: On time is already late. Present the rest of these to the team, and see what they further reveal to them about the heart of collaboration:

- Collaboration is not the only way, but it's the most direct way if you need innovation.

- Collaboration happens in present time; it exists only while you are doing it.

- To collaborate, you must know what you and your fellow collaborators bring to the party.

- To be full of love and enthusiasm for your work is a prerequisite for collaboration, a professional obligation; to be full of love and enthusiasm is a choice you make and a skill you learn and practice.

- If you have a problem and to solve it you need someone else to change, you don't understand your problem yet (Devin 2009).

A Refresher

Let's lock in the ideas from this chapter:

- Going from high-school garage band to symphony to string quartet takes practice. Give the team room to do so (and to produce some wrong notes along the way).

- Make a conscious decision with the team about whether they need collaboration to get their work done. If not, stick with cooperation and focus on getting that working well.

- Focus on individuals first when you start to build cooperation and, if needed, collaboration.

- For teams in collaboration conversations, intervene to offer a new skill or to help them practice.

- "Call it" when teams slide back into noncollaborative behaviors.

- As soon as possible, step out of the center, and let the team collaborate on their own.

- To an accomplished team of collaborators, reveal the heart of collaboration, and encourage them to discover their meaning behind each collaboration maxim.

Additional Resources

Austin, R., and L. Devin. 2003. *Artful Making: What Managers Need to Know About How Artists Work*. Upper Saddle River, NJ: Prentice Hall. The heart of the collaborative, artful mind-set lives in this book.

Avery, C., with M. Aaron Walker and E. O'Toole Murphy. 2001. *Teamwork is an Individual Skill: Getting Your Work Done When Sharing Responsibility*. San Francisco: Berrett-Kohler. Not only for helping individual team members create their collaboration ability, this book also includes many "team challenges" that can easily be adapted as eye-opening retrospective activities.

Tabaka, J. 2006. *Collaboration Explained: Facilitation Skills for Software Project Leaders*. Boston: Addison-Wesley. My copy of this book has notes in the margin, coffee stains, dog-eared pages, and scrap pieces of paper sticking out everywhere. That's how much I use it.

Tamm, J., and R. Luyet. 2004. *Radical Collaboration: Five Essential Skills to Overcome Defensiveness and Build Successful Relationships.* New York: HarperCollins. Beyond the Green Zone and the Red Zone, this book offers dozens of useful techniques to draw on when building a team's collaboration abilities.

Steinhardt, A. 1998. *Indivisible by Four: A String Quartet in Pursuit of Harmony.* New York: Farrar, Strauss and Giroux. This engaging memoir of the Guarneri String Quartet reveals the inner workings of a string quartet, specifically the innovative and emergent nature of practice and performance. In fall 2009, the Guarneri Quartet announced their retirement after continuously playing together for 45 years. We agile coaches have much to learn from their example.

References

Appelo, J. 2009. Self-Organization vs. Emergence. www.noop.nl/2009/10/self-organization-vs-emergence.html.

Austin, R., and L Devin. 2003. *Artful Making: What Managers Need to Know About How Artists Work.* Upper Saddle River, NJ: Prentice Hall.

Avery, C., with M. Aaron Walker and E. O'Toole Murphy. 2001. *Teamwork is an Individual Skill: Getting Your Work Done When Sharing Responsibility.* San Francisco: Berrett-Kohler.

Devin, L. 2009. Personal conversation during a collaboration session in which Lee Devin and Lyssa Adkins designed the Build Your Team's Collaboration Muscle seminar. Richmond, VA.

Godin, S. 2008. *Tribes: We Need You to Lead Us.* New York: Portfolio Hardcover.

Griffiths, M. 2007. Release and Iteration Planning with Innovation Games. Leading Answers blog. http://leadinganswers.typepad.com/leading_answers/2007/03/release_and_ite.html

Keitt, T. J., and T. Grant. 2008. *Serious Games Uncover Serious Requirements.* Cambridge, MA: Forrester Research.

———, and P. Jackson. 2008. *It's Time to Take Games Seriously.* Cambridge, MA: Forrester Research.

Mezick, D. 2009. Collaborative Intimacy: From Good to Great Collaboration. www.newtechusa.com/resources/CollaborativeIntimacy.pdf.

Senge, P., C. O Scharmer, J. Jaworski, and B. S. Flowers. 2004. *Presence: An Exploration of Profound Change in People, Organizations, and Society*. New York: Currency Doubleday.

Steinhardt, A. 1998. *Indivisible by Four: A String Quartet in Pursuit of Harmony*. New York: Farrar, Strauss and Giroux.

Tabaka, J. 2006. *Collaboration Explained: Facilitation Skills for Software Project Leaders*. Boston: Addison-Wesley.

Tamm, J., and R. Luyet. 2004. *Radical Collaboration: Five Essential Skills to Overcome Defensiveness and Build Successful Relationships*. New York: Harper-Collins.

PART III

Getting More for Yourself

Chapter 11

Agile Coach Failure, Recovery, and Success Modes

I know so much about the many ways agile coaches fail because I have failed by falling into the trap of every one of them presented in this chapter. I know a lot about agile coach success factors, too, because I have picked them up from watching others coach successfully, and I have asked those same coaches to tell me what I do that helps teams outperform even their wildest imaginings. (I often can't see that myself.) Over time, I have categorized common failures and successes as ways of operating, or **modes**. This chapter presents the various failure and success modes I have cataloged so that you can consider how they operate in your coaching.

It's probably human nature, but I have rarely recognized success modes in myself. The failure modes have been easy to spot. They sit right there in full view, like a zit on your chin. Instead of ignoring the zit or trying to cover it up, I paid close attention to it. I noticed each blemish, each failure mode, as it arose in my coaching, and over time, I was able to master it so that I could explicitly choose not to fall into its trap. As I fell into traps less and less, the teams I coached got "inexplicably" better results. Every time I noticed and named a new failure mode, I could then avoid it.

By the time you finish this chapter, you will be able to answer these questions:

- What are common agile coach failure modes?
- Where do failure modes come from, and how can I recover from them?
- What are common agile coach success modes? How can I recognize them in myself?
- What things can I do to help me express success modes more often?

When you fall into failure mode traps less, you have more time to notice the good happening in your coaching, the success modes. Noticing and naming these turn them into regular patterns, which makes them easy to remember and express more often.

Approach this chapter with a light heart. The failure and success modes are caricatures, gross exaggerations, and larger-than-life personas so that we can laugh through our tears as we recognize the truth they reveal in us.

Agile Coach Failure Modes

My firsthand experience with agile coach failure modes makes me an expert in them. At one time or another, I have been one (or more) of these personas in action. The accompanying figures offer a tongue-in-cheek view of these. See which describes you.

The Spy spends just enough time observing the team to pick up topics for the next retrospective and then slinks off into the night.

The Seagull swoops in at stand-ups, poops all over the team with well-intentioned observations or advice, and flies away again.

The Opinionator expresses opinions often, gets attached to them, and loses the objectivity needed to coach the team to have great discussions.

The Admin undermines team ownership by becoming an unnecessary middle man for meeting logistics, access requests, and other administrivia.

The Hub acts as the center of the universe for communication between team members and for task-level coordination.

The Butterfly flits around from team to team, landing just long enough to impart a pearl of wisdom or pose a philosophical question.

The Expert gets so involved in the details of the team's work that the forest gets lost in the trees.

The Nag helpfully "reminds" the team to start stand-up, update the storyboard, complete the tasks they committed to, and so on.

Which of these do you recognize in your coaching? C'mon, we all act out these modes or ones similar to them. We do it with the best of intentions. The team's design conversation seems stalled, so we jump in there with the Expert opinion. The team's burndown chart looks like a tabletop because they haven't updated the effort remaining on the tasks, so we Nag them to keep their task cards current. It's not the end of the world. None of these failure modes yields devastating consequences when done infrequently, but when done consistently (and unconsciously), they can sap the team's ability to self-organize. This is devastating.

Even though you have the best of intentions, maybe your coaching has been constantly invasive, like the Hub, for instance, and as a result, the team has come to depend on being micromanaged. Or, perhaps it's become regularly evasive, like the Butterfly, which creates in the team a sense of abandonment and leaves them alone to make agile up as they go along. In these cases, as with all the failure modes when done habitually, the coach's behavior somehow becomes central to the team's operation, a signal that damage from the failure mode may already be happening. The center of anything is the wrong place for a coach to be.

Where Do Failure Modes Come From?

Failure modes arise when a coach's ego or continuous partial attention (or both) are in play.

Judgment, intellect, planning, perception, and reality-awareness swirl around in an intricate dance in the ego, allowing you to be confident enough to risk speaking your ideas. Egos are normal, useful, and natural this way. We all have one, and we know its "I" focused voice when we hear it in our heads: What do *I* think? What should *I* do? What ideas do *I* have to contribute? What will people think of *me*?

When "I" thinking runs unchecked, it easily turns into "I" centeredness: Why can't they see what *I* see? What will *I* do if they don't do well? What will people think of *my* team? What will people say about *me*, as their coach?

Behind all this "I" thinking lurks fear: fear that the team really won't know the right way to go and fear that they will fail or not be good enough, feeding your fear that this will reflect badly on you. Fear breeds fear to the point that you may not give the team enough room to see what would happen, what they would come up with, and how good they really could be.

The Hub, the Admin, the Opinionator, the Expert, and the Nag do their damage when "I" thinking runs unchecked. Each of these failure modes inserts the coach into the team's operations in an attempt to ensure the team won't go too far astray and fail, which, in turn, makes the coach look bad. You pay a high price, though. The coach in the center ensures the team won't come up with amazing results, either.

Another harbinger of failure modes comes in the form of multitasking and its cousin, continuous partial attention. Both are fairly new, evolutionarily speaking, and scientists tell us clearly that the human nervous system may not be built to handle them (Kabat-Zinn 2006). You're probably well acquainted with multitasking—doing more than one thing at a time, usually with one task being simple that you can do it on autopilot. Although a more recent term, continuous partial attention is probably familiar, too. You may have experienced it sometime today: "I'm going to answer this e-mail while you tell me about your problem and while I look at my mobile phone/IM/e-mail device because it's chirping at me. Wait, someone is saying something I'm interested in. Will you say that again, please?"

It's like multitasking, but with a twist—the pressure of being "on" 24/7, constantly scanning the environment for who or what wants your attention next.

TRY THIS

If you feel comfortable doing so and the teams you coach are strong enough agilists, go ahead and coach two or three teams at once. Sometimes, coaching multiple teams can be healthy if you do it mindfully.

To make sure you don't fall prey to the failure modes that result from continuous partial attention, use a technique on yourself that you teach product owners: business-value-driven thinking. Keep your own backlog of team improvements, and prioritize them according to business value. When you don't know how to split your time between teams, let the backlog tell you. Work with the teams in business value order. Spend the most time with the team that's in the middle of the highest business value improvement and less time with another and maybe no time with the third (for today). When you are with a team, give that team your full, undivided attention and presence.

Continuous partial attention arises when the coach coaches multiple teams or is otherwise distracted, running from one team to the other. It leads to the Seagull, the Spy, and the Butterfly. These are all some version of doing just enough to make one's presence felt so it will look like you are coaching when you are really just barely there.

Recover from Failure Modes

A way to avoid or, at least, recover from the failure modes is simple and difficult: Replace fear with trust.

Put your trust in the people on the team. Trust that they really do know the right thing to do, even if it's different from what you would have them do. Trust that they can and will bounce back from blind alleys and approaches that don't pan out, so you need not save them from these disappointments. Trust that they will rise to the best in themselves to surprise and delight their customers (and you). Trust that if they fail, they will learn and be even better for it.

It's no small feat to get to a place where you trust. You have help, though. Agile frameworks have built-in mechanisms that help you trust because they at once encourage and contain failure. The battle cry of a team may be, "If we're going to fail, let's fail fast." They (and you) can adopt a cavalier attitude about failure because the timeboxed sprint ensures that no one fails very far or with very far-reaching results. And, if the failure reveals that the endeavor should have failed, then we'd rather know that now. This step toward trusting is provided for you by agile itself.

Now you take the next step. To make more room for trust, pay attention to what's actually happening on the team and what's *trying* to happen.

Trust + attention = good coaching (or, at least the foundation that makes good coaching possible)

Although no single right path gets you to a place of trusting and offering attention, here are a few things you might try to take steps in that direction: Cultivate mindfulness, get curious, get a broader view, pair, and practice success.

Cultivate Mindfulness

Anything to help you cultivate mindfulness helps avoid failure modes. Practicing mindfulness, you may learn to be fully present with teams, and you may find that your self-awareness increases. These two, presence and self-awareness, let you notice when a failure mode has taken hold.

For me, mindfulness means silencing the noise in my head so that I can think and, more important, observe clearly. To begin cultivating mindfulness, do nothing but breathe. Sit quietly and pay attention to the breath coming in and out of your body. If it helps, count your breaths from one to four, and then start counting at one again. When thoughts take over, as they will, simply notice them and then start counting breaths again. Focus on the breath; when your mind wanders, bring it back to the breath. Do this over and over again. Your mind does what it is wont to do; you are teaching it a new mindfulness skill. Persevere and your skill will develop. Then it gets easier (Devin).

> **SEE ALSO** You can find provocative challenges and practical advice for cultivating mindfulness in your coaching in Chapter 3, "Master Yourself."

After a while, you may notice that you have cleared space in your mind, and you can now tune in to what the team needs rather than what's going on inside you. With this additional capacity, you can see them and yourself clearly. Your failure modes become evident, and you can *catch* yourself falling into their trap faster and faster each time. This means you can *recover* faster and faster each time.

Get Curious

While observing a team as it works, get curious about what's going on. Ask yourself questions such as these: What's trying to happen here? Where is the team headed? What might the team find useful? Then, notice what's going on some more.

Take the time to see what's really there, to get the clear view of the team—the view uncolored by your judgments and assumptions. Then, notice what's going on with you. What failure mode is happening for you? What are you feeling? Is fear motivating you? Where is the trust? Where is your attention?

> **SEE ALSO** Just because you trust, this doesn't mean you take your brain on vacation. Still notice everything going on with the team and around the team. Use all of the skills offered in this book and let them come from a foundation of trust, even if you have to build that foundation all on your own. One way to build trust comes from getting curious, which also turns out to be a key method for solving problems, covered in depth in Chapter 8, "Coach as Problem Solver."

With trust and attention back on board and curiosity bringing you a clear picture of what's going on with them and what's going on inside you, the failure mode doesn't stand a chance.

Get a Broader View

If you imagined this team's life together as a gigantic landscape, what would today's view be? Perhaps you visualize a barren hill obscuring the horizon, a physical representation of how you feel about them today as you say to yourself, "I don't know what I'm going to do. They just don't care. They are lazy and unwilling to do anything special." Perhaps this view of them drives you to become the Nag.

Now step back. See this team's current circumstance in a broader timescale and in a broader setting. Imagine you are flying over the landscape of the team's life together. From this view, you see the barren hill below, but it's now just a sad dot in what is otherwise an interesting and varied landscape. You see what has come before, all those rocks and sinkholes of their early life together. You see what is to come, perhaps a flowing river coursing mightily over the land. Pitfalls exist there, too, in the future, make no mistake about it. But the whole is beautiful, just for itself.

Now come back to the team's shared vision statements. Drink from the well of what they said they wanted to be together. Refreshed, let this particular moment, today's circumstances, go. As you do, let the Nag, or whatever other failure mode has taken hold, go as well.

SEE ALSO Creating and using shared vision statements is included in Chapter 7, "Coach as Teacher."

Getting a broader view is a standard coaching skill, called **meta-view**, which you can use with yourself and with team members when they get stuck in today's circumstances (Whitworth et al. 2007).

Pair with Others

We teach team members to pair with one another because "two heads are better than one." Coaches benefit from pairing, too. Cultivate a group of colleagues you call on when you feel a failure mode start to grip you. These are people who commiserate with your predicament. They know how you feel because they have felt that same way before. They also remind you that you're going for high-performance—for a self-monitoring, self-adjusting team. And, with that renewed goal firmly in mind, put your "I-centered" thinking on the back burner, focus your attention, and get ready to coach from a place of trust.

Practice Success

On the road to recovery from the failure modes, as-yet unrecognized success modes appear. You'll find these success modes embodied in the things you do especially well, the things you notice improve the team's ability to self-organize and get work done. Look for them. Discover them in yourself and then name them and turn them into habits. Notice these and rejoice in them. They are your coach calling cards, your unique expression as a good coach and as a treasured and useful part of the team.

Pay attention to other coaches, and shamelessly steal their success modes. Practice these until they feel more natural to you than the failure modes. In so doing, they become your automatic, and most helpful, response.

Agile Coach Success Modes

Success modes don't announce their arrival loudly, so look for the small but mighty when you observe successful coaching in yourself or others. See which of these would make a difference in your coaching.

The Magician asks questions that—*voila!*—reveal what is there but could not be seen.

The Child genuinely wonders "why?" and is propelled by an insatiable curiosity about life and everything in it.

The Ear hears everything but gives people room to grow by not responding to all of it.

The Heckler keeps it fun and light and just a little off balance to jolt people out of complacency.

The Wise Fool asks the dumb questions that enlighten.

 The Creeping Vine makes small moves, imperceptible to the team, that relentlessly pull them back to the core of agile bit by bit.

 **The Dreamer** bravely gives voice to possible futures waiting to be created.

 The Megaphone makes sure all voices are heard, especially the voices of the oppressed.

To cultivate these, and other success modes, start with questions. Turn inward first, with this question: When would using each of these success modes feel natural to me? Then move outward, questioning the team and helping them question the status quo surrounding them. Table 11.1 offers some things you might say to them as you embody the various success modes.

TABLE 11.1   Questions help the success modes become common in your coaching

This success mode...	Sounds like this...
The Magician	"What is another reality here?"
The Child	"I'm curious…"
The Heckler	"Hey, Joe, tell 'em what you really think." "So, are we just gonna sit here, or are we gonna do something?"

Continued

TABLE 11.1 Questions help the success modes become common in your coaching (Continued)

This success mode...	Sounds like this...
The Wise Fool	"What makes it be this way?"
	"What is true here?" "Huh?"
The Dreamer	"What would it be like if it was exactly as we imagine it?"
	"What's happening now?"
	"What's struggling to emerge?"
The Megaphone	"What's another idea waiting to be said?"
	"Who is going to talk first?"

A couple of the success modes are also quiet. The Ear and the Creeping Vine work silently. When in play, team members recognize that a change has occurred but cannot pinpoint the cause. Over time, the space to be heard, quiet conversations that lead to revelation and dead-on comments from you that cut to the heart of the matter, create that change, yet no one thing is responsible. In each of them, though, the coach was working.

Which of these success modes will you adopt as your own? Which will you recognize and honor in yourself? Which will you notice and name in others?

Practice, Practice

Getting good at agile coaching means practicing. And failing. And getting up again to practice some more. You need not tear yourself away from a comforting failure mode overnight. You need not invent ten new success modes to be successful yourself. Just take the next step, whatever that is, and get better all the time. What you practice, you become.

Maybe noticing the failure modes in your coaching is enough of a change for you right now. Maybe just becoming aware of what trips you into a failure mode signifies a big leap forward. Go ahead, be aware. Be gentle with yourself. Trusting and paying attention may be new muscles for you—they certainly were for me.

Expect that you may revert to time-worn reflexes when stressful situations come up. If you pay attention, though, a new voice may speak to you a new truth: The stress behavior need not become your everyday behavior. With practice, eventually, even in stress, you can avoid the failure modes. But for right now, know where you are.

> *In order to succeed, your desire for success should be greater than your fear of failure.*
>
> —*Bill Cosby*

Just notice and pause. When you feel ready to recover, practice, practice.

Also remember that habits and attitudes are contagious. Team members pick up whatever you offer and propagate it far and wide. As you consider the failure and success modes active in your coaching, consider this: Which would you like them to catch? The Dreamer or the Nag? The Magician or the Spy? The Megaphone or the Opinionator? It's your choice.

A Refresher

Let's lock in the ideas from this chapter:

- Failure modes arise but need not consume your coaching.
- To combat failure modes, increase trust and attention.
- Notice and name success modes in yourself and others.
- Know where you are and take the next step. There is only practice.

Additional Resources

Kabat-Zinn, J. 2005. *Wherever You Go, There You Are: Mindfulness Meditation in Everyday Life*. New York: Hyperion. Any books or audio recordings on mindfulness meditation by John Kabat-Zinn are a great way to step into a mindfulness practice. This book was the one I tried first when it was initially published in 1995. More than ten years later, it still occupies an easily accessible place on my bookshelf.

Stone, L. 2008. Continuous Partial Attention—Not the Same as Multitasking. *Business Week*. www.businessweek.com/business_at_work/time_management/archives/2008/07/continuous_part.html.

References

Devin, L. A random collection of favorite acting exercises. Unpublished manuscript.

Kabat-Zinn, J. 2006. *Coming to Our Senses: Healing Ourselves and the World Through Mindfulness*. New York: Hyperion.

Whitworth, L., K. Kimsey-House, H. Kimsey-House, and P. Sandahl. 2007. *Co-Active Coaching: New Skills for Coaching People Toward Success in Work and Life, Second Edition*. Mountain View, CA: Davies-Black.

Chapter 12

When Will I Get There?

A journey of a thousand miles starts with a single footstep (Tzu), but certainly it should end at some point. Who wants to go on forever *becoming* an agile coach? As with most things that cause us to grow and change, no finish line gleams in the distance. No specific time or set of skills proclaim loudly "you have arrived" at agile coachdom. We agile coaches just keep learning and integrating new skills into our coaching for the sake of our teams' splendor. Certainly, we hit flat parts in the climb where we can catch our breath and rest in the skills and behaviors we have mastered thus far. When we take that well-earned pause, we look around and see the effect of our work on the teams around us. Yes, we have done well for them.

Yet, that further summit beckons. How long should we hang out here enjoying the view? There are so many things to learn and so much more to help teams accomplish. So, we take one final look at the good we have done and then motivate ourselves to move on, toward the next level of coaching mastery and then the next and the next.

The particular trail your agile coaching expedition takes will be unique to you. No two agile coaches approach their work the same way, and no two coaches will have the same coach-shaping joys and troubles.

By the time you finish this chapter, you will be able to answer these questions:

- When have I had enough experiences and built enough skills so that I can honestly claim the title of agile coach?
- What can I use to measure my effectiveness as an agile coach?
- How do I deal with the way my company measures my performance when that doesn't jibe with how agile works or what an agile coach does?
- How can I recognize my real value as an agile coach and help others to see it?

This chapter offers some trail markers that help you orient yourself during your coaching expedition. These markers, the skills and behaviors of agile coaching, indicate you are still on one of many trails that lead to good coaching. It also asks you to stop and enjoy the view when you have rightly earned a break.

Agile Coach Skills

When I coach apprentice coaches, I never give out the information I'm giving you now until the last part of our time together. In fact, I recoil at the idea of a "coaching checklist" to be used at the outset of an apprenticeship, as some kind of prescription for good coaching. So, please don't use the information in this chapter as such. Don't let it limit you. Instead, let your coaching be as big as a clear, blue Montana sky. Let your voice as a coach emerge through successes and failures alike. Don't let anyone's ideas of what an agile coach is, thinks, and does lead you to become less than you can and less than your teams need. Even mine.

Having conveyed to you my passion on the use and abuse of a checklist, I find that setting down in writing a set of basic agile coach skills can be informative, once you have already experienced coaching and have developed your unique coaching voice. From this foundation, the list can be used as an interim measure to answer this question: What do you want to strengthen next?

You know you have accomplished the basic range of agile coaching skills when you have done these things well:

- Instilled agile practices
- Started up agile teams
- Coached team members one-on-one
- Coached the whole team
- Coached product owners
- Coached outsiders
- Coached the team through change
- Instigated paths to high performance
- Accepted their ideas above your own
- Mastered yourself

- Modeled agile values and principles
- Navigated conflict
- Set yourself on a path of learning and growing
- Started giving back

Although greater summits await, having confidently integrated these coaching experiences and the skills needed to accomplish them, you receive a well-earned walk along a flat part of the trail with an amazing view. Enjoy it.

Instilled Agile Practices

Call yourself an agile coach when you have instilled in the team a desire to uphold agile practices and to keep the values of the agile manifesto alive, vibrant, and useful. You know this has occurred when the team does the following:

- Receives the expected benefits from the practices
- Keeps the agile manifesto and the 12 principles in mind when considering options about the product they're building or how they're working together (Beck et al. 2001)
- Ensures the agile manifesto and the inspect-and-adapt loop remain intact and vital for them as they alter agile practices

Table 12.1 provides a rundown of the main agile practices and some of their intended benefits. To make sure you have accomplished instilling the practices in agile teams, consider this list.

Started Up Agile Teams

Call yourself an agile coach when you have successfully started up agile teams. To do so, you have learned the objectives of team start-ups and have tried various agendas and activities to accomplish those objectives. You have planned and executed start-ups, and you have adjusted your approach for future sessions from the results. You know how to deliver a team start-up experience that stays true to agile and provides meaning to the team.

SEE ALSO For details about starting up agile teams, including specific teaching objectives and activities, see Chapter 7, "Coach as Teacher."

TABLE 12.1 Agile practices and their expected benefits

Product backlog	**Impediment removal**
All stories known at a given time are included.	Things to be fixed now; impediments don't sit.
Product owner has "sliced" business intent by prioritizing stories according to business value.	**Timeboxed sprint**
	Sense of beginning and ending.
A main prioritization driver is delivering business value as fast as possible, especially *first* business value.	Time period team can control.
	Sense of time pressure.
The backlog is alive, changing, frequently updated, and reprioritized.	Chance for leadership to change priorities or direction without jerking the team around (because this only happens between sprints).
Product owner ensures work is aligned with leadership's direction and product vision.	**Retrospective**
Sprint planning	Well-designed and facilitated meeting for the team to continuously improve.
Planned in order of story priority.	
All work is transparent.	Team thinks of themselves as a "well-oiled ecosystem" that they want to tune each time.
Team only works what has been agreed to.	
Sprint backlog/burndown chart	**Sprint review**
All work for the sprint is represented in sprint backlog.	Low tech, high impact.
Burndown chart is updated daily.	"Own up" to results with product owner and all outsiders (customer, sponsor, stakeholders, managers, and so on).
Burndown chart is used by team to spur conversations when it indicates they are not on track to "make it to zero" or they will burn to zero before the end of the sprint.	
Story/task board	**Release planning**
Actively used by the team to indicate overall status and convey each person's current commitment.	Everyone is clear on the incremental value each release will deliver.
	Everyone can talk to the future via the release plan.
Actively used by the team to spur coordination and sequencing.	Customer commitment is done via release, rather than sprint by sprint.
Stand-up	Customer interaction shifts from schedule-driven to value-driven.
Effective, supportive, constructive peer pressure is evident.	
Fine-grain coordination happens.	The release plan is trued-up frequently to adjust to current conditions such as team velocity and new features.
Team members raise impediments and ensure they get resolved.	

Coached Team Members One-on-One

Call yourself an agile coach when you have become fluent in the skills needed to conduct one-on-one coaching conversations; when you can conduct such conversations in an easy, informal way; and when the individuals in conversation feel a change in themselves as a result. You know you are doing this part of the job when you recognize "where" each team member is on their personal agile transformation and you activate in each person a desire to take their next step toward becoming an excellent agilist.

Coached the Whole Team

Call yourself an agile coach when you are fully living the vision of agile coaching: bulldozer, shepherd, servant leader, and guardian of quality and performance.

This may take the form of keeping the team focused one sprint at a time. Or paying close attention to team conversations to ensure they truly collaborate and move toward the simplest thing possible. Or calling out a destructive behavior so that others may have the courage to do so the next time such a behavior happens. Or reminding the team of their shared vision when they lose sight of it. Or a thousand other little things that you do constantly to help them all move toward becoming a healthy agile team that produces amazing results they are proud to call their own.

SEE ALSO	Chapter 5, "Coach as Coach-Mentor," covers the skills needed to coach whole teams, team members, product owners, and outsiders.
	The vision of an agile coach as shepherd, bulldozer, servant leader, and guardian of quality and performance is further defined in Chapter 7, "Coach as Teacher."

Coached Product Owners

Call yourself an agile coach when you have actively coached product owners to completely fulfill their important role. To do this, you probably will have coached the product owner on these topics:

Interacting with the team: The product owner can detect the fine line between challenging the team and bullying the team and back away when they have come close to crossing the line. You have encouraged the positive ways in which the product owner interacts with the team and also coached the product owner to curb behaviors that undermine the team's self-organization because it directly impacts their ability to deliver.

Practicing business-value-driven thinking: The product owner uses business-value-driven thinking in every decision, always asking, "What gives us the most business value now?" Things that don't meet the business value bar, such as unnecessary or unimportant meetings, decisions, or details, get pushed away or eliminated. The product owner stays laser-focused on doing only what it takes to create a great product, always keeping the long-term value in mind so that short-term decisions don't undermine and vice versa.

Creating, grooming, and using the product backlog: The product backlog is a living organism. The product owner uses it to adapt to new ideas and outside forces. It becomes more and more true to the actual need so that the team delivers the most valuable results as they become apparent. All stakeholders know where to view the product backlog to see how their desired feature compares with the others in terms of business value and, hence, the likelihood of getting created.

Removing impediments: The product owner gladly joins in with the team and agile coach to remove any impediment that threatens the momentum of the team or the quality of their results.

Managing stakeholders: The product owner uses an open and transparent product backlog to manage various stakeholders' desires for the product. The product owner constantly works with stakeholders to understand their needs as they relate to the vision for the product. The product owner corrals all those stakeholder voices and turns them into one single, unambiguous voice so that the team knows what to work on next and how that fits with the overall vision of the product coming to life.

You know you have coached the product owner well when the team views the product owner as a positive force propelling them toward a compelling vision and expecting greatness from them while also maintaining a strong grip on reality. Teams value such a product owner greatly.

Beyond the relationship between the team and product owner, you know you have created a positive and viable coaching relationship with the product owner when you get invited into the product owner's inner circle. You'll know this has happened when the product owner asks you to join key conversations about business situations and decisions that could affect the team.

Coached Outsiders

Call yourself an agile coach when you have engaged in many coaching conversations with sponsors, managers, and stakeholders outside the team. You have "laid down the law" about useful vs. hurtful interaction with the team, and you have helped outsiders see how they can best support the team's momentum and results. You have also taught them how to use agile to achieve a competitive advantage by building only the most essential and valuable and then moving on to the next higher-value endeavor.

Through the product owner, all outsiders are well aware of the team's plans, progress, and journey toward high performance. You have coached the product owner to represent the team and the product in this fashion, and through this, outsiders have come to expect that the product owner provides this valuable information.

Coached the Team Through Change

Call yourself an agile coach when you have watched a team wallow in the depths of despair over a change or unwanted circumstance and helped them get through the despair and emerge with a new plan for regaining their skill and vigor as a team. For sure, as soon as the team gets moving and grooving, something will happen to knock them back. They'll decide to add a new skill set to the team, a new direction will "come down from above," or the product owner will leave. If it's not one of these things, it is certain to be something else.

An accomplished agile coach knows how to coach within the team's current development stage, which often regresses during times of upheaval. Using agile principles, practices, and values, the coach shows the team ways to regain their lost footing, both as a whole team and as individuals.

SEE ALSO

Chapter 4, "Let Your Style Change," teaches you to detect the team's level of proficiency and match that with an effective coaching style.

Starting the team down a path to high performance begins when you set forth your expectation that they simply will be a high-performing team. To learn how to set this expectation, see Chapter 2, "Expect High Performance."

Chapter 6, "Coach as Facilitator," covers how to coach a team through conversations that generate ideas and result in decisions (and action).

Problems happen. See Chapter 8, "Coach as Problem Solver," to help you detect and guide the team through problems.

Conflict happens, too. For useful ways to deal with conflict and help it abate, see Chapter 9, "Coach as Conflict Navigator."

Instigated Paths to High Performance

Call yourself an agile coach when the teams you coach actively reach for higher and higher performance. When they take their journey toward performance into their own hands, you know you have instigated in them a path that will return benefits to each of them, the team as a whole, their product, and their company.

Accepted Their Ideas Above Your Own

Call yourself an agile coach when you willingly subordinate your ideas and decisions in deference to the team's ideas and decisions. It doesn't matter if yours were slightly better than what the team decided to do. Going for self-organization, it matters most that they learn ways to generate ideas and make decisions because they will whole-heartedly follow only those decisions freely chosen by them and inspirational to them.

Mastered Yourself

Call yourself an agile coach when you act from complete self-awareness to offer the team what they need in the moment, rather than acting from your own needs or unrecognized knee-jerk reactions. You are for them.

Modeled Agile Values and Principles

Call yourself an agile coach when the team sees you as a role model of a competent and successful agilist, when they can see the values of agile reflected in the way you approach situations and them, when they learn how to use agile well through your example, and when they acquire new or deeper skills that allow them to collaborate more fully to create astonishing results. These situations call forth the evidence that you have modeled agile well.

Navigated Conflict

Call yourself an agile coach when you have learned and used at least one conflict navigation model to help the team move through conflict and live amicably with conflict when it is unsolvable. You know you are doing this well when you mindfully choose when and how to intervene in conflict as it arises on the team, including the conscious choice to let conflict exist without intervening. Be quite proud of your coaching accomplishments when you notice the team navigating conflict all by themselves.

Set Yourself on a Path of Learning and Growing

Call yourself an agile coach when you have instilled in yourself an insatiable thirst for learning and an unquenchable desire to witness people and companies prosper beyond your imaginings. So many disciplines contribute to your effectiveness as a coach. Pick any of them and soak up what they have to offer. Integrate your newfound wisdom into your coaching, and watch your skills grow as you watch the teams you coach improve.

> *Live as if you were to die tomorrow. Learn as if you were to live forever.*
>
> —Gandhi

You know you have put yourself on a path of learning and growing when you set aside time to learn new skills and experience new mind-sets. This sacred time does not get put on the "back burner" when things get busy. Things will always get busy! You know this and keep safe the time needed to look up agile topics, to read blogs and let the hyperlinks take you into new realms of knowledge, to check out the latest agile books, or to read the presentation outlines for an upcoming agile conference and then go learn about the topics you encounter there.

As you reflect on your coaching ability and as you encounter new ideas, you take time to regularly measure your level of agile coaching proficiency. You measure yourself honestly and frequently and do what you have been coaching teams to do—reach for higher and higher performance all the time.

Started Giving Back

Call yourself an agile coach when you have started to share all those great lessons you've learned through your own trials and tribulations and through the new disciplines you've just read about. Be present in agile communities, locally if available or online. If no local agile group exists, create one. Get involved in agile conferences. At the very least, attend a conference, and contribute to the rich conversations happening all around you. If you have something to share, submit a presentation. Go for it! Join the ranks of other agilists working toward advancing the state of the art of agile. If you've been coaching, you have contributions to make. Make them.

Beyond a List of Skills

The list of skills is the "what" of agile coaching, in other words, the concrete things an agile coach does in the daily work of coaching. The "how" of coaching, the style and voice with which you coach, is just as important and often weighed just as heavily as the skills when people judge a coach's performance.

Measure Yourself as a Coach, Not as a Manager

Drive toward results. Direct the work of others. These are some phrases you might see in a managerial job posting or in a company's performance review criteria. Before becoming an agile coach, I even took a job that included this phrase: "Herd the cats."

The desire to control comes through loud and clear in the way most people's worth is measured by their company's performance management process. When it comes to performance review time, these controlling phrases crop up anew. Many successful agile coaches have been dismayed to learn that, despite the amazing results their teams produced and despite the new clarity and purpose that pervades the workplace, measuring their contributions still includes phrases such as "Herd the cats."

Agile coaching, done well, is impossible to see from outside the team and can be invisible even to the team members. It's hard for the people you coach to know how the thing you did with them contributed to their success. It's hard for a team to see that being coached by you translated into their ability to create more results better. It's close to impossible for management to see that your coaching was critical to getting the results they now enjoy from the agile teams.

This means that an agile coach may hear this from her manager, "Yes, I know the team performed far beyond anyone's expectation, but what did you do? What was your specific contribution to their success?"

If the coach is doing a good job, that question should be impossible to answer concretely. In fact, if any agile team member is doing a good job, that question should be difficult to answer for their own performance, even though they have all kinds of artifacts to point to and say, "See? That's my thing." The artifacts themselves—software code, new processes, and marketing plans—are shared to such a degree that team members cannot easily separate them into "mine" and "yours."

It's even harder for an agile coach because a coach's work products are invisible. Separating them from the overall success of the team cannot be done, yet performance review time often goads coaches into trying to do so.

Even though the way people measure the performance of managers and team leads doesn't translate to measuring a good (or bad) agile coach, the models exist and frequently get used for this purpose. Although woefully misdirected, they are simply the closest definition of "leader" readily available.

Changing the performance metrics your company uses for leaders and managers into ones suitable for agile coaching starts with you. When you embrace new and useful measures of good agile coaching and can articulate them, things can change. When you refuse to be measured by "directs the work of others" and instead stipulate "creates an environment where no one needs to be directed," you can make a change.

Think about your own abilities, style, and impact as an agile coach, and use the ideas in Table 12.2 to measure yourself on how well you are moving toward the essence of excellent agile coaching.

TABLE 12.2 Agile coach performance measures

Move away from	Move toward
Driving the team to get results Directing the work of others	Leading implicitly, creating an environment where the team naturally delivers great results without anyone having to "drive" them
Controlling the team's work to achieve predictability	Releasing the team to get the work done as they choose and holding them accountable for the results they promised
Following the company's rules	Challenging the company's rules every time they restrict value delivery
Immediately escalating problems to management	Working through problems within the people involved to fully resolve them and move on
Favoring options that are proven and safe	Creating safety for the team to experiment, fail, and learn
Delivering the product according to plan	Enabling the team to deliver the product according to their changing and increasingly accurate plan Letting business value delivered be the only metric that matters
Following time-tested strategies and procedures	Cultivating creativity and the team's ability to see each situation anew and to enhance the chance for a game-changing outcome even in familiar territory
Implementing agile by the book	Knowing when going "by the book" is best and when to sacrifice the most powerful expression of agile to get at least some improvement in an imperfect environment

When you start assessing yourself according to these agile-workable measures, others will start to do so, too. At the start of a new assignment, use these measures to set forth the expectation of what agile coaching entails and, therefore, what people will and will not see when the coaching works well. In so doing, you will help people know what to expect, and the way people measure you will begin to change.

If you work for a company with a deep-rooted performance management process, expect that receiving formal recognition for good agile coaching might take some time. During the wait, however, measure yourself, and be content with your teams' real accomplishments (and your very real contributions to them). When confronted with "You weren't <insert your favorite controlling adjective> enough," simply restate the results the team produced, and know that they would not have achieved them were it not for your work.

It will change, but only if you don't give up.

Claim Your Victories

They can't see your impact. Sometimes, you can't either. Your sense of personal worth and value can easily take a nose-dive if you don't make a regular habit of bringing your accomplishments to the surface.

Each week, sit down and write out a list of the value you delivered—just a little list of the things you helped emerge, the successes that people enjoyed because of your work, and the places where you outright rocked! Let this be a personal journal. Assume no one else will ever read it so that you can give yourself the permission to be unbridled in what you write there.

Figure 12.1 offers an example of a coach's typical weekly value check.

Having done this, you can honestly claim your victories. This reaffirms the value you personally delivered and helps you preserve your sanity when confronted with unworkable performance expectations. You also now have a fresh list of accomplishments to bring to mind when people ask, "What did you do this week?"

Making this list, week after week, shows the value your coaching has delivered and points out areas of growth and advancement. You may also be able to extract pieces from your value check to use with your manager. Perhaps this will help turn that performance management ship around.

Regardless of what happens with how others measure you, be sure to do your own measuring. When you leave a team or a group, look back over the whole time you have been with them. Conduct a personal retrospective, your own private inspect-and-adapt loop. Being honest with yourself, make some lists that consider your impact. Figure 12.2 shows an example of one coach's personal retrospective, looking back as a coaching engagement draws to a close.

TRY THIS

To step into the practice of considering your value, break it down into small chunks. For a week, at the end of every day, simply ask yourself, "What good have I been to anyone today?" And, then write down whatever comes to mind. In there, you may well discover the value you delivered but couldn't see.

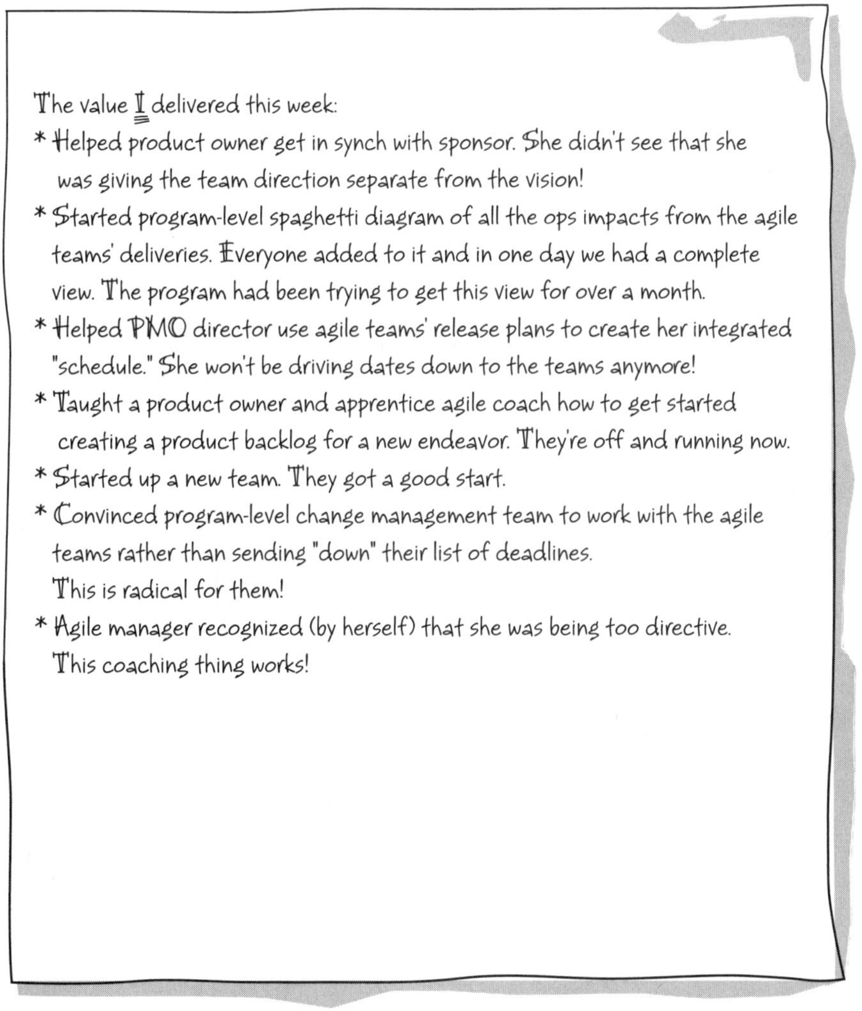

The value I delivered this week:

* Helped product owner get in synch with sponsor. She didn't see that she was giving the team direction separate from the vision!

* Started program-level spaghetti diagram of all the ops impacts from the agile teams' deliveries. Everyone added to it and in one day we had a complete view. The program had been trying to get this view for over a month.

* Helped PMO director use agile teams' release plans to create her integrated "schedule." She won't be driving dates down to the teams anymore!

* Taught a product owner and apprentice agile coach how to get started creating a product backlog for a new endeavor. They're off and running now.

* Started up a new team. They got a good start.

* Convinced program-level change management team to work with the agile teams rather than sending "down" their list of deadlines.
  This is radical for them!

* Agile manager recognized (by herself) that she was being too directive.
  This coaching thing works!

FIGURE 12.1 An agile coach's weekly value check

I know I have made a difference because...
* The team delivered huge changes that were accepted by
  leaders enterprise-wide. Managers say that, without agile, they would
  have likely delivered nothing.
* Three strong agile coaches have emerged from my coaching of them.
  One would have goten flattened by corporate politics if she hadn't
  discovered her talent for coaching agile teams.
* Two teams successfully weathered product owner change-outs.
* Teams are more often recognizing waste in things they used to blindly accept.
* I was a key influencer in helping a new (huge) program decide to go agile and
  do so with a very light program management team.
* An operations team now knows how to use agile to get ops work done faster
  to make more room for interesting project work.
* Two months after I left, I heard that all team members of a previously agile-
  hating team decided to continue with agile as they move into ops.
  Three of six want to try agile coaching. Wow. I never expected that!

I know I have not done enough because...
* Senior leaders don't know how to leverage agile teams' ability to deliver well
  and change fast. They still see agile as just a different way to
  manage projects.
* Newly minted agile coaches and product owners are left to struggle with high
  organizational walls by themselves, with no one to lend them a ladder.
* Senior leaders are not open to being coached or to take agile "to the next
  level." Instead, they are busy defining their custom version of agile which
  hides their dysfunctions.

I know I have grown...
* I positively impacted at least four people's lives (three agile coach apprentices,
  one product owner).
* I picked up a ton of new tools for conducting retrospectives and helping
  teams collaborate.
* I received many affirmations that I'm a good coach.
* I now have the ability to coach the management layers "above" the agile teams.

FIGURE 12.2   An agile coach's personal retrospective looks back on a coaching experience.

You don't have to wait until the end of a coaching experience to do a personal retrospective. Any time works well and can be especially revealing when done regularly.

Deliver Your Own Performance Review

A surefire way to know whether you have "arrived" as an agile coach requires you to do one simple thing: Notice your impact. When you interact with the team and offer an insight or a powerful question, notice what happens next. Do they come up with better or simpler ideas? Do they move into action with clarity? Do they ask for what they need and require the "powers that be" to provide it?

When you coach people one on one, notice the impact of your conversation on the person you are coaching. Notice both the impact in the moment and the effect days or weeks later. Also, work up the courage to ask people about the impact of your coaching on them. Ask the following: What has changed in the way you view the work? What new ideas have emerged? How has your ability to stay in action changed?

Deliver your own performance review by considering your impact as an agile coach, reveling in the things you do well, and squarely facing the places where you disappoint yourself or others. No one else will judge you more harshly or fairly. Only you know when you have "arrived."

A Refresher

Let's lock in the ideas from this chapter:

- The list of agile coach skills are markers along the trail of your own agile coaching expedition. Use them to orient yourself and to ensure you are on the trail of your choosing.

- Measure yourself as a coach, not a manager. Encourage others to do so as well by replacing managerial measures of success with agile-workable measures.

- Claim your victories so you can fully recognize the considerable value you add to agile teams.

- Frequently and honestly assess your coaching abilities and constantly reach for the next level of mastery.

Additional Resources

Strachan, D. 2006. *Making Questions Work: A Guide to How and What to Ask for Facilitators, Consultants, Managers, Coaches, and Educators.* San Francisco: Jossey-Bass. Personal retrospectives guide Ainsley Nies says that her work often results in people discovering the most pertinent questions to ask themselves, leading to a voyage of self-discovery and improvement. She recommends this book for helping find those pertinent questions.

References

Beck et al. 2001. Manifesto for Agile Software Development. www.agilemanifesto.org.

————. 2001. Principles Behind the Agile Manifesto. www.agilemanifesto.org/principles.html.

Tzu, L. *Tao te ching.*

Chapter 13

It's Your Journey

Every agile coach goes on a journey of their own making. Although there may not be much in common between people's journeys other than the agile frameworks themselves, there seems to be a common theme. For each coach, there comes a moment that unlocks the power and beauty of agile coaching. For some, it's the discovery of emotional intelligence and the realization that they have been pushing aside this part of their brilliance their whole career. For some, it's a structure that gives them a way to finally understand what makes human relationships work. For others, it's the realization that they can illuminate and guide without being directive. And for still others, it's the need to pay back for years of directing and squelching innovation in the name of driving results.

This chapter offers six stories from six very different agile coaches. Their backgrounds, experiences, and points of view diverge yet come together over this one idea—they each love agile coaching because it answers their call for a humane way of working that still delivers the tangible results businesses demand. As each one has undertaken their journey, they have developed their

---

By the time you finish this chapter, you will be able to answer these questions:

- What have other coaches' journeys toward becoming an agile coach been like?
- What has "unlocked" agile for them?
- How do I use what I've learned from their journeys to inform me on my journey?

unique voice as a coach—their own individual way of approaching teams and organizations to help them unleash the full potential of agile.

Come with me while we explore several agile coaches' journeys.

Agile Coach Journeys

In these stories perhaps you find something instructional or inspirational, something that helps agile coaching "click" for you. Perhaps you see yourself reflected in another's words. Or, perhaps you recognize why your story is different from all of these.

When you have a story of your own agile coaching journey, share it with others. Tell other agile coaches (and aspiring agile coaches) what makes agile work for you and why it matters.

Rachel's Journey: A Coach Finds Something Better and Champions It

Rachel Davies has been applying agile approaches since 2000 and is a well-known presenter at industry conferences. For several years, she has served the agile community as a director of the nonprofit Agile Alliance. She is the coauthor, with Liz Sedley, of *Agile Coaching*. Figure 13.1 depicts Rachel's agile coaching journey.

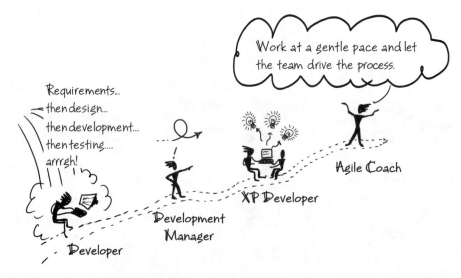

FIGURE 13.1   Rachel Davies' agile coaching journey

Here is Rachel's story in her own words:

My motivation for encouraging people to adopt agile is rooted in the 1990s. Back then, I saw teams working long hours applying traditional waterfall process, but when projects didn't deliver in time, then everyone's hard work was thrown away. So began my quest for an approach that respected people and enabled them to deliver software.

At the turn of the millennium, I stumbled upon Extreme Programming. I was fascinated and devoured everything I could find about this counterintuitive approach. I left my job as a successful development manager and joined an XP team as a developer so I could learn how to pair-program and apply test-driven development. Although there were days when I felt like a participant in a strange social experiment, what I loved about it was learning every day and being an integral part of a business that delivered software every week.

I became deeply interested in how and why agile approaches work. I went to user groups and conferences to learn from experts and practitioners. I wanted to share what I knew too and proudly presented my own experiences at these same events.

On the back of a conference presentation, I got my first assignment as an agile coach in 2003. Although I had plenty of theory and experience in implementing agile practices, I soon realized that I knew very little about coaching. I was way out of my depth. I saw well-known agile coaches get kicked out of the organization when they pushed teams to adopt "by-the-book" practices without taking time to understand the context.

Worse was to come; the team I was assigned to coach didn't care one iota about becoming agile. They were being pushed to adopt agile practices by their managers, and I was horrified to discover that the agile transition was tied up with staff reduction and relocation plans. Trust and morale were at rock bottom within IT.

How could I coach a team that wasn't interested in becoming agile? I looked to the agile community for inspiration. I attended the Agile Development Conference in Salt Lake City. It was exciting to talk with many of my agile heroes: Ward Cunningham, Alistair Cockburn, and Linda Rising. But James Shore's experience report struck a special chord with me. He helped me understand that change takes time and that a coach has to be patient and work in baby steps.

I decided to focus on a much simpler approach based on Scrum. I spent time with the team sharing everything I knew about how to write user stories, facilitate retrospectives, and make progress visible. I encouraged the development team to meet businesspeople and end users in the call center, and doing so helped them feel a stronger connection to the results of their work. Gradually, they started to absorb the techniques I showed them and to make them their own.

Over the next year, I moved from team to team, helping each team get a basic level of agility—I even coached teams at off-site suppliers. Along the way, I discovered that people really appreciated me taking time to listen to their concerns and help them identify possible courses of action rather than directing them on what to do. I was often able to put them in touch with other teams who had solutions to share. Communities of practice started springing up.

As the months passed, I grew to understand that these one-on-one interactions and team retrospectives are the times when an agile coach sows the seeds of change. I don't expect every single one to take root. I understand that each seed takes time to turn into a green shoot and further nurturing before it comes to fruition. For me, this is the essence of my coaching style—to work at a gentle pace and let the team drive the process.

—Rachel Davies

Dan's Journey: An Agile Coach Reflects on His Shu Ha Ri Progression

Dan Mezick is a man on fire about the things that make agile "click" for him: agile's entrepreneurial spirit and what he's learned from the allied discipline of group relations. A technical trainer and agile coach, Dan runs both the Agile

FIGURE 13.2 Dan Mezick's agile coaching journey

Connecticut and Agile Boston user groups, bringing the latest agile thought leaders to New England audiences. A real techie, Dan has absorbed just about every programming technology available. The same inquisitiveness that causes Dan to really understand programming has him focused on really understanding Scrum to answer the burning question, Why does Scrum work so well, anyway? Not one to do anything by half measures, Dan has brought agile into the world of youth hockey coaching where his Parent-Coach Timeout (PCT) framework allows parents, coaches, and players to get much more satisfaction and fun out of youth sports. Figure 13.2 portrays Dan's agile coaching journey.

Here's Dan's story in his own words:

> Since I am telling my agile journey story, you need to know a little bit about me. So here it is: I have a computer science degree with a minor in business. I have experience occupying a range of roles in software development, including nine years of professional programming. I have some software patents and also have direct experience managing multiple projects that include almost fifty programmers working through five direct reports. I have extensive experience teaching professional developers how to use the latest software tools. Lastly, I

have a long-running interest in the psychology of individuals and the psychology of groups.

In 2006, I brought all of this background with me when I attended Lowell Lindstrom's Certified ScrumMaster (CSM) class. Like everyone else who learns Scrum, I began to think I had it all figured out. Then some time passed, I gained experience, and I realized I did not really know very much about Scrum. This cycle repeated—and repeats again—to this very day. Along the way, I've had a few "a-ha" moments. The following are some of them.

As a newbie in Shu mode, during Lowell Lindstrom's CSM class, I suggested a way to tweak Scrum to solve a problem we were all discussing. Lowell asked me if I have any direct (empirical) experience with Scrum. I answered "no" and reflected on the very real value of direct, "here and now" experience.

SEE ALSO	Descriptions of the Shu Ha Ri stages of mastery and what they mean for coaching agile teams is covered in Chapter 4, "Let Your Style Change."

Later, when I attained some direct experience with Scrum, I realized that a lot of agile thinking is really the same as entrepreneurial thinking. The overlap is an empirical approach to working—learning by observation.

After digesting this experience and in Ha mode, I met Jeff Sutherland, cocreator of Scrum, at a conference, and I said to him, "True or false: Agile thinking is entrepreneurial thinking." Jeff pondered the question, looking down at the carpet for more than seven seconds. Then he looked up and answered, "True. In the *Harvard Business Review* article by Takeuchi and Nonaka, the authors say that the team literally 'acts like a start-up' when they work this way." That really confirmed my ideas and got me going. At the Agile 2007 conference, I gave a session on this topic, entitled Agile and Entrepreneurial Thinking Patterns.

A little bit later, still at the Ha stage of learning, I was offered an opportunity to do some coaching inside a large insurance company. During this coaching, I observed some odd behavior at the group level, so I started really getting into studying groups and group processes. I knew about Group Relations theory, which puts forth the idea that the primary and unstated task of a group is "to survive as a group." I attended a GR conference in 2009 and realized that Scrum's clear definitions for boundary, authority, role, and task (BART) properties are part of what powers Scrum. I later shared these insights about the Scrum/BART connection at the Agile 2008 and Agile 2009 conferences.

Just now, I figure I am in Ri mode. I know that as soon as I say this, I will gain some new experience, and then I will realize there's more to know and that I do not really know very much at all about agile and Scrum.

—Dan Mezick

Lyssa's Journey: An Agile Coach Atones

Lyssa Adkins, that's me. The last five years of my work life have been spent coaching agile teams and teaching agile. These years were preceded by almost 15 years of being a plan-driven project manager. If you've read parts of this book so far, you've already received bits of my coaching journey. The story you're about to read wraps it all up, puts it in order, and tells you more about what was going on inside me at every step in the journey.

Figure 13.3 shows my agile coaching journey.

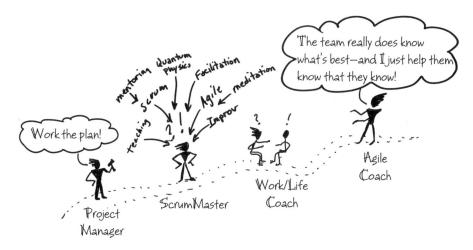

FIGURE 13.3 Lyssa Adkins' agile coaching journey

My journey to becoming an agile coach has been joyful, painful, and, above all, "revelationary." I started out as a project manager when the world was first formalizing project management and turning it into a repeatable process during the heyday of the Project Management Institute. I jumped on that bandwagon and became a great plan-driven project manager and, eventually, program manager and project management office director.

When I was a plan-driven project manager, I was driven—driven to be seen as someone who "has the whole thing under control." Even though I don't have any lasting physical illness from those experiences, the feeling of them lingers. We were always behind the eight ball, starting on "day one" already late, two hands tied behind our backs, never good enough. People were under constant and crushing pressure from not one but multiple projects. All of these projects were critical to the success of the business. At least that's what we were all told and what I let roll downhill as I drove them to work their tails off. I rode people hard. I was nice about it, no doubt, but the ways that people described me say it all. "She's like a pretty dog with a bone. She won't let you go." And "She wields a velvet hammer. Soft on the outside but steel inside." They said these things to my face, and I received them as compliments—being regarded as tough, driven, and serious was a badge of honor. In that era of my career, my slogan was "plan the work and work the plan."

I look back on it now, and I see the successes—project after project delivered on time, on budget, on scope (at least according to the last change request)—but not one delivered to a delighted client (although that wasn't part of the success criteria at that time). And, I see a long line of people who compromised their lives for those projects. They missed ball games, birthday parties, and lazy Sunday afternoons as they worked hours well beyond what anyone should reasonably expect. Although they made the decisions to sacrifice like this "on their own," I knew, deep down, that the system of which I was a part (and I was upholding) pressured them into making those choices. The divorces that occurred on my teams (about three a year), the nagging feeling that maybe those missed moments with families add up, the clients and company managers that drove me with their unrealistic expectations and "jump higher" demands—all these seemed to boil down to one idea: Work harder and ignore the personal costs.

And I drove myself to exhaustion, putting my young daughter to bed and falling into a fitful sleep beside her—still in my work clothes, with the dinner dishes in the sink and all the lights in the house still on. Getting just enough fitful sleep to do it all again the next day. Looking back, I think we all felt trapped in a way of working that did not support our best efforts or even care about our best efforts. Just churn out the next project; that's all the machine cared about.

This whole time, I received lots of kudos for being such a great project manager, not only from management and clients but also from team members. I look back on how I treated team members when I worked the plan-driven way and wonder why those same people would ever want to work with me as a project manager again. But they do (even today), so I can only surmise that while my actions were inhumane, they must have worked with project managers far more inhumane than me. Those project managers and the people on their projects probably think their way of working is "normal." Having never experienced any other way, they probably would not associate the word *inhumane* with the way they work, but it is.

Through an act of serendipity, I was told that my next project would be run using Scrum and that I would be a ScrumMaster. Through the help of my Scrum mentor, I learned to let go enough to let the team work. It was hard for me, almost painful, and so worth it. I was astounded at how proficient, quick, and quality-minded people could be in their work. I couldn't believe my eyes but felt somehow immensely relieved to find that teams really do know the right things to do—all without me "driving" them and all without them making personal sacrifices again and again.

I was in awe when the members of two different teams I ScrumMastered said, "No big deal that you have Lasik surgery scheduled on our release date. Go! We have this under control." And they did. I didn't even call in or find out what happened until I arrived back at work two days later, with new eyesight (in more ways than one). Both releases were successful, and the teams had moved on to the next highest value work—all without me telling them what to do or being there to orchestrate each person's move in the release process.

I was in awe when the most timid person on a Scrum team started talking out loud and was recognized for her (as yet, unseen) brilliance and then went on to become a leader in the group, taking her rightful place among the other leader/team members. Seeing her smiling face beam as she offered all her talents (not just the ones from her formal role) and feeling the life-renewing energy she was now giving the group, I was in awe.

I was in awe when a manager who had directed and forced throughout her career allowed herself to step back and create a void that invited the team to come forward. Under great pressure to "drive them," this was no small feat for her. She was richly rewarded as the team stepped into the void and filled it up to the brim with their ideas, direction, and considerable leadership. The very people she found so hard to manage and who had produced just so-so results in the past were now creating top-quality products that mattered. She was in awe of them. I was in awe of her.

All of these awe-full experiences led me to believe that there's something deeper going on with Scrum than just a new project management process. To capture the essence of this, I started to fill my head with lots of new ideas. I read various agilists' blogs and branched out from there to the subjects that inspired them and piqued their curiosity. As a result, I learned a little about many things: facilitation, theater, conflict mediation, improvisation, teaching, decision sciences, quantum physics, leadership, nonviolent communication, meditation, mentoring, servant leadership. I soaked it all in, letting each new idea marinate with the daily experiences I was getting ScrumMastering teams, by this time being referred to as an *agile coach*. As I started bringing these ideas to my teams, I was pulled up short by a feeling that offering them techniques and mind-sets from these various domains was just a new way to control. If I was not careful, I could drown them in so many new ideas that they would, once again, be paralyzed by someone else's direction for them. At the same time, a colleague said to me, "You call yourself a coach, but you're not really one."

Recognizing the truth in this, I took my first work/life coaching class and discovered a new world that offered skills 100% applicable to coaching agile teams. What a bonanza! And, I learned ways to let the team be in charge of their agenda, within which I could offer all these new ideas without knocking the team off their own path. From there, I shared what I had come to know as the depths of agile, bringing to them new ways of thinking to help agile come to life for them and make a difference in their lives. Now, I can clearly see that the team really does know what's best. My job as their agile coach is to help them know that they know.

—Lyssa Adkins

Martin's Journey: An Agile Coach Conducts a Personal Retrospective

Martin Kearns was one of the first three coaches to earn the Certified Scrum Coach designation, and he is also a Certified Scrum Trainer. I met Martin at the Scrum Gathering in the spring of 2009 and immediately knew that I wanted to find ways to work with him. Since then, he and I have shared our training and coaching tips and lessons with one another through video chats across vast distances and time zones, he in Australia and me in the United States. I find Martin to be a man of deep integrity, a quality that makes him a stellar role model while it challenges him to remain true to himself as he coaches teams. Figure 13.4 illustrates Martin's agile coaching journey.

FIGURE 13.4 Martin Kearns' agile coaching journey

Here is Martin's story in his own words:

> My journey as a coach has been quite emotional. My first step was to elevate myself above others with the title of "coach" without first stopping to assess my abilities. Was I really a coach?
>
> If anything, I gave myself the title of coach to massage my own ego, to have a title that carries built-in respect and says that I know more than others in the realm of agile. Secure within the hierarchical structure I had previously experienced, my role was simply to convince my direct reports of the efficacy of my solution, satisfy them with my explanation, and receive their support as we proceeded. I brought this mind-set to agile, replacing direct reports with team members but acting much the same way.
>
> It took me two years to realize that my ability to truly influence others to the agile way of thinking was constrained by my own attitude. People experienced me this way: "I know best. Listen to me. Bow to my superior agile knowledge." No wonder my ability to influence them fell short of my hopes.

I needed to learn more. After hours of researching human behavior and organizational dynamics, I finally found support for my own agile coaching journey in the writings of David Goleman on emotional intelligence (Goleman et al. 2003).

The realm of emotional intelligence (EI) helped me understand human motivation, expression, and dynamics on a new level. Now well recognized as an essential dimension for creating effective interpersonal relationships, it became evident to me that improving my EI quotient was fundamental to influencing others in an agile transition.

I realized that I needed to value the individual as the person that they are, respect their opinion, and learn more about their individual beliefs and personal goals. So, I began to concentrate on creating the type of relationship I needed to have with people in order to initiate change and have the influence I hoped I would. I applied Goleman's EI model through my own inspect-and-adapt cycles, and I learned many things.

Among them, I learned that being a coach requires a discipline of introspection, having the confidence and desire to examine one's state of mind and attitudes. When I first began to look within, I was not impressed with what I saw. I had been teaching the greatness of team-oriented approaches to software development and how productive (and enjoyable) a team empowered to determine how to resolve complex problems can be. What I realized was that I was acting more like an individual motivated by self-centered desires than the type of agile team member I was teaching and facilitating others to be.

I was really annoyed with myself and needed to start practicing what I teach. Therein I discovered the core of the problem: I was teaching more than coaching. There is a big difference between the two. To coach, one must be in sync with the emotions of a team and have complete resonance with their problems and opinions. The art of listening becomes particularly important. I reminded myself of this and began to listen to and understand what people were feeling and thinking and then ask questions that allowed all of us to know why.

As agile coaches, we need to remain keenly aware that change always has an upsetting impact. We must remind ourselves that when we enter a team's domain and experience a response to resist change, it has nothing to do with us. We should not take it personally. We must respect the past experiences of the people on the team and help them harness their strengths to establish an agile team mind-set.

The question an agile coach must then ask is, "How long should I invest in one person before concentrating elsewhere?" My answer lay in the realization that this question is not mine to answer. The coach educates people about agile concepts such as results-oriented approaches and shared ownership of the outcomes, good and bad alike. Through this, the coach provides the information people need in order to decide for themselves whether an agile way of working fits with their personal needs and beliefs. It's never an easy prospect to inspire in someone the desire to change their behaviors or mind-sets, yet that's what we coaches must do. I have found that the best way to achieve this is to lead by example. For example, be the first to observe the results of the practices we are adopting, respecting the opinions of every individual.

As I said before, being an agile coach has been an emotional journey, but it's been worth it. There are great benefits to being an agile coach. You get to help establish an environment where every team member is allowed to work to the best of their abilities and produce remarkable solutions that really answer business needs. There's nothing better than that.

Yet, even as you celebrate your teams' successes, you know your fate is to take the backseat at such times and never claim their success as your own. To really coach, your sense of success must truly lie with the team's increasing abilities and your impact on them. The attention for a job well done is all theirs. Instead, be delighted in how their success has bonded them into a stronger unit, capable of taking on new initiatives better than before.

The role of a coach is one I truly cherish. Once, before I became an agile coach, I coached athletes on a track team to a national league title. This was big stuff. For years we trained with one another, night after night without fail. To see the delight on my teammate's faces when we won and to feel without doubt that the hard work paid off was an experience

I will cherish forever. The win required a full team effort, each person giving it all, and resulted in an achievement we shared together. Now, with agile teams, the chance for this kind of greatness happens every day in my professional life. I am truly grateful to have the opportunity to work in the agile coach role where I get to re-live that gratifying feeling of real achievement over and over again.

My advice: Embrace the role of agile coach wholly, and the benefits will remain with you forever.

—Martin Kearns

Kathy's Journey: An Agile Coach Learns to Coach

Kathy Harman was known as "the best darn business analyst you'd ever want to meet" when she and I first crossed paths. A few years later, after losing touch with one another, our paths crossed again, this time in the context of professional coaching. During that period, we had each found our way to coaching and were "introduced" to one another by a mutual colleague in the coaching arena. Since then, Kathy and I have worked side by side as master agile coaches, helping people, teams, and organizations figure out how to best leverage agile to get the great results they desire. Figure 13.5 portrays Kathy's agile coaching journey.

FIGURE 13.5   Kathy Harman's agile coaching journey

Here is Kathy's story in her own words:

> I came to agile coaching in the same way that many others do: I was a project manager for years, was part of a couple of very successful agile teams, took the agile training, and became certified as a ScrumMaster. At that point, I felt ready to "lead teams to success." After all, I was great at motivating teams and keeping management informed and happy, could make Microsoft Project sing, and was experienced in agile methods. What else could I possibly need?
>
> I coached a couple of teams and found them devilishly hard to manage. They weren't nearly as compliant as the teams I'd worked with in the past! They didn't particularly want to conform to all the agile practices and didn't always do what I told them to do. I had to constantly nag them to do their stand-ups, and they weren't a bit interested in reviews or retrospectives. I took on more and more of the responsibilities of making sure the work got done. Agile coaching was hard work!
>
> Fortunately, I was sidetracked away from agile coaching by an intense interest in life coaching. I enrolled in the Success Unlimited Network coaching program and spent more than a year in deep study to attain coaching competencies. I was mentored as I coached clients and slowly absorbed the practices that form the backbone of life coaching such as active listening, powerful questioning, creating awareness, managing progress, and accountability. I soon realized why I had so much trouble with those agile teams: I was managing them, not coaching them.
>
> While in my training, I received a request to consider an agile coaching position. My first inclination was to decline, as I really enjoyed individual coaching. But then my curiosity kicked in: What would be the result if I applied the traditional coaching principles to teams in an agile environment? I accepted the position and had the good fortune to find an experienced agile and life coach already there, who had successfully planted the seeds of coaching agile using professional coaching techniques. I was able to slip in to an environment ripe for the kind of coaching I wanted to do.

I instantly felt a difference in my agile coaching abilities. Now that I'd been trained as a life coach, I better understood the agile ideal of coaching, of helping the team become self-managed. I was able to easily transfer individual coaching techniques to my team coaching: asking questions instead of giving suggestions, accepting that the team had the knowledge to succeed, and sustaining a positive outlook and approach. I saw how, when the team figured it out themselves, the lesson stuck. I helped teams understand the dynamics that made them successful (or caused them problems), and creating that awareness helped them to figure out how to celebrate their differences and create the unique Team Entity identity that makes them high-performing.

Rather than swooping in like an avenging "agile angel," spouting rules and absolutes, I watched how the team members acted, spoke, and interacted, and I let them find what would work. One team wanted team-building activities; another was not a bit interested in activities but wanted concrete processes to help them build a better team. For the former, I introduced games and exercises and helped them understand what they learned. For the latter, I coached them to create the process they wanted to be a high-performing team. They created the process, not me. I introduced tools and techniques to help them, but each time I asked if they wanted to use the technique and abided by their decision. It was their agenda, not mine! This approach resulted in very different teams, each with its own style, and both being high-performance agile teams. They embraced agile and were committed to team success. Communication was open, trust was high, and focus was laser-beam direct.

In the process, I learned as much as the teams did. Not everything I tried worked, and those things that didn't work taught me as much as those that succeeded. There is a rightness about coaching a team to success, sort of like conducting a symphony. Each team member plays an important part, but the true beauty is in the working of the entire team as a successful entity. There is a joyous letting go of the need to control, strong trust that the agile framework works, and an unconditional acceptance of the abilities of the team members to blend into a harmonious whole. I discovered a whole new and exciting world beyond individual coaching, equally as enriching and satisfying. And the best part? Being a real agile coach doesn't feel like hard work at all!

—Kathy Harman

Your Journey

The final of our six agile coach journey stories stars you. Where have you been? What have you learned? What cries out to you to be explored and integrated into your coaching? What's important about coaching agile teams to you?

Figure 13.6 stands ready, waiting for you to fill in the illustration depicting your agile coaching journey. Take a few moments to consider where you've been and where you're going and draw in the various coach events that have shaped your journey thus far. Go ahead, draw it in. Show your path ahead, too. What's the next summit for you to reach? What is your motto about agile coaching?

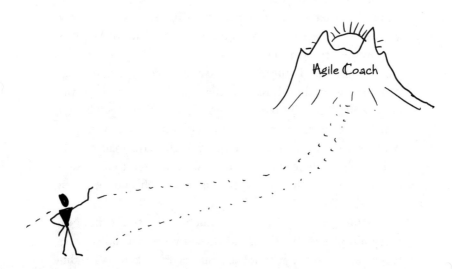

FIGURE 13.6 Your agile coaching journey

Then, share your journey illustration with others so they can support you on your way. You may also find that your story inspires them to further heights. What a gift that would be!

And, let me know what happens for you along the way, too. I can't wait to hear about your journey.

A Refresher

There's only one idea to lock in this time:

- It's your journey. Make it worthwhile. Dare to be a great agile coach.

Additional Resources

Sliger, M. Light Bulb Moments. www.sligerconsulting.com/lightbulb-moments. Agile coach, trainer, and coauthor of *The Project Manager's Bridge to Agility*, Michele Sliger calls the things that make agile "click" for people their light-bulb moments. She collects people's stories on her website.

References

Goleman, D., R. Boyatzis, and A. McKee. 2003. *The New Leaders: Transforming the Art of Leadership*. London: Sphere.

Index

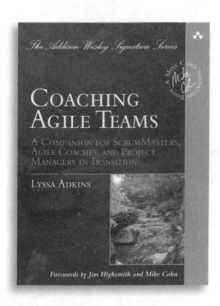

FREE Online Edition

Your purchase of **Coaching Agile Teams** includes access to a free online edition for 45 days through the Safari Books Online subscription service. Nearly every Addison-Wesley Professional book is available online through Safari Books Online, along with more than 5,000 other technical books and videos from publishers such as Cisco Press, Exam Cram, IBM Press, O'Reilly, Prentice Hall, Que, and Sams.

SAFARI BOOKS ONLINE allows you to search for a specific answer, cut and paste code, download chapters, and stay current with emerging technologies.

Activate your FREE Online Edition at www.informit.com/safarifree

> **STEP 1:**   Enter the coupon code: SHPIZAA.

> **STEP 2:**   New Safari users, complete the brief registration form.
> Safari subscribers, just log in.

If you have difficulty registering on Safari or accessing the online edition, please e-mail customer-service@safaribooksonline.com